INTERNATIONAL TAXATION

by

JOSEPH ISENBERGH
Seymour Logan Professor of Law,
University of Chicago

NEW YORK, NEW YORK
FOUNDATION PRESS
2000

COPYRIGHT © 2000 By FOUNDATION PRESS

11 Penn Plaza, Tenth Floor
New York, NY 10001
Phone Toll Free 1–877–888–1330
Fax (212) 760–8705
fdpress.com

ISBN 1–56662–870–9

 *TEXT IS PRINTED ON 10% POST
CONSUMER RECYCLED PAPER*

∞

SUMMARY OF CONTENTS

TABLE OF CONTENTS

PART I: BASIC ELEMENTS OF INTERNATIONAL TAXATION

International Taxation

Special Note on Sources and Citations

Here follows an overview of the principal sources of U.S. law on international taxation and a brief explanation of the conventions of citation and reference followed in this book.

Internal Revenue Code

The basic scripture of U.S. taxation is the Internal Revenue Code, a codification of the currently applicable provisions of income tax statutes extending back to 1913. The Code is a law of the United States; its provisions accordingly have full force to the extent consistent with the U.S. Constitution. The Code has been recodified twice since its introduction as the Internal Revenue Code of 1939. The Code currently in force is styled the "Internal Revenue Code of 1986." Provisions of the Code are cited in this book by section number only. E.g., "section 78" or "§78."

Income Tax Treaties

Income tax treaties between the United States and other countries also have the force of laws. There is no overarching priority or precedence between treaties and statutes. They simply coexist, and inconsistencies are resolved largely ad hoc, with the help of some partly codified rules. This book follows no special form of citation to income tax treaties, which are identified simply by the country with which they are in force.

Treasury Regulations

Expounding and expanding the Code (and many income tax treaties) are extensive regulations issued by the U.S. Treasury Department. The Treasury Regulations arise under a general grant of authority in the Code (section 7805) as well as under specific sections. Many regulations are interpretations of Code provisions, and contain mostly interstitial and illustrative matter. Some entire segments of U.S. tax law, however, exist principally as regulations issued under broad-framed (and sometimes skeletal) statutory mandates.

Treasury Regulations, to the extent consistent with the Code, have the force of laws. They can, however, be attacked by taxpayers and set aside as inconsistent with statutes or treaties. Courts show some deference to Treasury Regulations on close or doubtful questions, but taxpayers do succeed from time to time in persuading courts that specific regulations are inconsistent with the Code, overreaching, or otherwise invalid. Treasury Regulations are cited in this book as "Reg. §___". Regulations are usually numbered by "1." followed by the number of the Code section under which they arise. For example, "Reg. §1.902-1(a)" is a Regulation arising under section 902.

IRS Rulings

Below the Regulations in the hierarchy of official pronouncements on taxation stand IRS rulings. These contain positions taken by the Internal Revenue Service in response to specific transactions and situations. Typically they represent more narrowly focused applications of the tax laws than the Regulations. Rulings are issued in great numbers, with many fewer formalities than regulations. Rulings are valid only if consistent with the Code *and* the Regulations. They are frequently attacked by taxpayers as invalid, sometimes with success.

Rulings come in two types: published and unpublished.

Revenue Rulings. Published rulings (known as "Revenue Rulings") are collected in the Cumulative Bulletin of the Internal Revenue Service (cited here as "Cum. Bull."). A Revenue Ruling bears the number of the year and the order of its issuance. Similarly, the volumes of the Cumulative Bulletin are numbered according to the year in which their contents were issued. Thus "Rev. Rul. 78-113, 1978-2 Cum. Bull.__" is a citation to the 113th Revenue Ruling issued in 1978, contained in the 1978 volume (Part 2) of the Cumulative Bulletin. The Revenue Service acknowledges published Revenue Rulings as binding precedents.

Private Rulings. Unpublished or "private" rulings are issued directly by the Revenue Service to taxpayers who seek advance knowledge of the Revenue Service's position on transactions they are planning. These are known as "Private Letter Rulings" and have binding force only between the Revenue Service and the taxpayer to whom they are addressed. Similar to Private Letter Rulings are Technical Advice Memoranda concerning transactions already carried out by a taxpayer involved in administrative proceedings with the Internal Revenue Service.

Court Cases

Tax disputes can be heard before three different courts: the Tax Court, the Court of Claims, and the District Courts of the United States. The District Courts are constitutional courts of the United States under Article III of the Constitution; the other two are administrative law courts. Appeals can be taken from the decisions of all three, however, to the federal courts of appeals and ultimately the United States Supreme Court. Decisions of the Tax Court are cited here to the Tax Court Reports (abbreviated "T.C."); decisions of its predecessor, the Board of Tax Appeals (which sat until 1942), are cited to volumes of the "B.T.A." Reports.

Basic Elements of International Taxation

Chapter 1

U.S. Taxation in the International Setting

The Nature of International Taxation

A reader with no background in the subject would derive an imperfect idea of this book from its title. Strictly, there is no "international" taxation. Only nations and their subdivisions impose taxes. The subject known as "international taxation" involves mainly international aspects of tax systems originating in *national* environments.[1] The subject, furthermore, is rarely approached globally. Those contemplating investment or business operations in a foreign economic environment tend to focus narrowly on the tax system prevailing there. It is rare even for a practicing international tax specialist to be fully operational in more than one tax system. Those scattered around the world who use the label "international taxation" as a shorthand for their work are thus rarely talking about the very same subject. Rather, they concern themselves with indigenous adaptations of their own national tax systems to the international economic environment.

By any name, this book is mainly about *U.S.* taxation, albeit applied to economic activity with an international element. It is not, for all that, narrowly parochial. Because so much of the world's economic activity originates in the United States, and even more has the United States as its destination, a substantial part of the world's business transactions and investments are affected in some measure by U.S. taxation. Perhaps because it reaches so large a family of transactions, the U.S. system of international taxation is, I believe, the most fully elaborated of all. Its complexity and detail mirror those of U.S. taxation generally. Viewed at close range U.S. international taxation is a profusion of rules, mostly narrow and often impervious to apprehension through reading, bound together by no evident first principles or overarching themes. The subject cannot be derived in Euclidean fashion from basic postulates such as "Income should be taxed once, but only once, by the government with sovereign power over the place it is earned or the person earning it." Rather, the U.S. international tax system is made up of specific, piecemeal responses to the way investment or business operations are carried out across national boundaries. It is a Ptolemaic system, held together with epicycles added to the structure over time as national tax authorities come to grips with changing pathways of international investment and commerce.

---

[1]The subject is known by other names as well, among which are "Foreign Taxation," "Taxation of Foreign-related Transactions," and "Taxation of International Transactions."

That said, there is a family resemblance among the adaptations of different national tax systems to international economic activity, both in their content and their modes of enforcement. Someone conversant with the international elements of one tax system would likely recognize many of the features of another. Some of the recurrent elements of international tax systems reflect specific ways international business is conducted. Because international trade must bridge different economic and commercial environments, specialized intermediaries have arisen to narrow the span. More international commerce passes through independent agents, brokers, distributors, export-import specialists, and middlemen generally, than in purely domestic transactions. Joint ventures are more common, as is the use of separately chartered subsidiary corporations. Because it is typically harder and more expensive to take effective legal action outside one's native legal environment, specialized forms of financing and transfer of ownership—epitomized in the international sale financed by a letter of credit payable upon transfer of documents of title—have evolved to prevent goods and payment for them from resting simultaneously in the same hands. Concerns about the definition, scope, and protection of intellectual property may also induce different choices in the form of transfer of goods or intangible property than would arise within a single country. Governments too have different degrees of leverage (usually less) over enterprises operating largely beyond their borders, and have responded with separate mechanisms of enforcement and collection of taxes in the international setting.

The closest thing to a system of "international" taxation can be found in income tax treaties between different countries. A treaty by its nature is an element of the laws of more than one nation. Although the taxes affected by treaties are ultimately imposed by a specific country, the treasuries of the countries joining in treaties do make concessions from their habitual norms of taxation. The result is a tax regime arising under a treaty that may differ from the regime imposed by the laws of any one country. Here too the vantage point of this book is that of U.S. taxation; it is concerned almost exclusively with the income tax treaties of the United States.

"Inbound" and "Outbound" Transactions

From the perspective of the U.S. tax system, international economic activity falls in two broad classes: 1) investments or business undertakings of foreign persons in the United States, and 2) investments or business undertakings of U.S. persons abroad. Informally, these are known as "inbound" and "outbound" transactions respectively. More technically, the taxation of these two classes is called "taxation of foreign persons" and "taxation of foreign income." The most fully descriptive name for this book would be "U.S. Taxation of Foreign Persons and Foreign Income." A similar vocabulary is used in the international tax systems of other countries, with suitably reversed meanings, of course, for the terms "foreign," "inbound," and "outbound."

To approach the study of international taxation, a student needs little more than a reasonably well-formed notion of "income" and a basic knowledge of business and investment. Although the relevant statutes and regulations are riddled with mechanical complexities, they rest on the same essential elements as other areas of taxation. If you know about gross income, net income, inclusion, exclusion, credits, deductions, realization, recognition, timing, and basis, you already know the under-pinnings of international taxation. To gain a strong intuitive grasp of international taxation (as opposed simply to parsing its individual rules) requires in addition understanding the economic activity to which it applies—business and investment in the international setting. The great-est conceptual difficulties of international taxation lie in questions of characterization. These are even more acute than in taxation generally because of the greater opportunity in the international environment to maneuver transactions into different tax regimes, some more enjoyable than others. The real question in many cases ostensibly interpreting a provision of law is "What happened?" Questions of characterization are an undercurrent running through this book, and surface ubiquitously.

Matters of Terminology

There are some points of vocabulary. In referring to various beings, the language of taxation uses common terms in uncommon ways. In tax talk the term "person" includes entities *and* human beings. A "United States person," for example, may be an individual, a corporation, a partnership, or a trust. The term "individual" refers only to a flesh and blood human. Therefore in these pages the word "person" means any identifiable being or entity, while the word "individual" describes the likes of you and me. I use the terms "person" and "taxpayer" more or less interchangeably in this book. In places, when the context leaves no doubt, I sometimes use the word "person" to mean "individual."

Individuals and other persons whose legal status connects them closely to the United States are often described here by the term "U.S.," as in "U.S. resident," "U.S. corporation," "U.S. citizen," and more generally "U.S. person." The term "American" is sometimes used instead of "U.S.," as in "American citizen." For entities, the term "domestic" is used synonymously with "U.S.," as in "domestic part-nership" and "domestic corporation." The term "domestic" in this context has nothing to do with families. "Nonresident alien individuals" (the technical term for foreign nationals citizens residing outside the United States) are sometimes referred to here as "foreign individuals" or simply "foreigners." The term "foreign persons" refers to foreign individuals and foreign entities collectively.

The U.S. income tax system is administered by the U.S. Treasury Department. A division of the Treasury, the Internal Revenue Service, headed by the Commissioner of Internal Revenue, handles the day-to-day elements of this work. In this book, I make no distinction between the Treasury and the Internal Revenue Service. I refer here to the tax authorities of the United States variously and interchangeably as the "Treasury," the "Secretary," the "Internal Revenue Service," the "Revenue Service," the "Service," the "IRS," and the "Commissioner." No inference should be drawn from the changing vocabulary, which is meant only to relieve the tedium of uniformity.

The U.S. Taxing Power

The taxing power of the United States arises from Article I, Section 8, of the Constitution, granting Congress the power "to lay and collect taxes, duties, imposts and excises . . . ." This power is qualified in Article I, Section 2, requiring that "direct taxes" shall be "apportioned among the several states . . . according to their respective numbers . . . ," and in Article I, Section 9, requiring that "no capitation or other direct tax shall be laid, unless in proportion to the census . . . ." Under this last clause the Income Tax Law of 1894, was struck down by the Supreme Court as unconstitutional in Pollock v. Farmers Loan and Trust Co.[2] The adoption of the 16th Amendment in 1913, empowering Congress "to lay and collect taxes on incomes, from whatever source derived, without apportionment among the several states, and without regard to any census or enumeration," both eliminated all doubt on the power of the United States to tax income and left no evident limitation on that power.

The 16th Amendment has not, to be sure, prevented those who have felt aggrieved by U.S. taxation, both in and out of the United States, from raising constitutional objections. But, unlike aspirants to constitutional protection in other areas of law, they have generally fared poorly. The courts of the United States have taken the taxing power, within its stated limits, at face value, and have almost invariably upheld the validity of federal taxes, whether imposed on U.S. or foreign persons.

---

[2]157 U.S. 429, 158 U.S. 601 (1895).

The taxing power of the United States is exercised today through the Internal Revenue Code, a codification of tax laws spanning almost 90 years, styled since the Tax Reform Act of 1986 as the "Internal Revenue Code of 1986,"and known colloquially as the "Code." The Code imposes an array of taxes, of which the most important are the individual and corporate income taxes, payroll taxes on compensation from employment and self-employment, excise taxes on various goods and transactions, and estate and gift taxes. This book is concerned almost exclusively with the individual and corporate income taxes, imposed by sections 1 and 11 of the Code respectively, on "taxable income." The latter is itself derived through a plethora of specific provisions from a base of "gross income," defined in section 61.

Worldwide U.S. Taxation

You are probably familiar with the idea that the U.S. income tax is "worldwide." The worldwide reach of U.S. income taxation flows initially, simply enough, from the absence in the Code of any limitation on the taxation of U.S. persons. Section 1 imposes a tax on the taxable income of "every individual," and section 11 does the same for "every corporation." "Gross income," (the base from which taxable income is derived) is expressly defined in section 61 to include all income "from whatever source derived." Taxation of income from all sources is precisely what is meant by "worldwide" taxation. Indeed, it is not immediately obvious on first encounter with the Code that *any* person, regardless of nationality *or* residence, escapes worldwide U.S. taxation. You could easily conclude from section 1 by itself, which imposes a tax on the income of "every individual," that the Code purported to tax all human beings everywhere.

Its Limits in the Code

In order to find any limitation on the taxation of *foreign* citizens, you must read to section 2(d), which scales down the tax of section 1 for "nonresident alien individuals" as provided "in sections 871 and 877." The latter provisions in their turn expound a tax regime reaching mainly income related economically to the United States. A "nonresident alien" is a citizen of a foreign country residing outside the United States. There are similar provisions limiting U.S. taxation of foreign corporations in sections 881 and 882.[3]

---

[3]Nonresident alien individuals and foreign corporations make up a class often described collectively as "foreign persons."

This minuet of statutory cross-reference, only partly cued in the text itself, reveals the Code's true character: atomized, sprawling, and opaque. For much of the Code, at least on first encounter, the only way to know what it means is to know what it means.

Simpler Times

It was not always so. A century ago, the Income Tax Law of 1894 encompassed the entire U.S. income tax, both domestic and international, in a single nearly readable sentence:

> [T]here shall be assessed . . . and paid annually upon the gains, profits, and income received . . . by every citizen of the United States, whether residing at home or abroad, and every person residing therein, whether said gains, profits, or income be derived from any kind of property, rents, interest, dividends, or salaries, or from any profession, trade, employment, or vocation carried on in the United States or elsewhere, or from any other source whatever, a tax of two per centum on the amount so derived over and above four thousand dollars, and a like tax shall be levied, collected, and paid annually upon the gains, profits, and income from all property owned and of every business, trade, or profession carried on in the United States by persons residing without the United States.[4]

Another sentence in the 1894 law contains virtually the entire system of enforcement: "[I]n computing income [a nonresident] shall include all income from every source, but unless he be a citizen of the United States he shall only pay on that part of the income which is derived from any source in the United States." For all its endearing simplicity, the 1894 Tax Law was struck down as unconstitutional in 1895. Its basic framework, however, survives in today's law, embedded in a more than thousandfold increase in girth: 1) U.S. citizens and residents are taxed on their income from all sources worldwide, and 2) Nonresident foreign citizens are taxed only on income derived from the United States.

The Problem of Double Taxation

Worldwide taxation by the United States does not, needless to say, disarm the taxing power of other countries. Americans pursuing income outside the United States are bound to encounter tax collectors asserting their own national claims. The world is awash in possibilities of double, even triple, taxation. Countries to whom Americans are themselves foreign commonly tax foreigners (as does the United States) on the basis of the "source" of their income, a term widely used by national tax

---

[4]Act of August 28, 1894, §27.

systems to describe income within their reach. The short-lived 1894 Tax Law, as you may have noticed above, introduced the term "source" of income in the U.S. tax laws as a shorthand for the location of the property or business from which income is derived. This, however, is not the only plausible notion of the source of income, and other tax systems conceive the source of income quite differently. Consider the following scenario and variations.

A Contract in Kuwait

Suppose you are a lawyer practicing in New York City. One day your phone rings and a voice on the other end of the line, calling from Kuwait, asks you to do some research on a question and send your findings in the form of a memorandum. You decide that the caller, with whom you have mutual acquaintances, is creditworthy and you go ahead with the work, consisting of some reading, some thinking, and some writing, which takes in all 20 hours of your time. Your final product is a memorandum, which you send to your Kuwaiti client, along with a bill for $4,000 reflecting your hourly rate of $200. A check for $4,000 arrives by return mail, and you give the matter little further thought beyond wishing that your local clients were as easy to deal with.

Toward the end of the year you receive an official-looking letter from the Treasury of Kuwait, impressively adorned with a seal and crests, asking you to remit $2,000 in income tax to the Kuwaiti Treasury with respect to your $4,000 of Kuwait-source income, explaining that the rate of Kuwaiti income tax on the Kuwait-source income of foreigners from professional services is 50%. Although the arithmetic is sound, you are nonetheless taken by surprise. You know that your income from your work in New York is subject to U.S. income tax, but it has not occurred to you that a foreign country might attempt to tax it as well. You ask a friend who specializes in taxation if the demand of the Kuwaiti Treasury is kosher. Your friend tells you that in the *U.S.* tax system your income has its source in the United States, not Kuwait, because under U.S. tax notions income takes its source from the place of the economic activity that gives rise to it, and you did the work in the United States. You therefore write back to the Kuwaiti Treasury, pointing out that all the work that produced the $4,000 fee was done in the United States and that you don't think that it should be subject to Kuwaiti tax. The Kuwaiti Treasury responds in turn that *its* tax system identifies the source of income with the source of *payment* rather than the place the underlying work was done, adding the further explanation that the $4,000 came out of *Kuwait's* economy, reduced *Kuwait's* claims on the world's resources by $4,000, affected *Kuwait's* balance of payments, and that in any event its official determination is final.

International Taxation

Kuwait has won the narrow legal argument. As a matter of Kuwaiti law, you owe the tax. And while the tax does not comport with U.S. notions of the source of income, it is not self-evidently wrong. At this point one possible course for you is to pay the tax and move on with your life. On further reflection, though, you may not care who has won the argument. Depending on your anticipated future ties to Kuwait, you can just say no—simply not pay the Kuwaiti tax claim—without further ado. Kuwait can't do anything to you, unless you are planning to take your next vacation there. The United States will not enforce Kuwait's demand (or at least you don't think so). You therefore ignore Kuwait's tax claim.

Precisely because you can do so, and likely with impunity, the course of events just described will never occur. Kuwait's view of the source of your income in this vignette is entirely realistic (many countries take such a view), but Kuwait's relaxed approach to collection of its tax is not. Kuwait knows full well that it has little or no leverage to collect tax from *you*, and more than likely will not even attempt the vain act of doing so. Instead, you will receive from your Kuwaiti client a check for $2,000, along with an official form indicating that $2,000 of Kuwaiti income tax has been withheld by your client at the source and paid over to the Kuwaiti Treasury. You can engage in the same exchange of arguments with Kuwait as above, but now *Kuwait* does not care who wins the argument. It has the money. You cannot sue your client in Kuwait for the balance of your fee, because under Kuwaiti law you have been paid in full. Kuwait's requirement of withholding income tax at the source from payments of income to foreign persons has reversed the balance of power between you and the Kuwaiti Treasury. You cannot avoid the tax.

Given the inevitability of the withheld Kuwaiti tax, your next concern is how the United States will tax your fee in light of Kuwait's action. Assume for simplicity that the United States also imposes a 50-percent income tax. The worst possibility is that the United States Treasury might take no account whatever of the Kuwaiti tax, that is, deny you any deduction or other allowance for its payment. If so, your U.S. taxable income on account of the fee is $4,000,[5] and your U.S. income tax obligation $2,000 (at a 50-percent rate). The combined tax payments to Kuwait and the United States ($2,000 to each) have wiped out your income from the venture. This pathetic result is absolute double taxation, to wit, the taxation of the same income by each of two countries without any allowance by either for the tax imposed by the other. If it were

---

[5]Note that your U.S. income is the full $4,000 (and not the $2,000 cash you actually received) because your income includes amounts used to discharge *your* obligations, whether paid over to you or not. Remember Old Colony Trust Co. v. Commissioner, 279 U.S. 716 (1929).

10

common, double taxation of this sort would stop international economic activity in its tracks.

Another less disastrous possibility is that the United States will allow you at least to deduct the Kuwaiti tax from your U.S. taxable income. Without digging very deeply into the U.S. tax system, a deduction of the Kuwaiti tax might be defended as an expense of carrying on the business that generated the income. With a deduction for the Kuwaiti tax, your U.S. taxable income is reduced to $2,000, on which you owe the U.S. Treasury $1,000. Your combined total worldwide tax cost is $3,000. This too is double taxation, but in a milder form. While you have paid tax to two sovereigns, one of them (the United States) has made some concession for the tax paid to the other (Kuwait). The combined rate of tax is 75%, still a considerable surtax on international economic activity compared to purely domestic.

Better yet you might expect, especially if you have at some point heard of the foreign tax credit, to be allowed a full dollar-for-dollar offset of the Kuwaiti tax against your U.S. income tax. If a credit were allowed by the United States (assuming no deduction were also allowed), your U.S. taxable income from the venture would be $4,000, entailing a pre-credit U.S. tax of $2,000, reduced to *zero* by a tax credit of $2,000. With a U.S. credit the combined effect of Kuwaiti and U.S. tax is the same as the 50-percent rate imposed by either country. There is no double taxation.

If you expected a U.S. credit for Kuwaiti income tax in this situation, however, you would be disappointed. To be sure, the U.S. tax system normally pacifies international double taxation with a foreign tax credit, essentially a concession of the U.S. Treasury to the taxing power of the country of source. But the credit is accorded only for foreign taxes imposed on *foreign source* income. Recall that the Kuwaiti tax here was imposed on your fee for work done in the United States, which is *U.S.-source* income. True enough, Kuwait assigned Kuwaiti source to the income you received from your Kuwaiti client. But that was a matter of Kuwaiti tax law. The United States applies its own principles of source, not other countries', in allowing the foreign tax credit, which defers to the taxing power of the country of source only for income considered by the United States beyond its legitimate reach. The United States makes no such concession for foreign taxes imposed on income from law practice in New York. Nor will the United States change its mind upon hearing from you that Kuwait takes a different view of the source of this income.

Your last resort in this situation would be to attempt to characterize the income from your Kuwaiti client as some sort of foreign source income, so as to entitle you to U.S. credit for the tax paid to Kuwait. For example, since your work culminated in a memorandum sent to your client, you might try to cast the transaction as a *sale* of a written product in Kuwait, which the United States might acknowledge as generating foreign source gain. This attempt would likely fail: it would be hard to convince the U.S. Treasury (and more importantly a court) that you have been compensated principally for the transfer of a physical object. That such a maneuver could even be considered to the end of a better tax result, however, reveals the special importance of the characterization of transactions in the international setting.

This vignette of an international venture illustrates the main cause of international double taxation: inconsistent rules of source in different countries imposing overlapping taxes. Both the United States and Kuwait tax the same item of income as their own. Both have the power to tax in this instance—that is, both have a lever over the taxpayer—and so both can be "right" in the only sense that matters.[6] If all countries had perfectly consistent rules of source and a system of credits, there would be no double taxation. But they don't, and there is.

Territorial Taxation

Many countries practice what is known as "territorial" taxation, that is, taxation limited to income from sources within their boundaries, no matter who derives it. Territorial tax systems accommodate other tax systems in the simplest possible way—by not extending their own. In a territorial tax regime double taxation is tamed by taking no account of foreign income, whether earned by a citizen, resident, or anyone else. International economic activity originating in a territorial tax environment can sometimes elude the shoals of national taxation altogether. Returning to the vignette belabored above, suppose this time you are a consultant working in an office in *Kuwait*, and you are a Kuwaiti citizen and resident. Suppose further that Kuwait follows a strictly territorial method of taxation, that is, it taxes only Kuwaiti source income. A client in the United States asks you for some work, which you do for a fee of $4,000. Under the U.S. tax laws, you have foreign (i.e., non-U.S.) source income (for work done *outside* the United States). If the source rules in Kuwait turn exclusively on the origin of payment, however, you also have foreign (i.e., non-Kuwaiti) source income from the perspective of the Kuwaiti treasury. As a non-U.S. person you are subject to U.S. tax only on U.S.-source income (which in the U.S. Treasury's view, you do not have). Kuwait's territorial tax system reaches only Kuwaiti source income (which in the Kuwaiti treasury's view you also do not have). Economic activity involving only high-tax countries (50% in both

---

[6]There is, remember, no overriding international law of taxation.

Kuwait and the United States in this fantasy) escapes income taxation in either. This enjoyable possibility (as did overtaxation in the mirror-image example traversed above) flows from different and inconsistent source rules under U.S. and Kuwaiti tax law.

Therefore another possible (though somewhat unpredictable) consequence of the imperfect fit of national tax systems is opportunity. Inconsistent tax principles and source rules of different countries have been known sometimes to combine benignly—"underlap" if you will—and allow total escape from taxation by any country for those able to align their affairs artfully. Maneuvers of this sort are difficult for U.S. taxpayers, however, because of the worldwide reach of U.S. taxation.

The differences between territorial and worldwide tax systems are smaller than first appear. The combination of worldwide taxation and a foreign tax credit approximates in some respects the effect of territorial taxation. When foreign tax rates are roughly the same as U.S. rates, it matters little whether the U.S. Treasury simply ignores foreign income or allows an offset of its own tax by a comparable amount paid to foreign treasuries. Furthermore, few countries' taxation is unqualifiedly territorial, or absolutely worldwide. Rather, national modes of taxation fall within a range from territorial to worldwide. Some countries tax the worldwide passive investment income of their own residents, but not their foreign source business profits. Other countries tax the worldwide incomes of their own residents, but not of their citizens residing abroad. Yet others tax the worldwide incomes only of their citizens who are also residents. The United States, which pushes worldwide taxation as far as any nonsocialist country ever has, still leaves some income beneficially owned by U.S. persons beyond its grasp.

U.S. International Taxation in Brief Overview

The Inbound Regime

The United States taxes foreign persons under two different tax regimes, imposed respectively on passive investments and active business operations. Current flows of U.S.-source passive investment income—known in tax patois as "fixed or determinable income not effectively connected with a U.S. trade or business"—are taxed at a flat rate (generally 30 percent) without allowance for deductions. Business profits from the United States—known as income "effectively connected with a U.S. trade or business"—are taxed at the regular graduated rates, with allowance for the full complement of deductions and credits.

From this bare outline, it would seem that the U.S. taxation of passive investment is the more severe. To be sure, the highest marginal rates imposed on the net business incomes of foreign individuals and corporations (39.6 percent and 35 percent respectively) are somewhat higher than the flat 30% rate imposed on their passive investment income, but the allowance of deductions and credits in the taxation of business income would usually be more than enough to compensate for this relatively small difference in rates.

On closer scrutiny, however, there are gaps in the flat rate tax imposed on investment income, large enough to make it essentially benign. Gains from the sale of U.S. investment assets (other than interests in real property) by foreign persons, including capital gains from stocks, securities, and other financial assets, are not taxed at all. Even more importantly, interest from U.S. bank deposits and from U.S. "portfolio" debt (a class including most private and public bonds and other obligations) is exempt from U.S. taxation in the hands of foreign persons. On the other side of the scales, the tax on the branch profits of foreign corporations in the United States adds a potential extra 30% tax on their business profits when they are removed from the U.S. economic environment. This tax, dating from the 1986 Act, extends two-level taxation of corporate profits to a larger class of foreign business operations in the United States.

With these additional elements taken into account, the taxation of active U.S. business operations emerges as the more severe. It is rarely crushing in practical effect, however, by virtue of the combined effect of interest deductions removing earnings from the reach of U.S. taxation and the protections of various income tax treaties.

The Outbound Regime

The two essential—and often conflicting—elements of U.S. taxation of foreign income are the worldwide taxation of United States citizens and residents, and the status of corporations as separate taxable entities. The informing questions in the taxation of foreign income reflect one or the other of these elements, which arise respectively as the problems of double taxation and deferral.

The Foreign Tax Credit Since direct foreign investments and business operations of United States persons often attract foreign income taxes along with the baseline U.S. tax, the specter of double taxation is bound to haunt the pursuit of foreign income. The principal accommodation of the U.S. tax system to the possibility of source-based taxation imposed by other countries is the foreign tax credit. From a simple idea—a dollar-for-dollar reduction of U.S. tax for income taxes paid to foreign countries—the foreign tax credit has evolved into an elaborate statutory structure capable of engulfing an entire professional career.

Foreign Corporations and Deferral   The U.S. tax system generally recognizes the separate identity of corporations, even when they are owned and controlled by a single person or a small group. In domestic U.S. taxation, the separate identity of corporations is the occasion for two levels of taxation of the earnings of corporations, one imposed on the income of an entity and the other on dividend distributions received by shareholders. In international transactions, however, the separateness of corporations may permit escape from current U.S. taxation of the earnings of foreign corporations beneficially owned by U.S. persons. Because a foreign corporation is a separate foreign person, it is not subject to U.S. taxation on its income derived outside the United States. The earnings of foreign corporations are subject to U.S. taxation, in the normal course of events, only when distributed to U.S. persons as dividends. This regime is known as "deferral," because U.S. taxation is deferred until foreign earnings are paid to U.S. shareholders as dividends. Given that the distribution of a dividend is largely optional, deferral can go on indefinitely. Indeed, with the restatement to fair market value of the basis of shares at the death of a shareholder, deferral can become forgiveness.

Nearly unlimited in the early days of the U.S. income tax, the possibility of deferral is heavily circumscribed in the current U.S. tax system. For corporations owned or controlled by U.S. persons—known as controlled foreign corporations—deferral today remains only for a carefully qualified class of active business operations. For foreign corporations not controlled by U.S. persons, the possibilities of deferral are considerably greater. Even here, the incomes of foreign passive investment companies are subject to current taxation in the hands of U.S. shareholders, however small their holdings. And income attributable to intangible property originating in the United States is subject to current U.S. taxation, regardless of where or by whom it is used.

Complexity   This system may seem simple enough, even intuitive, when presented in broad overview. The devil, however, is in the details. And they, trust me, are satanic indeed. Particularly in the taxation of foreign income, the proliferation of rules (even of syllables) can be frightening. The reason for this complexity is the attempt to formalize distinctions between legitimate business operations outside the United States, generally enjoying full credit for foreign taxes, the deferral of U.S. taxation, or both, and maneuvers considered to be tax haven operations. The provisions governing the foreign tax credit and deferral thread a delicate path through unyielding imposition of U.S. taxation, to the possible detriment of international commerce, and excessive concession to taxpayers or foreign treasuries. Both sets of provisions are shot through with rules attempting to distinguish between legitimate overseas business operations, where the U.S. Treasury allows the foreign tax environment (harsh or benign) to prevail, and tax haven operations, where the U.S. Treasury steps in aggressively. The mechanics of these distinctions, real or imaginary, are often nightmarish.

Tax Havens and Income Shifting

Among the reasons for this complexity is the elusive nature of tax havens. A tax haven is not always immediately obvious. What makes a particular environment a tax haven is not invariably a low rate of tax, but relations with other tax regimes that permit the ultimate deflection of income to a low-tax environment with which the income may have little indigenous connection. The U.S. tax system has responded with rules treating as tax havens transactional structures where there is no necessary connection between the location of economic activity and the situs of its taxation or, more concretely, where activity and taxation occur in different places.

Until fairly recently, a prime tax haven was Holland, a country sometimes perceived as having pushed its own taxation to the edge of socialism and beyond. What made Holland a tax haven was its extraordinary network of income tax treaties, allowing income from high-tax environments to flow through a Dutch-chartered entity without tax on its way to some low-tax environment bearing a more conventional resemblance to a tax haven.

You should note that a low-taxed foreign business undertaking is not per se a tax haven. A resort hotel and casino owned and operated by a foreign subsidiary of a U.S. corporation in the Cayman Islands (a place of pleasantly benign weather *and* taxation) is not considered a tax shelter. If, however, the income from a Miami hotel is taxed (or more accurately, barely taxed) in the Cayman Islands and not in the United States, *that* is a tax haven operation. And if the mechanism to that end is a Dutch corporation, then the tax haven is Holland.

An essential pattern in many international tax sheltering operations is "income shifting," which consists of arranging for income to be taxed in a country different from the one where it arose as an economic matter. The latter is typically a high-tax environment; the former, not so much. A common ingredient in income shifting is artificial pricing in transactions between related persons, a problem known generally as "transfer pricing." There is a battery of provisions in the U.S. tax system aimed at artificial transfer pricing in international transactions, further discussion of which must await later chapters.

Chapter 2

Nationality and Residence for Taxation

Nationality

Of the essential bases of U.S. taxation, nationality raises the fewest difficulties. U.S. nationality (or citizenship—they are the same thing) is a status defined in longstanding nationality laws. The U.S. tax system, rather than impose a standard of its own, takes nationality as a given.[1] Tax disputes turning on nationality are not particularly common but, when they do arise, require extensive forays outside pure tax law. In the vast majority of cases the nationality of individuals is beyond doubt. Equally clear are the tax consequences for an individual of U.S. nationality: the United States taxes the incomes of its citizens[2] from all sources worldwide, whether they reside in the United States or abroad.[3] The validity of worldwide taxation of U.S. citizens was upheld by the Supreme Court in Cook v Tait.[4] Thus, along with whatever protections and benefits it confers, U.S. citizenship brings worldwide income taxation with it as its price, a quid pro quo expressly invoked in Cook v. Tait as justifying worldwide taxation of U.S. citizens. The problems that do arise in connection with nationality are typically at the fringes, involving dual nationality and loss of citizenship.

---

[1]The Treasury Regulations under section 1 of the Code contain a brief statement on U.S. citizenship, which does little more than refer to other laws: "Who is a citizen. Every person born or naturalized in the United States and subject to its jurisdiction is a citizen. For other rules governing the acquisition of citizenship, see Chapters 1 and 2 of Title III of the Immigration and Nationality Act . . . . For rules governing loss of citizenship, see sections 349 to 357, inclusive, of such Act . . . . "

[2]I use the terms "national" and "citizen" (as in "U.S. national" or "U.S. citizen") more or less interchangeably in this book. In some contexts, "citizenship" may not be exactly congruent with "nationality." The former term describes relations of allegiance to a range of political bodies, including cities, states, and even supranational entities. The latter term is more narrowly limited to fealty with a nation-state.

[3]A departure from worldwide U.S. taxation is the annual exclusion from income allowed in §911 to Americans living and working overseas. See chapter 18.

[4]265 U.S. 47 (1924). You may have noticed that early federal tax cases are often captioned as though they were disputes between two individuals. Suits for refunds of invalid or excessive taxes were originally brought against the individual Collector of each Revenue District (in this case Tait, the Collector of the District of Maryland), and challenges to assessments (nowadays Tax Court cases) were brought against the individual Commissioner of Internal Revenue (who for a long time was Guy T. Helvering). Helvering, Eisner, Bowers, Tait, and others who haunt the early reported cases, were not compulsively litigious tax cranks, but tax officials of the United States.

International Taxation

The Residence of Individuals

Individual residents of the United States, regardless of nationality, are exposed to U.S. tax on their worldwide incomes. U.S. taxation of nonresident aliens, by contrast, is largely limited to income from sources in the United States. Residence is therefore the first and most important touchstone of U.S. taxation for foreign nationals.

"Residence," as the term implies, is a measure of the extent and permanence of an individual's presence in a given place. The notion of residence, which has bearing in many legal contexts, quite early took on its own flavor in taxation. Even within taxation, the notion of residence is now made up of several separate strands. There is no across-the-board definition of a "resident" in the Code applicable to all individuals and entities for all purposes.[5] Rather, the terms "resident" and "nonresident" are attached to various persons for various purposes, with the result that there are several standards of residence germane to U.S. international taxation. The most important, and pervasive, is the residence of foreign nationals, which frames the boundary between worldwide U.S. taxation (imposed on foreign nationals residing in the United States, known as "resident aliens") and source-based taxation (imposed on foreign nationals residing outside the United States, known as "nonresident aliens").

Of lesser, but significant effect is the residence of U.S. citizens. Even though they are taxed on their worldwide incomes, U.S. citizens who reside outside the United States enjoy favorable taxation of part of their income earned outside the United States.[6] A different standard of residence determines the exposure of foreign nationals to U.S. gift and estate taxes. Yet another standard of residence, in section 865, determines the source of gains from sales of personal property. There is, finally, a separate definition (in regulations) of the residence of a partnership. The precise ingredients of residence are somewhat different in each of these cases.

Residence Before the Enactment of Section 7701(b)

Residence is, and always has been, a question of fact at its core. For the first 70 years of the U.S. tax system the "residence" of an individual was a factual determination shaped by accumulated administrative action and judicial decision. The notion of residence prevailing in tax questions

---

[5]The word "residence" appears ubiquitously in the Code, not as a generic touchstone of tax status, but (often accompanied by the adjective "principal" or "single-family") to describe a dwelling in the physical sense. See, e.g., §121.

[6]See chapter 18.

18

was an amalgam of common law notions of "residence" and "domicile" drawn from outside the realm of taxation. Residence for income taxation was physical presence in a place with the intention of remaining there indefinitely or for a substantial period of time. At the core of this idea of residence was the inner fact of intention, which can be apprehended only through difficult and uncertain inferences from external facts.

Practical determinations of residence under this common law standard came to turn on a checklist of external indicia of residence, which also served as a set of dos and don'ts for foreign nationals seeking to avoid U.S. residence. Important touchstones included the length of the stay, dwelling arrangements in the United States and abroad, family ties in the United States, and civic and social activity. Even lesser indicia of residence, such as the location of bank accounts and the place of issuance of driver's licenses, were invoked in close cases. The factors bearing on residence were not of equal importance, as well you can imagine. Length of stay and maintenance of a dwelling in the United States were the most important indications of U.S. residence. The fact remained, however, that determinations of residence reflected a hodgepodge of observable facts accorded weight in no perfectly settled rank or priority.

Individuals can control many of the routine elements of daily life, often at the cost of little more than inconvenience. Taxpayers therefore generally held the upper hand under this standard of residence. Foreign nationals willing and able to observe a few constraints could spend considerable time in the United States without exposure to worldwide U.S. taxation.

Section 7701(b)

Case-by-case inquiry into the indicia of residence was supplanted for foreign nationals by a largely arithmetic statutory definition of a "resident alien" added to the Code in 1984 as section 7701(b). The definition of a "resident alien" in section 7701(b) on its face applies only to foreign nationals and therefore does not govern residence for U.S. citizens. Section 7701(b) does, however, apply to foreign nationals for all purposes of the Internal Revenue Code other than the estate and gift taxes (which follow a notion of residence substantially the same as "domicile" at common law). Foreign nationals are thus now subject to a single standard of residence for U.S. income taxes, social security, and unemployment taxes.

Section 7701(b) is quite fully articulated. It contains more words than the entire Income Tax Law of 1894. U.S. residence under section

7701(b) is explicitly tied to two largely objective elements: the immigration status of foreign nationals, and the amount of time they spend in the United States. Section 7701(b) is not, however, in all respects a bright-line provision. At its core is a zone of indeterminacy in which the residence of foreign nationals still depends on case-by-case factual determinations.

Immigration Status: Lawful Permanent Residence

First, a foreign national who is a "lawful permanent resident of the United States" during a calendar year is a resident of the United States in that year.[7] A lawful permanent resident, known colloquially as a "green card" holder, is an individual entitled to remain permanently in the United States in accordance with the immigration laws.[8] Immigration status and tax status are now explicitly allied, and no one admitted to the United States as a permanent resident can avoid tax residence, however little time he spends in the United States.

"Substantial Presence" in the United States

The second major test of residence (entirely independent of immigration status) is physical presence in the United States. A foreign national present in the United States for 183 or more days during a calendar year is a United States resident in that year.[9] The core idea of this 183-day rule is extremely simple: 183 days is more (by a few hours) than half of a year. A foreign national who is in the United States for that length of time during a year therefore establishes a more important (or at least lengthier) connection with the United States than with any other country in that year.

The 183-day rule is known in section 7701(b) as the "substantial presence" test. Viewed at closer range, the substantial presence test has two forms, which can be thought of as "strong" and "weak" forms of the test.

Actual Physical Presence

Under the strong form of the test, U.S. residence results from the actual physical presence of an individual in the United States for 183 days or more during a calendar year. Actual presence establishes United States residence for the calendar year, and (unless specific exceptions

---

[7]§7701(b)(1)(A)(i).
[8]§7701(b)(6).
[9]§7701(b)(3).

apply) this determination survives any showing of intention or of a stronger or more permanent connection to another country.[10] This form of the substantial presence test is a straightjacket provision under which residence in the United States follows automatically from physical presence of 183 days. A taxpayer's intentions regarding U.S. presence do not come into play. A foreign national serving a prison term in the United States, and wishing every minute that he were somewhere else, might nonetheless be a U.S. resident under this test.

Substantial Presence by Carryover of Days

If residence in the United States turned on nothing more than physical presence for 183 days in any given year, it would be relatively easy to work around this test. By spending 180 days in the United States for several years in a row, for example, a foreign individual could maintain a substantial permanent connection with the United States without ever becoming a U.S. resident. Similarly, a stay of 182 days at the end of one year followed by an equal stay at the beginning of the next would add up very nearly to one full year in the United States without establishing U.S. residence; a full calendar year in the United States preceded and followed by six-month stays would permit nearly two years to be spent in the United States with only one year of actual tax residence. With this much flexibility, the careful timing of gains and losses could significantly reduce the tax cost of U.S. residence.

A second strand of the substantial presence test extends U.S. residence in many such situations. This form of the substantial presence test takes into account not only time spent in the United States during the calendar year, but also days spent in the two preceding calendar years, which are added to days in the calendar year in measuring substantial presence. The effect is to include periods of protracted but less intense connection with the United States as periods of U.S. residence.

Days from the preceding two years are accorded less weight in arriving at the total than the days of the actual calendar year. Specifically, the tally of days spent in the United States (to be counted toward the 183) is determined as follows: 1) days from the current year are counted at their full value; 2) days from the first preceding calendar year are counted as 1/3 of a day; and 3) days from the second preceding calendar year are counted as 1/6 of a day.[11] The following illustration may help:

---

[10]§§7701(b)(1)(A)(ii), 7701(b)(3).
[11]§7701(b)(3)(A).

> A foreign national (who has never before been to the United States) spends 90 days in the United States in 2000, 150 days in the United States in 2001, and 120 days in the United States in 2002. In applying the substantial presence test, the individual is treated as having spent 180 days in the United States in year 2001 (the 150 days actually spent in 2001 plus 1/3 of the 90 days spent in 2000). Because this amount is less than 183, the individual is not a United States resident in 2001. In 2002 the individual is treated as having spent 185 days in the United States, consisting of the 120 days actually spent plus 1/3 of the 150 days spent in 2001 (or 50 days) and 1/6 of the 90 days spent in 2002 (or 15 days). [120 + 50 + 15 = 185.] Therefore the threshold requirement of the extended form of the substantial presence test is crossed in 2002.

Another way of looking at this test is that every day spent in the United States potentially contributes $1\frac{1}{2}$ days (i.e., 1 + 1/3 + 1/6) to the count of days used in measuring substantial presence over the succeeding years.

It follows that the greatest constant-level number of days that can be spent in the United States year in and year out without triggering United States residence is 121. Repeated annual stays of 121 days eventually become measured as $181\frac{1}{2}$ under this extended substantial presence test —still below 183.[12]

United States residence cannot, however, result entirely from days carried forward from earlier years. A minimum physical presence of at least 31 days in the United States is required before substantial presence is ever triggered.[13] Without this limitation, a year following two full years of U.S. presence would be a year of U.S. residence for someone who spent only a few minutes of January 1 in the United States.

Closer Connection and Tax Home in a Foreign Country

The upshot of this extended formulation of substantial presence is that an individual can spend fewer than 183 days in the United States in any given year, or even fewer than 180 days consistently over a period of years, and still be treated as a United States resident. This possibility is rendered less likely, however, by a qualification of the substantial presence test when it is met only by carryover of days. For individuals who meet substantial presence by carryover of days during a calendar year, but are actually present fewer than 183 days in the United States, the application of the 183-day test is not absolute. Under an

---

[12]On a ski lift in Aspen a few years ago I met a woman who expressed annoyance (in an accent that sounded somewhat indeterminately European—and rich) about her accountant's nagging reminders of the 121-day limit, which, if ignored, might cost her dearly in U.S. taxes and, if heeded, might cause her to miss some the year's best snow.

[13]§7701(b)(3)(A)(i).

"exception" provided in section 7701(b)(3)(B) an individual actually present in the United States on fewer than 183 days during a calendar year, despite an extended count of days exceeding 183, is not treated as a U.S. resident if it is established that for the year the individual 1) has a "tax home" in a foreign country and 2) has a "closer connection" to that foreign country than to the United States.

The overlay of such notions as "tax home" and "closer connection" necessarily reduces the certainty of this strand of the substantial presence test. There remains a numerical threshold, but for individuals physically present fewer than 183 days, substantial presence by carryover of days creates in effect a presumption of United States residence, which can be turned back by someone whose personal epicenter is demonstrably in another country. The determination of a "tax home" raises problems that in domestic tax litigation have bordered on the talmudic and have never been fully resolved.[14] For its part, the determination of the country to which an individual has a "closer connection" requires specific focus on that very individual, which in turn calls up many of the indicia of residence invoked under prior law. Sheer duration of stay is no longer an uncertain factor, to be sure, but all the others, including the place of principal residence, social, economic, and family ties, retain some force in this determination.

Exceptions

There are exceptions from the arithmetic of substantial presence for certain individuals, extending in favor of foreign nationals (diplomats and students, among others) whose presence in the United States, even if lengthy, does not generally imply permanence. Mechanically, these exceptions operate by excluding days spent in the United States with an exempted status from the days counted as presence in the United States.[15] Among the protected group are full-time diplomats and consular officials, teachers or trainees, and students.[16] Also excluded from the count are days spent in the United States by an individual unable to leave because of a medical condition that arose there.[17]

---

[14]The notion of a "tax home," incidentally, is imported into section 7701(b), with a detour through section 911, from section 162(a)(2), which allows (as you may remember from an introductory income tax course) the deduction of expenses incurred while traveling "away from home" in pursuit of a trade or business.

[15]§7701(b)(3)(D). A day in the United States with an exempt status also does not enter into the count of days carried forward as fractions under the weak form of substantial presence.

[16]§7701(b)(5)(A).

[17]§7701(b)(3)(D)(ii). Note that days in the United States *do* count for a foreigner who goes there expressly for medical treatment. Only foreigners who cannot *leave* on account of sudden illness are shielded by this exception.

There is a pitfall in these exceptions. A foreign national who holds an exempt status during part of a year is not thereby inoculated against U.S. residence for the year, but may become a U.S. resident in that year by spending enough days in the United States *without* the exempt status. Consider a full-time student who graduates on June 1 from a degree program. Graduation may well bring the exempt status to an end. If the student then stays on in the United States for business or pleasure until the end of the year (another 213 days), the count of substantial presence will be more than met.[18]

Entities, Associations, and Partnerships

In the U.S. tax system there is no feature of associations or entities (partnerships, corporations, and trusts) that corresponds exactly to the "nationality" or "residence" of individuals.[19] For most organizations, however, there is a place—or at least an identifiable legal environment—that establishes their existence and identity. For corporations, it is the place of incorporation (or "charter"). For partnerships, similarly, it is the place under the laws of which they arise. For trusts, it is the legal system in which they are acknowledged as such and which governs relations among grantors, fiduciaries, and beneficiaries. This place, which is sometimes called an entity's "situs," bears importantly on its taxation.

Corporations

In the Code the situs of corporations and partnerships is signaled by the terms "domestic" and "foreign." A "domestic" entity (which includes a partnership or a corporation) corporation is one "organized in the United States under the laws of the United States or of any State."[20] All other corporations and partnerships are "foreign."[21]

---

[18]Furthermore, U.S. residence so acquired may extend to the *entire* year, including the months with student status.

[19]Many foreign legal systems do have a notion of corporate "residence," identified variously with a corporation's seat of management or principal place of business. Entities classified differently in different legal systems are sometimes known as "dual resident corporations."

[20]§7701(a)(4). Colloquially, "domestic" corporations are often called "U.S. corporations," a usage I often follow here.

[21]It follows from these definitions that a corporation or partnership organized under both foreign and U.S. law (not a conceptual impossibility, at least for some corporations and most general partnerships) would be "domestic" but not "foreign."

The situs of a corporation has momentous tax consequences. A domestic corporation is subject to U.S. tax on its worldwide income; a foreign corporation only on income derived from U.S. investment or business. Because a corporation in the end is nothing more than a piece of paper with the official seal of a government conferring a separate legal status on a particular undertaking or body of assets, some commentators have questioned the formalism of having large tax consequences turn on which of several eligible sovereigns issues the document. But no other basis for taxing corporations—including the nationality of their beneficial owners or the principal place of their operations or management—meshes as simply with the U.S. system of worldwide taxation. Furthermore, a number of other elements of U.S. tax law have blunted the distinction between foreign and domestic corporations in various settings.[22]

Partnerships

While the situs of a partnership is defined similarly to that of a corporation, the actual determination of situs is more obscure. If a Frenchman and a Mexican agree to do business as partners in several states of the United States and provinces of Canada, under what law is the partnership "organized"? It is perhaps fortunate that the situs of partnerships usually matters little for tax purposes. Because partnerships are not themselves taxable entities—they are "fiscally transparent" in tax parlance—it is the nationality or residence of the individual partners that generally governs U.S. taxation of the partnership income.[23] There is also a vestigial notion in the U.S. tax system of the residence of a partnership apart from its status as domestic or foreign, which comes into play only in connection with the source rules for interest.[24]

Trusts

The situs of trusts flows from the definition of a "United States person" in section 7701(a)(30). A trust is a "United States person"(and hence subject to worldwide U.S. taxation) if 1) the trust is subject to the authority of a court within the United States *and* 2) the fiduciaries

---

[22]Among these are various "look-through" rules concerning the source of income, discussed in chapter 3, and the the special regime of taxation of U.S. shareholders of controlled foreign corporations and foreign personal holding companies, discussed in chapter 15.

[23]One situation where the situs of partnerships does matter is in withholding. Withholding of U.S. tax is required from payments of income to foreign, but not domestic, partnerships.

[24]See chapter 3; Reg. §301.7701-5.

in control of the trust are United States persons. All other trusts are foreign trusts. A foreign trust escapes U.S. taxation on its non-U.S. income. U.S. beneficiaries of foreign trusts, however, are ultimately subject to full U.S. taxation on any trust income from which they benefit.

The Source of Income

Source in General

The concept of source of income is essential mortar—if not the keystone—in the U.S. system of international taxation. The source of income bears centrally on the taxation of both foreign and U.S. persons. With a few narrow exceptions, foreign persons are subject to U.S. tax only on their income from sources within the United States. For U.S. persons, the source of income shapes the contours of U.S. taxation by setting limits on the foreign tax credit.

The "source" of income is not a self-defining notion. There is no immutable, metaphysically correct notion of source of income. Within broad limits, national tax systems frame the source of income according to the desired reach of their taxing power. Nonetheless, the association of income with a place as its "source" generally does rest on some actual connection between the place and the income. And while there is no universal touchstone of that connection, there are recurrent patterns in the source of income. The developed countries, and in particular the United States, tend to associate the source of income with the economic activity giving rise to it. The source of compensation for services, for example, is the place the services are performed. A limitation on this principle is that the relation between economic activity and resulting income may be diffuse. Royalties for the use of intellectual property, for example, can reasonably be attributed both to the effort and investment of creating it and to its day-to-day uses in the production of income. When matching income with economic activity is difficult, as with interest income, other elements—such as the place of residence of the person paying or receiving the income—have come to serve as proxies for its economic center of gravity. Some tax systems (usually in countries that are heavy importers of capital) engage in no dissection of the economic origins of income, but simply ask from whose pocket it was paid. In their view the source of income is the source of its payment.[1] None of these notions of source is followed with unyielding consistency. And of course the source rules must also (and do to a considerable extent) reflect the practical possibilities of collection of tax.

The term "source" of income made its first statutory appearance in the ill-fated 1894 Act, where it served as shorthand for the property or business activity from which income was derived. It soon became

---

[1] The U.S. tax system itself follows this approach in determining the source of some scholarship and fellowship grants. See Reg. §1.863-1(d).

apparent that the source of a given item of income cannot be derived with certainty from broadly stated general principles. By 1921, the tax laws contained a detailed schedule of source rules for income of the most common types. Today extensive rules of source of income are collected in sections 861-863 and 865; many other provisions affecting specific questions of source are widely scattered in the Code.

Skim through Code sections 861 through 865. Even a quick perusal of the source rules reveals how elaborate they have become. There are separate source rules for interest, dividends, rents and royalties, compensation for services, gains from sales of property, and many other items. The rules further separate items of income into those with a single source and those with multiple sources (such as income from compound processes of production and sale). Questions of source are further articulated (indeed excruciatingly so) in sprawling regulations on the allocation and apportionment of deductible expense.

Income from a Single Source

The core provisions on source in the Code, sections 861 and 862, enumerate several classes of income and assign them a source. The enumeration in these sections deals mainly with items of income that can readily be classified as belonging to a single type (such as interest, dividends, or royalties), and that have their source entirely within or without the United States.

Interest Income

As a general rule, interest paid by individuals, partnerships, and trusts takes its source from their place of residence, while interest paid by corporations has its source in the place of incorporation.[2] Thus interest paid by individuals, partnerships, and trusts that are "residents" of the United States has U.S. source, as does interest paid by domestic corporations. This rule is a proxy (and a rough one at best) for a matching of interest with the activity that generates the income from which it is paid.

In particular, the rule placing the source of interest paid by an individual in the individual's place of residence doubtless reflects the broad expectation that a borrower is most likely to put borrowed money to work where he resides and pay the interest from funds available at that

---

[2] §§861(a)(1), 862(a)(1).

place. This is by no means the only rule one could imagine. Interest could, for example, derive its source from a tracing of the proceeds of borrowing to their actual place of use. Such a tracing rule would not necessarily be more accurate, however. Money and credit are for the most part fungible and a borrower's ultimate borrowing capacity probably depends as much on the extent and location of his assets overall as on the use to be made of a specific borrowing. It is therefore entirely tenable to treat the residence of an individual payor of interest as the locus of his "credit." Although reasonable, this source rule does have consequences that both borrowers and lenders will occasionally find somewhat startling. For example, a foreign bank lending to a U.S. resident may receive U.S.-source interest, even if the loan is initiated outside the United States and finances operations entirely outside the United States.

There is both difficulty and opportunity in the day-to-day operation of this source rule. A threshold problem is determining the residence of the payor of interest, which may be anything but apparent to a lender of money whose dealings with the borrower are limited. The residence of *foreign* individuals is governed by a set of explicit tests codified in section 7701(b). These tests, as you may remember from chapter 2, are tied to immigration status or length of time spent in the United States. Both elements may not only be difficult for a lender to ascertain but may change from year to year. While there is no express statutory standard of residence for *U.S.* citizens, the Treasury also follows the tests of section 7701(b) in determining the source of interest that they pay.

Marcel's U.S. Venture

Once past the question of residence, the source rule for interest paid by individuals can produce surprisingly gratifying results. Because interest paid by *nonresident* individuals has *foreign* source no matter how intense or farflung their economic activity in the United States,[3] interest deductions on what is essentially self-owed debt can shield U.S. business income from taxation. Suppose for example that Marcel, a citizen and resident of Fredonia, has the opportunity to acquire for $1 million a U.S. business producing $150,000 of income per year. If Marcel simply buys the U.S. business directly with his own funds, the annual income of $150,000 will attract U.S. income tax of roughly $45,000. Instead, Marcel borrows $800,000 of the purchase price at 12 percent interest from a foreign corporation of which he owns all the

[3]This assumes, of course, that their presence in the United States does not push them past the threshold of U.S. residence.

stock and to which he has previously transferred the funds as a contribution to capital, securing the loan from the corporation with the U.S. business assets. The pattern in outline is the following:

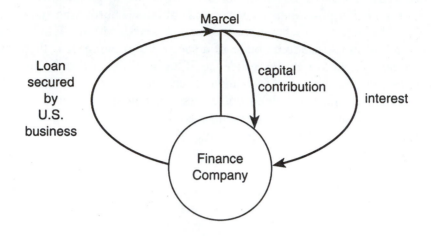

Under the source rules, the interest Marcel pays to his foreign corporation has *foreign* source. As such it is not exposed to U.S. taxation in the hands of its recipient (Marcel's wholly-owned foreign corporation) unless it is attributable to the *recipient's* U.S. business. Marcel's foreign corporation, however (unlike Marcel), is not itself engaged in a U.S. business. Merely holding debt secured by property in the United States does not of itself constitute a U.S. business.[4] Marcel's payments of interest, on the other hand, *are* deductible from the income derived by Marcel from the U.S. business.[5] With annual interest deductions of $96,000 (12 percent of $800,000) Marcel's taxable income from the U.S. business is reduced from $150,000 to $54,000, and Marcel's U.S. income tax from roughly $45,000 to roughly $13,000. This is a strikingly good result for an exercise that entails little more than a day or two's paperwork.[6]

---

[4]Even if the corporation did have a U.S. business, the *foreign*-source interest it received from Marcel would still not be subject to U.S. tax unless derived from the activities of a U.S. *office*.

[5]Under the Regulations on interest allocation, "interest expense incurred by a nonresident alien shall be considered to be connected with income effectively connected with a United States trade or business . . . to the extent that interest expense is incurred with respect to liabilities that [are] secured by assets that generate such effectively connected income." Reg. §1.861-9T(d)(2)(i).

[6]I mean by this the time and effort of forming the foreign corporation and documenting the various loans and security interests.

But why stop there? It may seem that Marcel could eradicate *all* U.S. taxable income by borrowing the full purchase price of $1 million at *15* percent interest from his foreign finance company. This, however, would be costly overreaching. First, the rate of interest charged on loans between related persons is subject to revision by the Revenue Service if it departs from arm's length standards. Second, the allowable interest deduction in such patterns is limited, under Regulations on the allocation of expenses to U.S.-source income, to interest on debt not exceeding 80 percent of the assets of the U.S. business paying the interest.[7]

Earnings-Stripping Tax Shelters   A notable consequence here of the source rule for interest (which, please remember, extends only to interest paid by individuals) is the reduction of U.S. taxable income by the deduction of interest paid by Marcel that is at the same time excluded from U.S. taxation in the hands of its immediate recipient, a person related to Marcel. This maneuver is known in the tax lexicon as "interest-stripping" or "earnings-stripping" because taxable income is stripped away from the U.S. tax environment by interest deductions. The reader should study and thoroughly understand this pattern built around a simple source rule. It contains the essential element of all international tax-haven operations: the deflection of deductions that reduce a stream of income otherwise subject to substantial taxation to an environment where they are less heavily taxed, while remaining under the same beneficial ownership.

If you have some experience in taxation (or have taken a tax course or two), this pattern may leave you faintly uneasy. There are decided cases, such as *Gregory*[8] and *Aiken*,[9] with which the Revenue Service might question the reality and business purpose of the foreign corporation interposed by Marcel to channel funds to his U.S. venture. The pattern is surprising resilient against attack, however. Marcel's corporation is neither transitory nor a pure conduit. It has permanent assets and owns and retains the interest it receives from Marcel. The structure can be strengthened against attack by enlarging the range of economic activity of Marcel's foreign corporation. If it engaged in business or invested elsewhere in the world, financed other projects of Marcel's, lent to venturers other than Marcel, borrowed from other sources, and above all had other owners besides Marcel, it could not even plausibly be set aside as a conduit.

---

[7]"Interest . . . is not considered to be connected with effectively connected income to the extent that it is incurred with respect to liabilities that exceed 80 percent of the gross assets of the United States trade or business." Reg. §1.861-9T(d)(2)(ii)(A).
[8]Gregory v. Helvering, 293 U.S. 465 (1935).
[9]Aiken Industries v. Commissioner, 56 T.C. 925 (1971).

International Taxation

For Marcel the simple rule for the source of interest has become an international tax shelter. I don't mean to overstate, however, the allure of Marcel's earnings-stripping plan. It only works for U.S. business operations directly owned by foreign individuals. Marcel's acquisition of the U.S. business through a corporation, U.S.-chartered or foreign, would be fatal to the tax shelter. As you will see below, interest paid by a domestic or foreign corporation has U.S. source if attributable to the operations of a U.S. business.[10] Marcel must therefore trade the tax benefits for the advantages of the corporate form, consisting of limited liability, anonymity, and insulation from U.S. transfer tax. Marcel's plan is limited in practice to small and medium-sized businesses that lend themselves to individual or family ownership.[11] The plan cannot be used for a petrochemical plant or automobile assembly line. The opportunities for earnings-stripping through elaborate offshore structures built on tax treaties and tax havens have become so sharply constrained in recent years by counterattacks from Washington, however, that tax averse-foreign persons may begin to look longingly at Marcel's simple plan.[12] We shall revisit this earnings-stripping pattern at the very end of this book, after considering far more elaborate types of international tax shelters.

Foreign Taxes The analysis thus far deals only with U.S. taxation. For Marcel's tax shelter to work, both the U.S. and Fredonian systems must permit it. What the United States offers is the particular source rule that allows escape of some business profits from the U.S. tax environment as deductible interest. If Fredonia (Marcel's country of residence) imposes low or no income tax, U.S. tax is the only concern. The source rule by itself is all that is needed is to defeat the Scylla of U.S. taxation. If Fredonia is a high-tax country, though, then Marcel still has to avoid Charybdis. The plan will avail little unless by chartering his finance company in a low-tax environment Marcel can keep its income beyond the reach of Fredonian taxation. The Fredonian system therefore must respect the separate, untaxed, status of Marcel's finance company and not subject its income to current taxation in Marcel's hands. In other words, when Fredonia is a high-tax environment, the structure works only if Fredonia does not reach or look through foreign-chartered entities owned by Fredonian persons. This raises another

---

[10] For reasons discussed in chapter 5, interest paid to Marcel or to his wholly-owned foreign finance corporation also would not be exempt "portfolio interest."

[11] And with a family-owned business, you have to watch for the creation of a partnership.

[12] The recently adopted "check-the-box" rules on the tax character of entities, furthermore, has enlarged the range of forms that Marcel's tax-favored investment ownership of a U.S. business can take. See chapters 10, 24.

problem in international tax haven operations: the extent to which national income tax systems look through separately chartered entities owned by persons subject to their taxation. You will remember from chapter 1 that when Fredonia respects the formal separate identity of the foreign finance company, the resulting tax regime is known as "deferral."[13]

The deduction of interest expense from a stream of business income otherwise subject to U.S. taxation is the active ingredient in virtually all international tax haven operations. The other leg of the haven is the deflection of the interest, free of further U.S. tax, to some benign low-tax environment. Notice that if Marcel has borrowed the capital used in Fredonia, he may get a double dip, i.e., deductions in both the United States and Fredonia against high-taxed income, with an offshore build-up of untaxed income in between.

If you get to the bottom of this pattern and understand exactly what makes it tick, you will have the U.S. system of inbound taxation in your pocket.

The 80-percent Rule

In an exception to the general source rule, known as the 80-percent rule, interest received from an alien *resident* individual or from a *domestic* corporation has *foreign* source nonetheless if 80 percent or more of the payor's gross income during the three years preceding the year of payment was itself "active foreign business income."[14] "Active foreign business income" is foreign source income attributable to the active conduct of a trade or business outside the United States.[15] A domestic corporation meeting the 80-percent foreign business requirement is commonly known as an "80/20 company," even if foreign business accounts for more than 80 percent of its income.[16]

U.S. branch Interest of Foreign Corporations

Under the general rule of section 861(a)(1), interest paid by a foreign corporation has foreign source. Under section 884(f)(1), however, "[i]n the case of a foreign corporation engaged in a trade or

---

[13]Deferral would not be available to a *U.S.* person in Marcel's situation (so don't get any ideas) because the U.S. tax system looks through offshore tax haven companies and taxes their passive investment income to their U.S. shareholders. See chapter 15.

[14]§§861(a)(1)(A), 861(c).

[15]§861(c)(1)(B).

[16]In determining the status of a corporation as an 80/20 company, the operations and income of its own controlled subsidiaries are taken into account. Id.

business in the United States ... any interest paid by such trade or business in the United States shall be treated as if it were paid by a domestic corporation ... ." Put more simply, interest paid by a U.S. branch business of a foreign corporation has U.S. source. Such interest is known as "branch interest." The branch interest rule treats a U.S. branch more or less as though it were a separately chartered U.S. corporation.[17]

The 80-percent rule and the branch interest rule are known as "look-through" rules, because they look through the formal place of charter of a corporation (which normally governs the source of interest that it pays) to its underlying operations. Look-through rules serve, among other ends, to counter somewhat the arbitrariness of corporate situs. Viewed at closer range, the 80-percent rule and the branch interest rule cut in nearly opposite directions. The former softens the inflexibility of the source rule, while the latter closes off an easy escape from U.S. taxation. These and other look-through rules have in basic respects weakened the separate identity of corporations. There are so many look-through rules for so many purposes in the Code that you will eventually know where to expect them.

The Source of Dividends

In its basic statement the source rule for dividends is both simple and intuitive: the source of dividends is the place of incorporation of the corporation that pays them. Thus U.S. corporations generally pay U.S.-source dividends and foreign corporations pay foreign source dividends. As with interest, the source rule for dividends is modified by a look-through rule.

The 25-Percent Rule

If more than 25 percent of a foreign corporation's gross income is "effectively connected"[18] with a U.S. trade or business, then the dividends it pays have *U.S.* source in the same proportion that its

---

[17]This raises an intriguing possibility. Suppose a foreign corporation with a U.S. branch business would be an 80/20 company if it were U.S.-chartered (because, for example, its U.S. branch is small in relation to its worldwide business operations, which generate more than 80 percent of its income). Is the branch interest now foreign source interest paid by an 80/20 company? Literally, section 884(f)(1)(A) should have that effect. Treasury Regulations under section 884(f), however, brush the possibility aside. Reg. §1.884-4(a)(1).

[18]"Effectively connected" income is discussed in chapter 7.

effectively connected income bears to its total income.[19] Put more simply, if more than 25 percent of a foreign corporation's income consists of U.S. business profits, dividends paid by the corporation have U.S. source to the extent of those business profits.[20] Thus if half of the income of a foreign corporation consists of U.S business profits, 50 cents of every dollar it pays in dividends has U.S. source. This rule, known as the "25 percent rule," looks through the formal place of charter of a corporation to its underlying operations and income, and assigns source to its dividends accordingly. The entity in a sense becomes transparent. Were it not for the 25-percent rule (and similar look-through rules generally) the formality of the place of charter would govern the entire international tax consequences of corporate operations.

The 25-percent rule has an important corollary. During much of the history of the U.S. income tax the 25-percent rule, by assigning U.S. source to some part of dividends paid by foreign corporations, could trigger U.S. tax on those dividends even when paid to their *foreign* shareholders. The resulting tax was known as the "second tax on dividends." The second tax was hard to enforce, given that the event triggering it was a transfer to foreign persons that might be made entirely outside the United States. It was often toned down or called off altogether by income tax treaties of the United States with other countries. It was nonetheless a major concern of foreign investors in the United States.

Today the second tax has faded into insignificance, having been almost entirely supplanted by the branch profits tax of section 884, introduced in 1986, which also imposes a second layer of U.S. tax on U.S. business profits of foreign corporations.[21] The branch profits tax is imposed more uniformly, however, and is easier to enforce. There is more on the branch profits tax in chapter 9.

Constitutional Interlude

The second tax on dividends was the occasion for the courts to consider the constitutional boundaries of the U.S. taxing power when applied to foreign persons. In two cases before the Board of Tax Appeals (the predecessor of today's Tax Court) foreign taxpayers urged that the second tax on dividends could not constitutionally be imposed on them. For want of a better place, I discuss these cases briefly here.

---

[19] Section 861(a)(2)(B).

[20] Below the 25-percent threshold, however, no part of the dividends paid by a foreign corporation has U.S. source.

[21] See chapter 9.

In Lord Forres v. Commissioner,[22] the IRS had sought to tax dividends paid by a U.K.-chartered corporation to a shareholder, Lord Forres, who was a U.K. citizen and resident. The dividends were paid from U.S. business profits of the U.K. corporation, the entire operations of which were in the United States. Forres put up several constitutional objections, among them that the tax reached so far beyond the territory of the United States as to deny him due process of law. It may not immediately strike you how, if at all, due process of law is implicated in this pattern. Forres was invoking a doctrine you may have encountered in a civil procedure course to the effect that the that a government cannot validly exercise "jurisdiction" over property and persons outside its territory. The argument went nowhere. The U.S. courts had power beyond question over assets in the United States beneficially owned by the taxpayer. The U.K. corporation's earnings were derived from a U.S. business and the dividends were paid entirely from those earnings. Given that, it was neither unreasonable nor unfair (and hence not "undue" in the constitutional sense) to assign the dividends U.S. source,[23] with the consequence of extending the U.S. taxing power to a foreign citizen and resident who received them.[24]

In a later case presenting a slightly different pattern, Ross v. Commissioner,[25] the taxpayer was a citizen and resident of Canada who owned the shares of a Canadian holding company, which in turn owned shares of stock of several U.S. corporations. Under the source rules in effect at the time, the dividends Ross received from the Canadian corporation had U.S. source[26] and were subject to U.S. income tax. The imposition of U.S. tax on dividends received by Ross from the Canadian company was upheld as constitutional, even though the Canadian company had no activity in the United States and quite possibly Ross had never set foot there.

---

[22] 27 B.T.A. 154 (1932).

[23] That is the effect of the 25-percent rule, remember.

[24] It further weakened Forres' position that a U.S. corporation doing business in the U.K. would itself have been treated as the time as a *U.K.*-resident corporation and would have paid *U.K.*-source dividends to a U.S. shareholder. If the United States simply followed the U.K. rule of corporate residence (which is also the worldwide norm) Forres's corporation would have been a U.S.-resident corporation in the first place.

[25] 44 B.T.A. 1 (1941).

[26] Under older source rules dividends paid by foreign corporations had U.S. source to the extent paid from *any* U.S.-source earnings. Today, under the 25-percent rule discussed above, dividends paid by foreign corporations have U.S. source only to the extent paid from U.S. business profits, not U.S.-source income generally. Since the dividends received from U.S. corporations by Ross's Canadian holding company were not business profits, but passive investment income, the subsequent dividends paid to Ross by the Canadian company would now have entirely *foreign* source.

Ross's holdings were as follows:

Ross

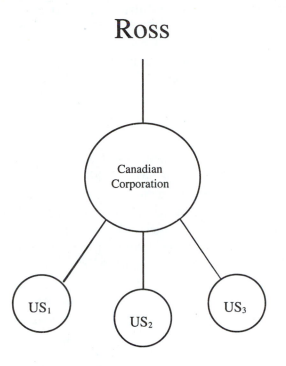

For Ross the outcome of the case was a severe and dismal result. The earnings of the U.S. corporations had undoubtedly been subject to U.S. corporate income tax. The dividends received from them by Ross's Canadian holding company had U.S. source and were accordingly subject to U.S. tax in the Canadian company's hands. The U.S. tax imposed on the dividends paid by the Canadian corporation to Ross individually was therefore the *third* layer of U.S. taxation on the underlying earnings. But *Ross* was not a case about what was sensible or humane. While acknowledging the severity of the result, the court thought the case governed by *Lord Forres*. The dividends received by Ross were derived from assets in the United States beneficially owned by him. For this reason the income was related to the United States in a significant way and, equally important, the tax was ultimately collectible. That Ross could have chosen a more tax-efficient form of ownership of U.S. assets did not make the tax unconstitutional.[27]

Lord Forres and *Ross* suggest that there is little constitutional constraint on the power of the United States to tax the incomes of

---

[27]A spirited dissenting opinion in *Ross* dwells emphatically, but ultimately unpersuasively, on the unfair burden of the U.S. tax.

foreign persons.[28] Note, however, that for a number of reasons—among them a concern not to create self-defeating obstacles to foreign investment—the United States does not press this power anywhere near to the limit. The tax upheld in *Ross* has long since been repealed by Congress, and today passive foreign investors in the United States generally face a benign tax regime.

Source of Income from Services

The source of income from personal services is the place where the services are performed.[29] Taken in broad overview this source rule is readily fathomable. Compensation for labor or personal services performed in the United States has U.S. source; compensation for other services has foreign source. The rule is also reasonable. Added value from services generally arises in the vicinity of their performance. In its specific application, though, there are some difficulties.

Before venturing into those difficulties, I should mention the "90-day" exception to the source rule. Compensation for services by a foreign individual present in the United States for 90 days or less during the taxable year has *foreign* source if 1) the services are performed for a foreign person not engaged in business in the United States and 2) if the total compensation for the services is $3,000 or less.[30] Sometimes known as the "commercial traveler exception," this exception is designed to enable foreign individuals to make short business or professional trips to the United States without U.S. tax consequence. The $3,000 limit, while perhaps adequate to this end when first introduced in 1936, has faded into insignificance through inflation. Few engineers, accountants, executives, or even traveling salesmen, would find shelter under this provision if they spent more than a few weeks in the United States. As a practical matter, the statutory rule has been supplanted by more accommodating provisions in income tax treaties between the United States and the countries of origin of many business travelers.

With the 90-day exception out of the way, a specific difficulty in applying the source rule is matching compensation with services

---

[28]There are acknowledged constitutional limitations on the power of the individual states to tax other states and their citizens. These limitations, however, arise in the interest of harmony among the several elements making up the American nation, and are not germane to the taxation of foreigners by the United States itself. See United States v. Bennett, 232 U.S. 299, 306 (1914) (the limitation on the taxing power of the states "has no application to the Government of the United States so far as its admitted taxing power is concerned.").

[29]§861(a)(3).

[30]§861(a)(3).

performed in different places. If services are performed only in the United States, or if compensation is expressly earmarked for identifiable services performed in the United States, then source is straightforward.[31] Often, however, an individual or firm receives an aggregate of compensation for services performed in a number of places, among which is the United States. A business executive, for example, may work all over the world for a package of salary and stock options that are not explicitly allocated to services in different locations. It may seem obvious to assign source to compensation in such a case according to time spent in different places, but following through with this idea can be tricky. First, you must record or remember how much time is spent where. Second, the nature and intensity of work done may differ in different places. Should the U.S.-source component of the compensation be determined by the total time spent in the United States during the year taken as a percentage of the entire year, or by a comparison only of the number of actual days of work inside and outside the United States, or on some other basis entirely? A three-day round-the-clock merger negotiation in New York, as an economic matter, likely accounts for more of a corporate lawyer's compensation than a three-day weekend in Bermuda cradling a brief business meeting. The 90-day rule resolves only a tiny fraction of these situations for foreign taxpayers and none for U.S. persons.

This type of source problem has recurrently afflicted professional athletes, especially players in the National Hockey League, which has teams distributed widely in the United States and Canada. Athletes paid by the year have to figure out what part of their salaries have what source. Depending on how they do this, the part of any salary attributable to the offseason might have a different source from the part attributable to playing games. Add training camp, possible playoff games, and occasional postseason exhibitions into the mix, not to mention sign-on bonuses and the like for rookie players, and the question of source can turn downright messy. It may come as no surprise, therefore, that the source of the compensation of NHL players has devolved into a saga of perennial litigation. There are rulings and an Augean series of cases (over 200 docketed in U.S. courts in the 1970s, some of which are still wending their way through appeals) on questions

---

[31]Fortunately, it is rarely if ever necessary to make particularized allocations of compensation for services to sources within *different foreign* countries. Compensation need only be assigned U.S. or foreign source. For most foreign persons, therefore, the important question is how much compensation has U.S. source. For a U.S. person, the proportion of foreign source income is usually all that matters.

of source of income concerning 1) Canadian players who want to minimize their U.S.-source income exposed to U.S. tax and 2) U.S. players who want to maximize their foreign source earned income.

Matching compensation with services is even more difficult when the services are performed through groups or associations of individuals (such as partnerships) or by firms whose employees engage in different tasks and receive widely varying compensation. Under well-established notions of agency firms are deemed to "perform" services through their employees or agents. The source of the resulting income—the place of performance—is therefore the place where the corporation's employees or agents perform the services. But while an employer can reasonably be treated as spending time in a place through the presence there of employees, the length of time spent by employees in performing services in a place is not a self-evident basis for assigning source.[32] Activities in some places might produce more income than in others, especially if different types of work or projects are involved. Even within a single project, more productive activity might well be reflected in higher compensation for some employees. Therefore the source of the services income of a firm with farflung operations could plausibly be assigned according to the payroll costs incurred by the firm in different places, rather than a pure "time" basis, so that a firm engaged in performing services both in and out of the United States would have U.S.-source service income in proportion to its payroll costs in the United States.

The Treasury Regulations on source once determined the source of income from services, both for individuals and firms, entirely on the "time" basis, that is, the number of working days spent in different places. The Service then had the sorry experience of attacking its own regulations, unsuccessfully, in a case where allocation solely by time was favorable to the taxpayer.[33] In the Regulations currently in effect, the source of income from services performed both in and out of the United States "shall be determined on the basis that most correctly reflects the proper source of income under the facts and circumstances of the particular case," with the further provision that "in many cases" the facts will make apportionment "on the time basis ... acceptable ... ."[34]

---

[32]Note that the question here is not the source of *employees'* income received for the services—that can often be assigned a source according to time *they* spend in different places—but the income of the *employer* derived from the employees' efforts.

[33]Tipton & Kalmbach v. United States, 480 F.2d 1118 (10th Cir. 1973).

[34]Reg. §1.861-4(b)(1).

Source of Rentals and Royalties

Under section 864(a)(4) "rentals and royalties from property located in the United States" have U.S. source. An immediate corollary is that rentals and royalties from property outside the United States have foreign source. This rule applies to all classes of property—real, personal, tangible, intangible—and embraces income from the full range of transfers of the use of property, including leases, licenses, rentals, bailments, and the like. Thus lease payments for an equipment rental in the United States have U.S. source, as do film rentals from the distribution of a motion picture in the United States and royalties from the use of a patent in U.S. manufacturing operations.

The location of tangible property—real or personal—is generally straightforward. So, therefore, is the source of rentals and royalties for its use. Real property is where it is, and rents from buildings or land and royalties from mineral resources take their source unambiguously from the location of the property. Most tangible personal property is similarly easy to locate. When property is used both in and out of the United States, an allocation of source is made according to the amount of time the property is used in different places, unless different rental rates can clearly be associated with different locations.

The location of intangible property is more elusive. Unlike tangible property, it is not confined to one place at a time. Where it is located is in fact more a metaphysical than a physical question. Reflecting this uncertainty, section 861(a)(4) extends U.S. source to income "for the use of or for the privilege of using" intangible property in the United States. The source of income from intellectual property thus depends on where it is used. While the place of use of intangible property may be more fathomable than the abstract notion of its location, that place too is far from self-evident. This may explain the further extension of U.S. source in section 864(a)(4) to income from the "privilege" of using intangible property in the United States. Reflecting the different ways in which intangible property contributes to income, this provision may imply U.S. source for income from rights in property that are not literally "used" in the United States. For example, the writer of a play produced in the United States might license the U.S. film rights in the work to the producer of the play for the duration of its theater run to protect the play from competition in other media. Royalties from this license of film rights, even if they were measured by the use of the literary property as a play and no film were actually created or used in the United States,[35] would have U.S. source.

Gains from Sales of Property

The source of gains from sales of property is harder to wrap into a single formula than other source rules. This is so in large part because the term "sale" is a rubric covering a range of economic activity. Some sales entail only transfer of ownership, perhaps anonymously, while others imply an extended economic relationship between seller and buyer in which various types of added value may arise. For many years, the source rules themselves made no distinctions between any classes of sales, and treated the sale of a gold bar where title passed on delivery in New York in the same manner as door-to-door sales in New York of imported cosmetics.[36]

Real Property

The simplest source rule is for gains from the sale of real property. The gains have their source where the property is located, usually a matter beyond doubt. Until 1980, this rule as stated in Code section 861(a)(5) assigned U.S. source to gains "from the sale or exchange of real property located in the United States." Because the rule was framed in terms of sales of the actual property, it did not then reach many transfers of interests in real property held in a form other than direct ownership. For example, a sale of shares of a corporation owning real property in the United States produced gain subject to the source rule for sales of stock, a form of *personal* property. Such relatively simple devices as incorporation once permitted transfers of U.S. real estate with no resulting U.S.-source income.

Today section 861(a)(5) assigns U.S. source to all "gains, profits, and income from the disposition of a United States real property interest." A "United States real property interest" is a term of art, defined (in section 897(c)) to include, along with all directly owned real property, holdings of stock in *domestic* corporations with substantial holdings of U.S. real property. Section 861(a)(5) therefore reaches gains

---

[35]You might also think of this as a defensive "use" of the film rights to protect the income stream from the stage rights.

[36]Both types of sale originally gave rise to U.S.-source income. Where the U.S. tax system treated these undertakings differently was in their classification as a "trade or business," which brought them under correspondingly different tax regimes. See chapter 6.

from sales of shares in certain U.S. corporations along with gains from sales of actual real estate.[37]

Personal Property

For nearly 70 years, the Code contained a single short statement on the source of gains from the sale of personal property. Section 861(a)(6) assigned U.S. source to "gains, profits, and income derived from the purchase of personal property without the United States . . . and its sale or exchange within the United States."[38] This is known as the "place of sale" rule because it assigns U.S. source to property sold in the United States, even if purchased outside. Section 861(a)(6) is still in the Code, although it applies today only to sales of *inventory*.

Sales of all other types of property are now governed by section 865, which was added by the 1986 Act and is as discursive as the prior rule was laconic. Section 865(a) states the general rule that:

> [I]ncome from the sale of personal property—
> (1) by a United States resident shall be sourced in the United States, or
> (2) by a nonresident shall be sourced outside the United States.

The basic principle here is that gains from sales of personal property take their source from the place of "residence" of the seller. The quotation marks around the term "residence" are not an attempt on my part to be cute. A "resident" is a specially defined notion in section 865 for purposes of this source rule. Section 865(g) defines a "United States resident" individual as 1) any U.S. citizen or resident alien with no "tax home" outside the United States,[39] or 2) any nonresident alien with a "tax home" *in* the United States. A "tax home" entails either a substantial residential or business presence in a given place. The "residence" of an individual for this purpose is thus akin to an economic center of gravity. Within this definition a *resident* alien individual (as defined in section 7701(b)) can be a *nonresident* for purposes of the source rule of Section 865, by maintaining a "tax home" outside the United States while a nonresident alien can be a "resident" within section 865, by having a U.S. "tax home."[40]

---

[37]Note that section 861(a)(5) does not affect the source of gains from sales of shares of *foreign* corporations holding U.S. real estate.

[38]I.R.C. §861(a)(6) (1986).

[39]§865(g)(1)(A)(i).

[40]Also, U.S. citizens and resident aliens are not treated as nonresidents with respect to any sale of personal property unless they pay to a foreign country an income tax

An immediate—and notable—consequence of section 865(a) is that most sales by foreign persons of stock, securities, or commodities held as investments, even if made on U.S. securities or commodities exchanges, generate *foreign* source income. This effect is of central importance in the taxation of passive investment of foreign persons in the United States.

Sales of Inventory

The most important aspect of section 865 is what it does not do. "Inventory property," is excluded from its reach by section 865(b), which defers to the source rule of section 861(a)(6). Section 861(a)(6) in turn assigns U.S. source to "gains, profits, and income derived from the purchase of inventory property ... without the United States ... and its sale or exchange within the United States."[41] For inventory the old "place of sale" rule therefore survives. Until the 1986 Act, as noted above, this was the universal source rule for all gains from sales of personal property. Now, by virtue of the addition of the word "inventory," it is the source rule only for sales of inventory. The latter, however, are not only by far the largest class of sales, but outweigh all others combined in economic importance.

Section 861(a)(6) governs only income from the purchase *and* sale of inventory. It deals with pure selling (retail and wholesale distribution and marketing) as opposed to selling that arises as the culmination of some other economic activity, such as manufacturing or processing. On its face, section 861(a)(6) applies only to gains from the sale *within* the United States of property purchased *outside* the United States.[42] Other combinations of purchase and sale are obviously possible. Although section 861(a)(6) does not literally say so, gains from the purchase and sale of inventory entirely inside the United States also have U.S. source, and conversely gains from the purchase and sale of inventory entirely outside the United States have foreign source. Section 861(a)(6) must be understood, in short, to fix the source of gains in the place of sale without regard for the place of purchase.

---

equal to at least 10 percent of the gain derived from the sale. §865(g)(2). Therefore U.S. persons derive U.S.-source gains from sales of property in tax havens, regardless of their economic center of gravity.

[41]"Inventory property" is broadly defined to include stock in trade and any other property held for sale to customers in the ordinary course of business. §§861(a)(6), 865(i)(1), 1221(1).

[42]The corresponding provision of §862(a)(6) assigns foreign source to gains from the purchase of inventory property inside the United States for sale outside the United States.

The Place of Sale—Passage of Title

What brings a sale "within" the United States, as opposed to somewhere else? In other words, how does one determine the place of sale? Section 861(a)(6) does not say, and it is far from obvious.

Sales of goods involve a mix of physical and legal events. Generally there is both an agreement (sometimes implicit) and an actual transfer of goods. When these events occur in the same place, there is no problem. But in international sales they are often dispersed. Negotiations may occur in one place; the agreement may be executed in another; the goods may be delivered at yet another place; legal title may pass at another still. Any one of these could be taken as the place of sale, or a weighing of all might determine the place to which the sale relates most intensely—a "center of gravity" test in effect.

After some fits and starts, in which various tests for the place of sale were followed at different times, the U.S. tax laws have come to rest on one operative event—the passage of legal title—as the touchstone of the place of sale. Initially adopted because it was simple and easy to administer, this test of source is most notable today for the high degree of control it leaves with taxpayers over the source of income from sales. The reason for this control—which was not intended by the U.S. Treasury when it adopted the passage of title test in the 1940s—is the changed meaning of passage of title in commercial law. The very concept of "title" has become largely irrelevant in commercial law. In the Uniform Commercial Code (which was adopted by most states only *after* the establishment of passage of title as the touchstone of source in tax matters), the transfer of rights and burdens in connection with sales no longer turns on the passage of title. The only provision in the UCC concerning the vestigial notion of "title," in fact, is that where title is germane for some purpose *other* than commercial law, it passes where the parties to a sale specify in their agreement.[43] This makes the source of gains in a range of situations a matter of the stroke of a pen, by which the parties to a sale can specify a place of passage of title that is advantageous for tax purposes. Let me add that taxpayers' control over source, while considerable, is not wholly unfettered. Under regulations, the Treasury can disregard the place of passage of title if it is artificial or has been manipulated primarily for tax avoidance.[44] That means that a Canadian seller and an American buyer cannot specify, for example, that title passes in some remote tax haven such as Fiji. The residence of the seller or the buyer is almost always germane to a transaction of sale,

---

[43]UCC. §2-401(1). Absent specific agreement between the parties, title passes as a general rule where the seller completes performance of delivery. UCC §2-401(2).
[44]Reg. §1.861-7(c).

however, so that passage of title in either place is very likely to hold up. Often that leaves taxpayers enough room to maneuver.

The advantage to taxpayers from control over source is obvious in some instances. You can readily appreciate why a foreign merchant would prefer to have foreign source income from sales of goods destined for the United States.[45] Let's suppose that our friend Marcel has become a wine merchant in his country of Fredonia. If Marcel ships wine to distributors in the United States, he should make certain that title to the goods passes in Fredonia before transport (or perhaps in some sales office Marcel maintains in a third country). Marcel's gains will then have *foreign* source from the perspective of the U.S. tax system and likely escape U.S. taxation. Assume further that the Fredonian tax system follows a "center of gravity" test in determining the source of gains from sales of goods. If the agreements were negotiated and executed in the United States, the gains might then have *foreign* source in Fredonia (bearing in mind that U.S.-source income is foreign source income in Fredonia). If Fredonia has a territorial tax system, it may not reach Marcel's "foreign" source gains. Artful handling of the different source rules in two countries may thus leave Marcel's gains beyond the reach of any tax.

The advantage to a U.S. person of being able to create foreign source income at will by steering passage of title outside the United States is less immediately fathomable. U.S. persons are, after all, subject to full U.S. income tax on income of any source, domestic or foreign. But keep this pattern in mind when you come upon the foreign tax credit in chapter 11, and all will be clear.

Income of Mixed Character

The source rules canvassed thus far deal either with income from a single source, or with income of a single type (such as compensation, rentals, and royalties) with components of different sources. Much income, however, consists of bundled gains of different types and sources, even though realization of the income may be triggered by a single event. The activities of a integrated international oil company, for example, may consist of extracting oil from the ground in one place, refining the oil into gasoline somewhere else, and selling the gasoline to a motorist at a pump in yet another place. The company may also do its

---

[45]To be sure, as we shall see, even U.S.-source gains from sales of goods are not subject to U.S. taxation unless "effectively connected" with a U.S. business. But U.S.-source income is far more likely than foreign source income to be taxed as effectively connected.

own shipping of unrefined and refined products. Within conventional U.S. income tax concepts, the first—and only—event of "realization" occurs upon the sale of gasoline at the pump. The aggregate gain from the transaction ("gross income" in tax parlance) is the difference between the proceeds of the final sale and the cost of gasoline sold (arrived at by measuring and allocating all costs incurred along the entire chain of production and distribution).

This gain is made up of several elements, each reflecting value added by significantly different operations of the taxpayer. Exploration and extraction yield crude oil of ascertainable value that is tied economically to the place the natural deposits are found; refining creates value from a process itself separately identifiable; and the marketing and distribution of the finished product are a final element in the total gain. The single realization event unlocks a gain built up over time, properly attributable to several sources.

Such elements are implicit in virtually all combined operations of production and sale of goods. Although production and sale can take highly specialized forms requiring different business skills, both are commonly carried out by the same enterprise and, not infrequently, across national boundaries.

Section 863(b)

The present statutory provisions and regulations governing transactions of this type have come to rest, through a long history, at a place of relatively benign simplicity. The entire statutory scheme for income of compound type is contained in section 863(b), which provides only a broadly sketched framework and leaves the specifics to regulations:

> In the case of gross income derived from sources partly within and partly without the United States, the taxable income may first be computed by deducting the expenses, losses, or other deductions apportioned or allocated thereto and a ratable part of [other expenses]; and the portion of such taxable income attributable to sources within the United States may be determined by processes or formulas of general apportionment described by the Secretary.

This general statement is followed by a partial list of types of income of compound source. The most important of these is income "from the sale … of inventory property produced … within and sold … without the United States" or vice versa.[46] More colloquially, this is income from the production of property in one country and its sale in another.

---

[46] §863(b)(2).

If only because most economic activity culminates in a sale of some kind, virtually all manufacturing operations have the potential to generate this kind of income. Whether combined or not, production, distribution, and sale are easily distinguishable activities. There is, however, a wide spectrum of undertakings of combined production and sale, with sales of very different types of income embedded in them. Sales by manufacturers at the point of production are usually wholesale transactions, amounting to little more than simple transfers of ownership, which leave most of the marketing and distribution still to be done. Other producers, however, involve themselves fully with the ultimate sales to consumers.[47] The proportion of added value attributable to the sales varies greatly along this spectrum. It may, furthermore, reflect uneven abilities of an enterprise. It is one thing to manufacture a mattress in a factory and quite another to sell it to a customer in a department store. The manufacturing processes of an enterprise may be highly efficient, and therefore potentially gainful, while its distribution and selling remain ineffective. Conversely, a marketing wizard may be a mediocre producer.[48] In either case, a preponderance of any gain from the combined activity should be ascribed to the activity that is efficiently conducted.

Thinking about the problem from scratch, it would seem plausible to disengage the several elements of the transaction and determine a notional arm's length intermediate price; that is, to assume a wholesale transfer at the place of manufacture by a producer to an independent distributor, for resale at a point further along the stream of commerce. Thus dissected, the transaction can be viewed as a sale by a manufacturer to an intermediary at the place of production, followed by a subsequent resale in a different place. The gain from the initial sale (at the place of production) is a manufacturing gain, and should draw its source from the place of manufacture, while the gain derived from the subsequent sale on the basis of the intermediate price should have its source in the place of sale (given that that is what governs the source of gains from sales of inventory). The two separate items of gain (or loss) will always add up to the total income from the transaction.

---

[47]The operations of Avon Products (cosmetics) and McDonalds (fast food) come to mind.

[48]It may seem that integrated enterprises with widely uneven capacities in different lines of work would rationally break themselves up and recombine with other firms. But it doesn't always happen.

The 50/50 Method

While permissible in some cases, however, pursuit of an arm's length intermediate price is not the first-line approach of the Regulations under section 863(b). Instead the Regulations prescribe an apportionment formula, known as the "50/50 method":

> Under the 50/50 method, one-half of the taxpayer's gross income will be considered income attributable to production activity ... . The remaining one-half of such gross income will be considered income attributable to sales activity ... .[49]

The source of income within each half is then apportioned according to the location, respectively, of the taxpayer's "production assets" and "sales activity."[50] This is not as complicated as it may seem on first encounter. In the relatively simple case where production occurs entirely in one country and sales entirely in another, the apportionment formula splits the gain equally between both sources, hence the term "50/50 method." For example, suppose an enterprise manufactures computer memory chips entirely in the United States in plants wholly owned by it and sells its entire output in Japan, but owns no assets or facilities there. Then under the formula one half of the resulting income would be from sources within Japan (apportioned to the location of "sales activity") and the other half from sources within the United States (apportioned to the location of "production activity").

While simple, this apportionment of source cannot claim any particular economic plausibility. The formula assumes equal contribution to income from production and sales, and further apportions that contribution according to their location. While the location of production is tied to physical assets, the location of sales is tied, as we have seen, to the passage of title, an element of little economic significance. Here, as in the simpler case of combined purchase and sale of inventory, taxpayers have considerable control over the source of their gains.[51]

---

[49]Reg. §1.863-3(b)(1)(i).

[50]Id.; Reg. §1.863-3(c).

[51]This is because of the ease with which U.S. producers can arrange their export sales in such a way that title to their products passes outside the United States. Here also, the tax advantage of this control for U.S. persons arises in connection with the foreign tax credit, discussed in chapters 11-14.

Independent Factory Price

A taxpayer may elect, in lieu of the 50/50 method, to determine the source of income under the "independent factory price" (or "IFP") method, "if an IFP is fairly established."[52] To do so the taxpayer must "regularly [sell] part of its output to wholly independent distributors or other selling concerns in such a way as to reasonably reflect the income earned from production activity."[53] An IFP, in other words, is an arm's length intermediate price as discussed above. It cannot, however, be entirely notional, but must be based on actual sales of output to independent buyers.

Sales by Foreign Persons Attributable to a U.S. Office

There is a separate source rule for certain sales through a U.S. office. Section 865(e)(2)(A) provides that gain of a foreign person from the sale of *any* personal property has U.S. source, "notwithstanding any other provisions [of the Code]," if the sale is attributable to a U.S. office or other fixed place of business maintained in the United States. Note, first, the sweeping extent of this source rule. It applies to *all* sales (not just of inventory) and overrides *all* other source provisions. For foreign persons' sales through a U.S. office of goods produced abroad the beneficial "50/50" allocation of gains between U.S. and foreign source otherwise allowed under section 863(b) does *not* apply.[54] Instead, the entire gain has U.S. source.

This source rule brings gains attributable to *foreign* production within the reach of U.S. tax, with the result that direct sale and distribution in the United States of goods produced outside the United States may be unattractive, if not prohibitive, for foreign persons.[55] The 50/50 allocation formula under section 863(b)(2) creates incentives for *U.S.* persons to *export* manufactured goods. Section 865(e)(2), for its part, is an obstacle for foreign manufacturers exporting to the United States. It is not insuperable, but requires careful handling. Foreign producers selling in the United States generally avoid creating a U.S. office, and deal if at all possible with independent distributors and brokers.[56] Those that must have their own distribution operations in the

---

[52]Reg. §1.863-3(b)(2)(i).

[53]Id.

[54]Nor does it matter where title in the goods passes to the buyer.

[55]Income tax treaties, however, often mitigate this hazard. See chapter 21.

[56]Marcel, the Fredonian wine merchant from a few pages back, should in no circumstances establish his own sales office in the United States, at the risk of exposing his entire gains to U.S. taxation.

United States[57] (such as the Japanese electronics and auto giants) often create separate U.S. distribution affiliates, to which they sell their produced inventory *outside* the United States. The U.S. distribution affiliate derives U.S.-source gain from its resales of products in the United States, but the foreign producer derives no U.S.-source gain from its production and sales outside the United States. This pattern quells the problems of source and allocation under sections 865 and 863, but raises instead transfer pricing questions under section 482.[58]

Source and Characterization

Conceptually prior to the technical problem of applying the source rules outlined above is the question of classifying the income to which they apply. You can assign a source to income only if you know what it is. Ubiquitous in taxation, the problem of characterization is especially pervasive in determining the source of income. For example, a gain that could either be profit from a sale of property or a fee for brokering a sale between others will not reveal its source until its character has been resolved.[59] Many of the decided cases on the source of income ultimately turn on its classification.

Some questions of characterization are fairly tractable: interest, dividends, rents from real property, and social security benefits are in the main readily identifiable. Other types of income—such as compensation for services and gains from transfers of rights in intellectual property—molt into each other at uncertain and overlapping boundaries.

Services or Transfer of Property?

A free-lance writer who "sells" a story is usually treated as having transferred an identifiable property right—the copyright—while another writer (a staff reporter on a newspaper, for example) may be viewed as performing services (writing) for compensation. The boundary between these situations has been a perennial matter of dispute, both in

---

[57]Outfits like Sony and Toyota cannot as a practical matter channel all their U.S. sales through independent agents.

[58]See chapter 4. There is, however, no antidote against excess of bureaucratic zeal. During the 1980s one part of the U.S. government (the IRS) pursued Toyota-U.S. (the U.S. distribution affiliate) under §482, alleging that the transfer prices of cars from Toyota-Japan (the foreign producer) were so high as to shift excessive income to Japan. At the same time another part of the U.S. government (the International Trade Commission) was bringing a dumping complaint against Toyota-Japan, alleging sales of cars in the United States below cost.

[59]A classic case of this type is Balanovski v. United States, 236 F.2d 298 (2d Cir. 1956), *cert. denied,* 352 U.S. 968 (1957).

domestic and international tax settings. To a large extent, the distinction between services and transfers of intangible property has turned on whether or not the creator (writer, artist, inventor, etc.) had rights in an asset separately identifiable as "property" apart from tax law. It follows that changes in the legal regime of intellectual property itself have affected this boundary.

Ingram v. Bowers

A seminal case in this area is Ingram v. Bowers,[60] which illustrates both the importance of characterization in international taxation and the limitations of the process. The case concerned income of Enrico Caruso. Under a 1911 agreement with the Victor Company, Caruso performed several songs at the company's recording studio in New Jersey. By the terms of the contract, Caruso was undertaking simply to sing songs, which the Victor Company would record. Victor made a master recording and then made template copies from which individual records were made and sold around the world. Caruso received a royalty from the sale of each individual record by Victor.[61]

The songs were all recorded at the Victor Company's studios in the United States. The Revenue Service accordingly took the view that Caruso's "royalty" arrangement was simply compensation for services (consisting of singing) performed in the United States. It made no difference to the IRS that the compensation for the services happened to be tied to the value of those services to Caruso's employer. So viewed, Caruso's entire income from the arrangement was U.S.-source compensation, including the contingent amounts received from sales of records *outside* the United States.[62] Caruso's estate (he was dead by the time of the case) sought, in contrast, to characterize the transactions as licenses by Caruso to the Victor Company of rights in the recorded songs for use around the world. This characterization did not affect the source of the income from record sales in the *United States*, which would in any event have U.S. source as royalties from the "use" of property in the United States, but would have recast as foreign source income the royalties received by Caruso on account of the *foreign* (i.e. non-U.S.) sales.

---

[60]47 F.2d 925 (S.D.N.Y. 1931), *aff'd,* 57 F.2d 65 (2d Cir. 1932).

[61]These terms were modified in 1919. Caruso was to record 40 songs and to receive a royalty of 10 percent of the list price of all records sold, or a guaranteed minimum of $100,000 per year. Under the 1919 agreement, Caruso also undertook to record songs for no other company.

[62]The contingent element, in this view, affected only the measure, but not the nature, of Caruso's compensation.

Siding with the Treasury, the district court found the overall arrangement to be compensation for services. Caruso had agreed to sing and had been compensated for singing and, therefore, "the place where the work [was] done, and not the place where the later event fixing compensation occurs, is the source of the income, in cases where the income is from the exercise of a profession or vocation as in this case."[63] On appeal this decision was affirmed (in an opinion by Learned Hand) on the ground that the agreements between Caruso and Victor gave Caruso no interest in the matrices and the records themselves, nor any rights in the nature of a copyright. There being no interest in intellectual property to be licensed, the characterization as a license could not stand.

As a matter of economic fundamentals, the courts could plausibly have found that Caruso's income was not, at least in substantial part, compensation for services. True, Caruso sang songs for money, but what made the singing so valuable was the unique quality of Caruso's voice. That would make Caruso's huge income akin to a rent from his exclusive control over this rare attribute. Economists view the incomes of superstar performers or athletes as rents of a sort, like the income derived by the owner of a uniquely fertile patch of land. An economist might suggest as an example of this type of rent Babe Ruth's $100,000 compensation from the New York Yankees in 1927, when his 60 home runs exceeded the output of any other *team* in baseball. Without his particular combination of eyesight, wrist strength, and coordination, Ruth could hardly have earned more than $2,000 as a laborer in 1927. The $98,000 difference can be thought of as a rent from Ruth's unique physical attributes. The economic return to Caruso's singing voice can be thought of in much the same way.

Rather than attempt to fathom the basic economic character of the income, however, the courts characterized Caruso's income according to the *legal* category into which his contractual arrangement with Victor fell. They focused narrowly on the terms of Caruso's contracts with Victor, and in particular on the absence of any express transfer of rights in intangible property. The courts' approach does not betoken any intellectual failure on their part. Both the trial and appellate judges understood that Caruso's royalties fell uneasily into the class of compensation for services and reflected to a considerable extent his ownership of a unique asset. Much compensation for services, however, embodies some element of rent or return to human capital, albeit in varying degrees. A case-by-case dissection of compensation into rents and pure returns from labor is impossible. The courts could not remove

---

[63]47 F.2d 925, 927.

Caruso from the class of recipients of compensation for services, because within the law of intellectual property as it stood Caruso's contractual arrangement did not frame any rights in intellectual property.

Further Implications of Ingram v. Bowers

Ingram v. Bowers has some intriguing corollaries. A practical consequence of the case (that the U.S. Treasury probably did not anticipate) is a golden (or even platinum) opportunity for foreign recording artists with a following in the United States. Where Caruso went wrong was in doing the actual singing in a New Jersey recording studio. That gave his entire compensation (the "royalties" as they were called) U.S. source, no matter where records were sold to consumers. If Caruso had recorded *outside* the United States, none of his compensation would have had U.S. source. This point was not lost on star performers of later generations. Many of the iconic foreign rock stars of the 1960s recorded in places like the Bahamas (where income taxation bears as lightly as the gentle breeze). Their huge incomes from these recording arrangements, thanks to Ingram v. Bowers, had no U.S.-source component, even though overwhelmingly the largest market for sales of their records was the United States.[64]

Another implication of Ingram v. Bowers is that a change in the underlying intellectual property arrangement—for example, if the agreements with Victor had created for Caruso identifiable rights in the songs—might have changed the tax consequences. This possibility was both confirmed and limited in Boulez v. Commissioner.[65] Boulez, an orchestra conductor who had received "royalties" under an arrangement similar to Caruso's, argued that amendments of the copyright laws in the 1970s established the existence of property rights of performers in recorded works. The court agreed that under present-day copyright laws a performer may retain a property interest in recorded works, but noted as well that the possibility arises only from express contractual agreement, which Boulez in particular had not obtained. Boulez

---

[64]You may perhaps associate some of these superstar groups with such high-tax countries as Great Britain and wonder what they gained by avoiding U.S. taxation, given the fiercely high taxes in their countries of nationality. The answer lies partly in the territorial taxation of such countries—implying no tax on foreign-based business operations of their own citizens—and partly in the possibility of surrender of citizenship of a high-tax country and the acquisition of citizenship in a country with a laid-back fiscal culture. Monaco, for example, is a longstanding haven for the fiscally challenged. One of the world's best-known athletes in the 1970s was a Swede in language and culture, but a Monegasque in civil status.
[65]83 T.C. 584 (1984).

therefore lost. But it is strongly implied in *Boulez* that the taxpayer *could* have retained intellectual property rights in the recordings by contract.

Ingram v. Bowers and *Boulez*—two taxpayer defeats—therefore contain the seeds of a favorable U.S. income tax regime for foreign performing artists. Those who have the flexibility or bargaining power to record in a place of their own choosing outside the United States can leave their agreements with record companies as silent as Caruso's on the question of the artists' property rights, and thereby remove their entire incomes from the reach of U.S. taxation. Those who record in the United States are worse off from a tax standpoint; but by retaining specified property rights in their agreements they can impart foreign source at least to their share of gains from record sales outside the United States.

A Brief Note on Products, Services, and Software

Another boundary of characterization with implication for the source of income lies between tangible products, intangible property, and services. If I transfer a product embodying protected intellectual property, such as a computer disk or a CD, have I transferred rights in intellectual property or a physical article embodying protected intellectual property? It makes a difference in the source of my gains. In the latter case (more than likely a sale of inventory) the place of passage title would govern source; in the former, section 865's rule of residence. There are few overarching rules on the question.

Consumer goods are generally treated as items of inventory. A copyrighted book is simply a book; a patented vacuum cleaner an appliance; and an electronic game player complete with CD/ROMS a toy. Computer software raises particular problems, because it is transferred 1) in consumer markets, 2) in connection with long-term service agreements, and 3) everything in between. The Service has issued Regulations on the classification of transactions involving computer programs. The transactions fall in four classes: 1) transfers of copyrights in a computer program; 2) transfers of copies of the program (copyrighted articles); 3) provision of services for the development of a program; and 4) provision of know-how relating to computer programming.[66] The first of these, the transfer of a copyright, is a sale or a license depending on the extent of the rights transferred.[67] The second, the transfer of a copyrighted article, is similarly a sale or a rental

---

[66]Reg. §1.861-18(b)(1).
[67]Reg. §1.861-18(f)(1). See also chapter 5.

according to the extent of rights transferred.[68] The remaining two are different types of services.[69]

---

[68]Reg. §1.861-18(f)(2).

[69] There are numerous examples in the Regulations fleshing out these general principles. Reg. §1.861-18(h).

Chapter 4

International Transfer Pricing

A thread running through international taxation is the problem of "transfer pricing." The term refers to the pricing of goods and services transferred between related persons not dealing at arm's length.

Prices charged after bargaining between unrelated persons are called "arm's length" prices. A price charged between related persons that approximates the result of independent bargaining is also called an "arm's length" price.

When unrelated persons deal at arm's length, the prices at which they transact reflect both prevailing competitive conditions and the specific course of bargaining between them. By contrast, among related persons —for example within a group of corporations under common control or beneficial ownership—transfer prices answer to no overriding economic pressure. They may reflect a largely unconstrained decision by the transacters to adjust accounts among themselves. A group of corporations under common ownership and control is a single economic enterprise. Only the terms of transactions with unrelated persons outside the group affect the economic gain or loss of the group as a whole. If a subsidiary corporation engaged in production within a group sells its output to a separate marketing subsidiary of their common parent corporation, a higher price between the two related companies will shift more of any overall gain to the producing company; a lower price will shift gain to the marketing subsidiary. Transfer prices, in short, affect the distribution but not the absolute amount of gain or loss among related persons.

Transfer Pricing and Taxation

With taxation in the picture, there may be advantage in artful adjustment of transfer prices within corporate groups constituting integrated enterprises. If entities within a related group face different tax environments, or different rates of taxation within the same tax regime, transfer pricing may bear decisively on tax consequences. One affiliate may be tax-exempt, for example, or have recoverable losses, or be exposed to taxation at special rates. In the international setting the variety of tax environments is greater, and hence the possible gains from artificial transfer pricing. Departures from arm's length prices between affiliates organized in different countries may shift taxable income to a low-tax environment and deductible expense to a high-tax one. Wholly discretionary transfer pricing would let firms adopt in some measure the tax environment of their own choosing. They might simply establish an affiliate in a tax-advantaged place and channel transactions through it, at prices matching the booked results of operations with the most advantageous features of the indigenous tax regime. A simple example of such a scheme is the diversion of maximum profit to an affiliate organized in a low-tax or no-tax jurisdiction, with concomitant reduction of the profit exposed to higher tax elsewhere.

An Example

To make this more concrete, consider the following two-corporation parent-subsidiary group:

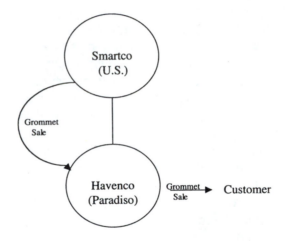

Smartco is a U.S. corporation subject to high income tax. Smartco produces grommets at a cost of $1 each and can sell them in Paradiso (a zero-tax country) for $2. If Smartco sells the grommets in Paradiso directly, its gain is fully subject to U.S. tax. Instead Smartco sells the grommets to its Paradisan subsidiary Havenco for $1.01. Havenco (which is untaxed, remember) in turn sells the grommets to unrelated Paradisan customers for $2.00, realizing a profit of $0.99 on each sale. The two-corporation group headed by Smartco makes a $1 gross profit per grommet, of which 99 cents is not taxed.

If the arm's length wholesale price of grommets is $1.50, Smartco's low price to Havenco has shifted 49 cents of profit per grommet from Smartco to Havenco—which, significantly, is from a high-tax to a low-tax environment. If Smartco had charged the arm's length price in the intra-group sale, it would have had taxable gain of 49 cents. As a pure accounting matter, Smartco's loss is Havenco's gain. As a tax matter, Havenco's gain is the U.S. Treasury's loss.

Section 482

The U.S. tax authorities have never not known about transfer pricing. From the earliest days the U.S. tax laws have had provisions designed to strengthen the Treasury's hand in dealing with artificially priced transactions between related persons. The core provision in the present Code is section 482, which reads in part:

> In any case of two or more organizations, trades, or businesses (whether or not incorporated, whether or not organized in the United States, and whether or not affiliated) owned or controlled directly or indirectly by the same interests, the Secretary may distribute, apportion, or allocate gross income, deductions, credits, or allowances between or among such organizations, trades, or businesses, if he determines that such distribution, apportionment, or allocation is necessary in order to prevent evasion of taxes or clearly to reflect the income of any of such organizations, trades, or businesses.

Pursuant to this one-sentence mandate, the Treasury has issued extensive regulations. The version currently in force dates largely to 1994. The Regulations cover nearly the full range of transactions between related persons, and are as discursively articulated as section 482 itself is laconic.

Section 482 is aimed at the unilateral advantage related taxpayers could otherwise obtain through unchecked transfer prices. Its goal, broadly stated, is to recast transactions among affiliates on arm's length terms and adjust U.S. taxation accordingly. On its face, section 482 is not prescriptive. It does not literally obligate taxpayers to any particular course of action. Rather, section 482 empowers the Commissioner to reallocate income and expense in transactions among related persons. In practical effect, however, section 482 is a formidable weapon, among other reasons because it is backed up by an array of penalties that can be imposed on taxpayers that have strayed from the virtuous path in transfer pricing.

Section 482 prescribes allocation of income and expense between related persons to prevent tax avoidance and "clearly to reflect" their income. Across nearly the full range of transactions, the Regulations under section 482 identify clear reflection of income with arm's length pricing between unrelated persons. That is, transactions between related persons on terms that differ substantially from similar transactions at arm's length between unrelated persons are subject to immediate and unanswerable revision by the IRS. Conversely, when related transacters can point to substantially identical arm's length transactions between unrelated persons, they are nearly immune from molestation under section 482.

Arm's Length Pricing and Gains from Integration

For those of you who crave an academic digression, let me point out *en passant* that in pure theory the arm's length standard is not conceptually perfect. More specifically, arm's length pricing between related taxpayers is not exactly the same as clear reflection of income. Transactions between related persons are part of an integrated process of production and distribution subject to command. The transacters are part of a single economic enterprise, or "firm" as it is known to economists. An arm's length price is what an unrelated person would charge or pay after bargaining. The incomes of related persons within an integrated firm, however, reflect their non-arm's-length relationship. Integration in a single enterprise trades the cost of market transactions, including bargaining and the maintenance of the resulting contractual relations, for the costs and benefits resulting from the exercise of common control. Absent regulatory or other constraint, firms integrate when they stand to gain from shaping their transactions by internal command, and conversely do not when arm's length bargaining under the regime of market exchanges is less costly. The incomes of integrated firms should therefore tend to be greater, by the amount of gains from integration, than the combined incomes of unrelated transacters. There is no certain way to allocate the gains from integration within a firm on the basis of arm's length dealings by strangers.

I should add that this observation casts no doubt on the validity or wisdom of the Regulations under section 482. The arm's length standard is almost surely the best practically attainable. No other method subject to a degree of empirical verification is more accurate. Because an economically perfect determination of income is rarely if ever available to taxpayers and tax administrators, the realistic alternatives to a standard of arm's length pricing are various formulas of allocation and apportionment. In the current transfer-pricing regime, these come into play as second-line methods when arm's length prices are elusive.

The Elusiveness of Arm's length Prices

The real problem with the arm's length standard lies not in any theoretical shortcomings, but in the day-to-day difficulty of giving it effect. An arm's length price has in common with a policeman that as often as not you can't find one when you need one.

Except for sales of commodity-type fungible goods, most transactions involve goods, services, or assets in which there is some element specific to the transaction. Goods may embody unique designs and other proprietary elements. The value even of laundry detergent may be tied to a brand name. It is hard to compare the terms of a transfer of a Royce-Rolls and a Ferrari on the same footing. First, you would have to find transfers of generic "brand X" luxury cars, then strip away the differentiated features of Royces and Ferraris. The first step is impossible, because there is no generic luxury automobile market; the second leaves open much room for argument.

The Regulations under Section 482

Despite the difficulty, the Regulations under section 482 embrace arm's length pricing as the test of clear reflection of income,[1] and unflinchingly hold up the banner of arm's length pricing: "In determining the true taxable income of a controlled taxpayer, the standard to be applied in every case is that of a taxpayer dealing at arm's length with an uncontrolled taxpayer."[2] The Regulations press hard to come up with arm's length touchstones for intra-family transactions. To this end, they establish transfer prices based on a hierarchy of identity, similarity, or even mere analogy with arm's length transactions, before retreating to arbitrary formulas and safe harbors.

Related Persons

Neither section 482 nor the Regulations assert a precise test of what makes taxpayers "related" (or, as the Regulations put it, "controlled taxpayers"). A "controlled taxpayer means any one of two or more taxpayers owned or controlled directly or indirectly by the same interests, and includes the taxpayer that owns or controls the other taxpayers."[3] Remaining above the arithmetic fray, the Regulations further provide: "It is the reality of the control that is decisive, not its form or the mode of its exercise. A presumption of control arises if income or deductions have been arbitrarily shifted."[4] A rule of thumb is that common beneficial ownership or voting control of 50 percent or more may set the stage for an allocation under section 482. Usually the degree of common ownership of related persons reined in by section 482 is higher, because transacting persons with substantial nonoverlapping

---

[1]Reg. §1.482-1(a)(2) ("The purpose of section 482 is to ensure that taxpayers clearly reflect income attributable to controlled transactions, and to prevent the avoidance of taxes with respect to such transactions. Section 482 places a controlled taxpayer on a tax parity with an uncontrolled taxpayer by determining the true taxable income of the controlled taxpayer.").
[2]Reg. §1.482-1(b)(1).
[3]Reg. §1.482-1(i)(5).
[4]Reg. §1.482-1(i)(4).

unrelated owners would find it difficult to practice artificial transfer prices without protest from outside owners.[5]

Arm's Length Results

The arm's length standard is initially defined in the Regulations with reference to the results of the same transactions between unrelated persons: "A controlled transaction meets the arm's length standard if the results of that transaction are consistent with the results that would have been realized if uncontrolled taxpayers had engaged in the same transaction under the same circumstances."[6] The arm's length standard is, notably, cast here in terms of arm's length *results*, not merely prices (as in earlier regulations). A "result" can easily encompass the profit earned in arm's length transactions, as well the prices charged. This statement implies virtual identity between the controlled and uncontrolled transaction. On this score, however, the Regulations immediately concede that "because identical transactions can rarely be located, whether a transaction produces an arm's length result generally will be determined by reference to the results of comparable transactions under comparable circumstances."[7]

Methods: the "Best" Method

In pursuit of arm's length prices in "comparable" transactions, the Regulations expound several transfer pricing "methods" applicable to different transactions such as sales of property, services, loans, and rentals.[8] There is no fixed hierarchy among these methods, but the Regulations require the use of the "best" method, or more precisely "the method that, under the facts and circumstances, provides the most reliable measure of an arm's length result."[9]

The two principal factors in determining the best method are "the degree of comparability between the controlled transaction (or taxpayer) and any uncontrolled comparables, and the quality of the data and assumptions used in the analysis."[10]

---

[5]If enterprise *A* shifts income to enterprise *B*, and only half of each enterprise is owned by the same interests, the outside owner of *A* (who is losing equity for someone else's tax advantage at most) is likely to speak up.

[6]Reg. §1.482-1(b)(1).

[7]Id.

[8]Reg. §§1.482-2 through 1.482-6.

[9]Reg. §1.482-1(c)(1).

[10]Reg. §1.482-1(c)(2).

Comparability

It follows that the operative standard of the Regulations as a practical matter, is *comparability*. Comparability depends on "all factors that could affect prices or profits in arm's length dealings."[11] And within comparability, there are gradations. Roughly, the Regulations seek out "exact" comparable transactions before settling for "inexact" comparable transactions.

The factors underlying comparability are 1) the economic functions carried on by the taxpayers, 2) the contracts between them, 3) the risks they incur, 4) prevailing economic conditions, and 5) the nature of the property or services over which they transact.[12] Transactions need not be identical to be comparable, but the uncontrolled transaction must provide a "reliable measure" of an arm's length result.[13] Adjustments must be made to account for differences in the results of transactions that also have significant underlying comparability.[14] The greater the number of adjustments, however, the less reliable the conclusion of comparability.[15]

Transfer pricing methods, and the standard of comparability, are fleshed out in connection with specific types of transactions between related persons. There follows here a brief outline of three transfer pricing methods for sales of goods (among several others). The point of this exercise, by the way, is not for you to try it at home, but to give you some slight sense of the inner plumbing of the Regulations,

Sales of Property between Related Persons

Comparable Uncontrolled Price Method

As the Regulations put it: "The comparable uncontrolled price method evaluates whether the amount charged in a controlled transaction is arm's length by reference to the amount charged in a comparable uncontrolled transaction."[16] Even though there is no formal hierarchy of methods, the Regulations do take on a special glow when expounding the comparable uncontrolled price method as "the most direct and reliable measure of an arm's length price for the controlled transaction" if there are no differences or only minor differences between the con-

---

[11]Reg. §1.482-1(d)(1).
[12]Id.
[13]Reg. §1.482-1(d)(2).
[14]Id.
[15]Id.
[16]Reg. §1.482-3(b)(1).

trolled transaction under scrutiny and a comparable uncontrolled transaction.[17]

The Resale Price Method

The resale price method approaches a sale between related persons from the perspective of a buyer who will resell the goods to an unrelated person: "The resale price method evaluates whether the amount charged in a controlled transaction is arm's length by reference to the gross profit margin realized in comparable uncontrolled transactions."[18] The "arm's length" transfer price under the resale price method is determined "by subtracting the appropriate gross profit from the applicable resale price for the property involved in the controlled transaction under review."[19] The "appropriate gross profit" is then computed by multiplying the applicable resale price by the gross profit margin (expressed as a percentage of total revenue derived from sales) earned in comparable uncontrolled transactions.[20]

Cost Plus Method

The "cost plus" method is concerned with properly compensating the *seller*'s contribution to a sale of goods between related persons: "The cost plus method evaluates whether the amount charged in a controlled transaction is arm's length by reference to the gross profit markup realized in comparable uncontrolled transactions. The cost plus method is ordinarily used in cases involving the manufacture, assembly, or other production of goods that are sold to related parties."[21] Under this method the arm's length price is the seller's cost of the property sold to a related person, increased by an appropriate markup, reflecting the value of the seller's role as producer: "The cost plus method measures an arm's length price by adding the appropriate gross profit to the controlled taxpayer's costs of producing the property involved in the controlled transaction.'[22] The "appropriate gross profit" is "computed by multiplying the controlled taxpayer's cost of producing the transferred property by the gross profit markup, expressed as a percentage of cost, earned in comparable uncontrolled transactions."[23] Whenever

---

[17]Reg. §1.482-3(b)(2)(ii)(A).
[18]Reg. §1.482-3(c)(1).
[19]Reg. §1.482-3(c)(2)(i). The "applicable resale price" is the price charged to unrelated persons after sales within a group. Reg. §1.482-3(c)(2)(ii).
[20]Reg. §1.482-3(c)(2)(iii).
[21]See Reg. §1.482-3(d)(1).
[22]See Reg. §1.482-3(d)(2)(i).
[23]See Reg. §1.482-3(d)(2)(ii).

possible, the gross profit markup should be derived from comparable uncontrolled sales made by the taxpayer involved in the controlled sale. In the absence of such sales, an appropriate gross profit markup may be derived from comparable uncontrolled sales of other producers.[24]

Transfers of Intangible Property

The Regulations propound a similar array of methods of determining taxable income from a transfer of intangible property between related persons. An additional, unique, element in transfer pricing of intangible property arises from the second sentence of section 482: "In the case of any transfer (or license) of intangible property ... the income with respect to such transfer or license shall be commensurate with the income attributable to the intangible." This sparely phrased provision is shot through with difficulty. Known as the "superroyalty" provision, this sentence, greatly simplified, allows for continuing annual adjustments after transfers of intangible property to make the results "commensurate with income."

Literally, the superroyalty provision applies after the fact, measuring income attributable to a transfer of intangible property and imputing the income back to the transferor as compensation for the transfer. The reason for it is concern that related persons could easily undervalue transferred intangible property with an uncertain future and claim later that the transferee was just lucky. The provision does not so much assert a strict arm's length standard as revise the terms of a transfer based on subsequent results.

The Regulations provide in a broad range of situations for annual adjustment of the consideration charged for intangible property between related persons to ensure that it is commensurate with the income attributable to the property.[25] There are a number of exceptions. Most important, no periodic adjustments are made if the same intangible asset was transferred to an uncontrolled taxpayer on the same terms and under substantially the same circumstances as those of the controlled transaction.[26]

---

[24]See Reg. §1.482-3(d)(3)(ii)(A).
[25]Reg. §1.482-4(f).
[26]Reg. §1.482-4(f)(2)(ii)(A).

Advance Pricing Agreements

A development in the past decade is the issuance by the IRS of advance pricing agreements ("APAs") on intercompany transfer pricing under section 482. In the IRS's own words:

> An APA is an agreement between the Service and the taxpayer on the [transfer pricing methodology] to be applied to any apportionment or allocation of income, deductions, credits, or allowances between or among two or more organizations, trades, or businesses owned or controlled, directly or indirectly, by the same interests. The [transfer pricing methodology] thus represents the application to the taxpayer's specific facts and circumstances of the best method within the meaning of the income tax regulations under section 482 of the Internal Revenue Code ... as agreed pursuant to negotiations between the Service and the taxpayer.[27]

The advantage of an APA for taxpayers is certainty. But certainty comes at both transactional and substantive cost. The submissions and supporting analysis required to obtain an APA are extensive. Equally if not more important, the best a taxpayer can hope for in an APA is a middle-of-the road result. The IRS is unlikely to confer its blessing on transfer prices at the aggressive end of the arm's length range.

---

[27]Rev. Proc. 96-53, 1996-2 Cum. Bull. 375. This Revenue Procedure expounds general guidelines for APAs.

II

Inbound U.S. Taxation

Chapter 5

U.S. Taxation of Foreign Persons: Passive Investment Income

Thus far we have worked through several of the building blocks of U.S. international taxation—nationality, residence, and the source of income, among others—but haven't yet woven them into a complete canvas of taxation of foreign persons and foreign income. This and following chapters lay out the actual U.S. tax regime applicable to inbound and outbound transactions.

Generalities on Inbound Taxation

The tax environment facing foreign investors and foreign-owned businesses in the United States reflects two conspicuous, and often conflicting elements of the U.S. fiscal and economic landscape in recent decades: thirst for tax revenues and thirst for foreign capital. Impounding these dual concerns, U.S. taxation of foreign investment is a patchwork of severe and benign provisions.

There are two different tax regimes within the U.S. system of inbound taxation, that apply respectively to passive investment income and active business profits from the United States. At the boundary between these regimes is the notion of a U.S. "trade or business"—a measure of the character and extent of economic activity in the United States.

In broad outline, foreign persons are taxed 1) at a flat rate of 30 percent on the *gross* amount of their U.S.-source passive investment income (known as "fixed or determinable" income) and 2) at full graduated rates on *net* business profits (known in tax parlance as "income effectively connected with the conduct of a trade or business in the United States.")[1]

From this bare outline, it may seem that the U.S. taxation of passive investment is the more severe. While the highest marginal rates imposed on the net business incomes of individuals and corporations (39.6 percent and 35 percent respectively) *are* somewhat higher than the flat 30 percent rate imposed on passive investment income, the disallowance of deductions and the absence of lower rate brackets in the flat tax regime often make a flat 30 percent of *gross* income a greater amount than the portion of *net* gain bitten off at the regular graduated rates.

---

[1] §§871(b), 882(a), 884.

Closer scrutiny reverses this first impression. There are large holes in the flat rate tax on investment income of foreign persons. Capital gains from the sale of U.S. investment assets (other than real estate) are not taxed at all. More important, interest from U.S. bank deposits and from U.S. "portfolio" debt (a class including most private and public obligations) is also exempt from U.S. taxation. Because capital gains and interest represent the overwhelming bulk of income from passive investment in the United States, the tax regime on passive investment income is not fearsome in the end. On the other side of the scales, there is an additional tax of 30 percent on the branch profits of foreign corporations in the United States when they are removed from the U.S. economic environment. This tax, dating from the 1986 Act, extends two-level taxation of profits to most business operations of foreign corporations in the United States.

The overall pattern of U.S. taxation of foreign persons that emerges from these provisions is relatively benign taxation of passive investment income (represented mainly by interest and capital gains derived from financial assets) and more aggressive taxation of active business profits. This tax regime reflects, I believe, the combination of the large U.S. appetite for foreign capital that has developed in the last three decades and an accompanying wariness of surrendering day-to-day control over economic activity in the United States to foreigners. The need for foreign capital is the aftermath of American profligacy, both at home and abroad, that has transformed the United States since World War II from the world's largest exporter of capital to its largest importer. The uneasiness over foreign control of U.S. business assets is a concomitant defensive reaction, a sort of economic nationalism that recoils at the thought of being an economic satellite of any other nation. We prefer the claims of foreigners to be general (in the form of bank deposits, noncontrolling corporate debt, Treasury obligations, and the like) rather than specific (such as waterfront landmarks, heartland farms, or icons of American industry). Let me add that a similar ambivalence about the different forms of foreign investment is revealed, often more saliently, in the tax systems of many other countries.

The difference in tax cost between the two U.S. income tax regimes imposed on foreign persons can be seen as a sort of tax toll-charge on the exercise of control over economic activity in the United States. And in this context the threshold of control is low. An ownership stake of only 10 percent by a foreign person in a U.S. enterprise, for example, either as a shareholder or as a direct owner of equity, is enough to remove the interest received by the person from the enterprise from the class of exempt portfolio interest.

Even these second-order impressions of the U.S. tax system must be further refined. The actual level of U.S. taxation of foreign-owned business operations in the United States is not crushingly high. Reasons for this include the network of income tax treaties and various artful structures of ownership cultivated by foreign owners. In broad outline, the art of planning over the years for U.S. operations by foreign persons has been the conversion of U.S. business profits into a stream of passive income enjoying some Code-favored or treaty-favored regime. More graphically, it is to shoehorn the results of active business operations into the form of passive investments. Such maneuvers, and the U.S. Treasury's countermeasures, are discussed further in later chapters.

The Flat Rate Tax

Sections 871(a) and 881 impose U.S. tax at a flat 30 percent rate on the U.S.-source passive investment income of foreign persons. The flat rate tax has its own separate base, which departs substantially from the general pattern of U.S. income taxation. It is collected by withholding at the source.[2] Overall, the flat tax regime is not designed to be subtle but to reach a large class of U.S.-source income with a simple tax that lends itself to withholding.

The flat rate tax is imposed on *gross* income, which means that it permits no deductions.[3] Allocable expenses therefore produce no tax benefit. What is commonly known as "investment interest," for example, is not deductible by foreign persons to any extent.

"Fixed or Determinable" Income

The flat rate tax regime applies to items of income enumerated in section 871(a)(1). The core of this income consists of

> interest . . . dividends, rents, salaries, wages, premiums, annuities, compensations, remunerations, emoluments, and other fixed or determinable annual or periodical gains, profits, and income

to which a few similar items are added in other provisions. The flavor of this enumeration is inclusive. The drafters clearly wanted it to reach comprehensively a certain type of income. The catchall phrase at the end

---

[2]§§1441, 1442.

[3]The denial of deductions results by inference from sections 873 and 882(c), which limit the deductions of foreign taxpayers to those attributable to income "effectively connected" with a U.S. trade or business.

("other fixed or determinable annual or periodical gains, profits, and income") picks up similar types of income (such as royalties) not explicitly listed. This entire category of income is routinely described by tax lawyers as "fixed or determinable" income, which has become the standard shorthand.

On first reading, however, the statutory enumeration does not appear universally inclusive. Both the explicit terms and the coda could be read as limited to income occurring in flows or regular increments. One might reasonably conclude from the language of the statute that "annual or periodical" gains did not extend to purely isolated or fortuitous ones, such as found money, for example, or the proceeds of a single wager or prize fight. A number of rulings by the IRS in the early days suggested this possibility,[4] but were later set aside.[5] It is now well established that "fixed or determinable" income includes virtually every type of gain, whether arising in a lump sum or periodic flows, whether one-of-a-kind or from recurrent transactions, and whether arising in a steady, intermittent, or erratic stream. The proceeds of a single wager, the prize from entering a horse in a single race, or even found money, fall within the class.[6]

A further characteristic of most of the enumerated items of fixed or determinable income is that the tax base is readily identified. Most rents, royalties, and wages, and all interest and dividends, come in measurable amounts that have the character of gross income. Typically (but not always) these amounts arise without substantial expense by the recipient, and therefore have a large component of net gain. This is at least in part the justification for taxation at flat rates without allowance for deductions. Perhaps the simplest way to understand fixed or determinable income is that it includes all gross income that can be measured by the person paying it.

Gains from Sales of Property

From this it follows that there is one crucially important type of income that is *not* fixed or determinable income: gain from the sale of property. The amount received by a seller of property is more akin to

---

[4]E.g., S.M. 975, 1 Cum. Bull. 184 (1919) (winnings of horses at a race track not annual or periodical income); O.D. 907, 4 Cum. Bull. 232 (1921) (commission on single transaction not annual or periodical income); G.C.M. 21575, 1939-2 Cum. Bull. 172 (prizes awarded to foreign artists for best pictures at exhibition not annual or periodical income).

[5]Rev. Rul. 58-479, 1958-2 Cum. Bull. 60 (revoking S.M. 975, O.D. 907, G.C.M. 21575, above).

[6]The period that satisfies the "periodical" element is apparently *one*, which makes even once-in-a-lifetime income "periodical" income of a sort.

gross receipts than gross income. From the buyer's side there is no way to tell whether the seller has gain (which would constitute gross income) or loss. The amount of tax that a buyer should withhold from the purchase price of property is indeterminate. Congress accordingly decided to leave gains from sales of property beyond the flat rate tax when it was adopted in 1936. Capital gains of foreign investors from pure investment assets therefore are generally free of U.S. tax.

Withholding

Withholding at the source from fixed or determinable income is different in basic respects from wage withholding that you may have encountered as an employee. The latter is a down payment of tax; there is a subsequent reckoning with the IRS (by filing a return) in which there may be a refund or additional tax due. In the flat rate tax, the tax and withholding are so thoroughly intertwined as to be congruent. Withholding is set at the same rate as the tax itself and falls on the same tax base—the gross amount of fixed or determinable income from sources in the United States. From this amount there is a ready computation of gross income.

In this system withholding and the flat rate tax have become essentially coextensive. Indeed, in the patois of international tax lawyers the term "withholding tax" is often used to describe the flat rate tax itself.[7] A foreign taxpayer from whom the correct amount has been withheld has nothing more to pay and can expect to get nothing back. The taxpayer and the Treasury are thus quit of each other, and there is no need even to file a return.[8]

Interest from Passive Investments

Interest is the first inclusion among the enumerated items of fixed or determinable income subject to U.S. taxation in section 871(a)(1). Little U.S.-source interest paid to foreign persons, however, is actually subject to U.S. tax. Various exceptions and exemptions shield from U.S. tax virtually all interest received by foreign persons from passive investment. Interest paid to foreign persons on deposits of all kinds by U.S. banks and other financial institutions is exempt from U.S. tax in section 871(i).

---

[7]This habit is so engrained that some international tax lawyers refer to any flat rate tax as a "withholding" tax, even if it is paid by return.

[8]The Code itself in fact requires foreign taxpayers to file returns even when the appropriate amount of tax has been withheld. §6012(a)(1). The Treasury Regulations, however, waive this requirement when tax has been withheld under §1441 and paid over to the Treasury in an amount sufficient to satisfy tax liability in full. Reg. §§1.6012-1(b)(2), 1.6012-2(g)(2)(i).

"Portfolio Interest"

Even more important, since 1984 U.S.-source interest from almost all types of debt obligations has been exempt from U.S. tax for foreign persons by virtue of sections 871(h) and 881(c) of the Code. These provisions exempt from flat rate tax what they term "portfolio interest" received from U.S. sources by foreign taxpayers.

Exempt "portfolio interest" includes the bulk of interest paid on passive debt obligations. Broadly, it is interest on a debt obligation held for investment by an identifiably foreign person. The design of portfolio interest in the Code aims to assure 1) that the exemption is enjoyed only by actual foreign investors and 2) that relationship between borrower and lender is genuinely passive, i.e., that the interest truly is "portfolio" interest and not the product of some active business.

We can get a more precise picture by picking apart the Code's definition of "portfolio interest," which is interest paid on an any "obligation" either 1) in registered form with a foreign owner or 2) if in bearer form, issued with restrictions on U.S. ownership.[9] Within these limitations, which are designed to prevent exempt portfolio interest from falling into the hand of U.S. beneficial owners, almost any kind of debt obligation can qualify, including bonds, notes of all kinds, and even debt on open account if it is properly recorded and is not a business loan made in the ordinary course of a moneylending business.

The exemption of portfolio interest eliminates U.S. income tax on much of the return to passive foreign investment in the United States. So amiable a tax regime would naturally induce all sorts of economic activity, including some highly entrepreneurial, to don the cloak of passive investment. Dressing ownership of U.S. business assets as ostensible debtholdings has become an obvious temptation. Section 871(h) contains a battery of provisions designed to keep the wolves from donning sheep's clothing.

Exceptions, limitations, and Restrictions

10-Percent Shareholders

Exempt portfolio interest does not include interest received by a "10-percent shareholder" of the issuer.[10] The point of this limitation is to deny an exemption for U.S.-source interest paid to owners and

---

[9]§871(h)(2).
[10]§871(h)(3).

substantial equity holders of an enterprise. Foreign owners of U.S. businesses cannot (unless they are widely dispersed small shareholders) cast their holdings in U.S. businesses in the form of debt yielding an untaxed flow of interest. Without the 10-percent limitation for equity holders, foreign investment in U.S. businesses would routinely be structured with the highest sustainable levels of debt in order to remove the underlying business profits from the U.S. tax environment as tax-free portfolio interest.

The denial of exemption for interest paid to 10-percent shareholders means that foreign capital will not find as favorable a U.S. income tax regime when it is invested in controlling interests in U.S. businesses as when it is invested in passive financial assets. By allowing foreign investors to enjoy a tax-free regime for U.S. investment only up to the point they become large equity holders of U.S. businesses, the tax system attempts to favor foreign investment in economic activity that remains under American control.

A "10-percent shareholder" (despite the use of the term "shareholder") includes holders of partnership interests as well as corporate stock. For debt issued by corporations, a 10-percent shareholder means any person owning 10 percent or more of the combined voting power of all classes of stock of the corporation. The status of 10-percent shareholder of a corporation is tied to voting power rather than beneficial ownership. Foreign owners willing to leave control to others can thus expatriate U.S.-source business profits in the form of exempt portfolio interest by capitalizing their ownership of U.S. business enterprises with a combination of nonvoting equity and debt.[11]

To grasp the import of the 10-percent shareholder rule it may be helpful to revisit Marcel's tax-sheltered U.S. business operations from chapter 3. There the interplay between the source rule for interest paid by individuals and a particular form of self-loan allowed Marcel to divert part of a stream of U.S. business profits to a low-tax environment through interest deductions. Generically, this is known as an earnings-stripping tax shelter. Marcel in that pattern must own the U.S. business assets directly, as a proprietor. For non-tax business reasons, though, we noted that Marcel might well prefer to own the business in a corporation. If the exemption of U.S.-source portfolio interest were wholly unqualified Marcel could simply acquire his U.S. business through a corporation in which he held both debt and equity, and exclude the interest from income as exempt portfolio interest. The business, remember, produces $150,000 of income a year. If Marcel were in a

---

[11]In the case of a partnership, however, a 10-percent shareholder is any person who owns 10 percent or more of the capital or profits interests in the partnership. §871(h)(3)(B).

low-tax environment he could, for example, hold his U.S. business in a U.S. corporation funded with $800,000 of 12-percent debt and $200,000 of stock. Assume, as in the diagram below, that Marcel uses a domestic U.S. corporation.

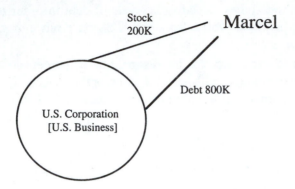

The interest of $96,000 is deductible from the corporation's income, leaving $54,000 of taxable income in the corporation, subject to U.S. corporate income tax of $8,500.[12] If the interest is exempt portfolio interest in Marcel's hands then $96,000 of Marcel's U.S. business profits would escape U.S. taxation.[13]

Because, however, Marcel is a 10-percent shareholder of the corporation paying the interest, the interest is not exempt portfolio interest in this case and is subject to U.S. flat rate tax of 30 percent. There is now only a slight tax advantage at best over direct ownership.[14] Nor would it help for Marcel to hold the debt of the U.S. corporation indirectly, so that no literal 10-percent shareholder would receive the interest. Consider the use of a foreign finance company, as on the facing page.

Here the foreign corporation is not directly a 10-percent shareholder (or any kind of shareholder) of the U.S. corporation. Still, the interest paid to F is not exempt portfolio interest. Attribution rules in section

---

[12]If Marcel received the $150,000 directly as a proprietor, his U.S. income tax would be roughly $45,000.

[13]The earnings remaining in the U.S. corporation would eventually be subject to a second layer of U.S. taxation (30 percent, unless shielded by treaty) upon their distribution to Marcel as dividends with respect to on his stock, but the distribution can be deferred for a long while, or Marcel can eventually capture the value of the accumulated earnings by selling the stock, at no U.S. income tax cost.

[14]It would avail Marcel little to use a *foreign* corporation to hold his U.S. business. Interest paid by the corporation would have U.S. source under the rule of section 884(f)(1) and, being paid to a 10-percent shareholder, would not be exempt portfolio interest.

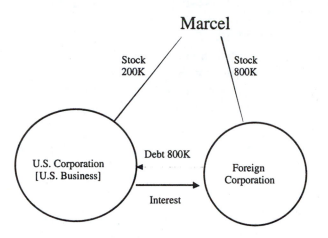

871(h)(3)(C) treat the foreign corporation for this purpose as the owner of the shares of the U.S. corporation directly owned by Marcel, thus making it a 10-percent shareholder by attribution. This is yet another form of look-through rule.

What Marcel cannot do alone, however, can be done with a second investor. If, for business reasons, Marcel must own the U.S. business in corporate form, another unrelated foreign investor, say Odette, could lend to Marcel's corporation and receive exempt portfolio interest. If, however, Odette were related to Marcel (married to him, for example) then by attribution under the rules sketched above Odette would be treated as a 10-percent shareholder and interest paid by Marcel's corporation would not be exempt portfolio interest in her hands and would be subject to U.S. flat tax. Therefore, even if Marcel and Odette are very very fond of each other, they should nonetheless (from a tax perspective, be it understood) live together rather than marry.

Interest Paid to Foreign Banks

The unrelated debtholder in this pattern, moreover, cannot be a bank or similar full-time professional lender. In another important exception, interest received by a bank "on an extension of credit made pursuant to a loan agreement entered into in the ordinary course of its trade or business" is *not* exempt portfolio interest.[15] The premise of this treatment of bank loans is that a bank loan generally is more like a business transaction than a passive investment and should be taxed

---

[15]§881(c)(3)(A).

accordingly.[16] The rule also prevents foreign banks from gaining a competitive advantage over U.S. banks in making loans to United States persons outside the United States.

Taxpayers have attempted in various ways to maneuver around the restrictive rules for bank debt. For example, an unrelated person such as Odette might borrow from a bank and re-lend to Marcel's business corporation on similar terms, as follows:

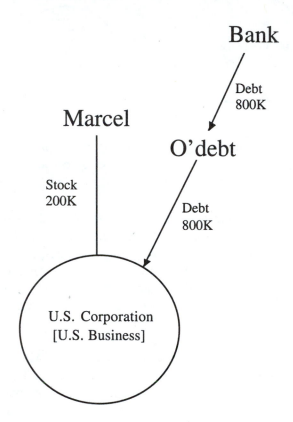

This pattern, known as back-to-back (or mirror image) debt, is central to many international tax shelters and earnings-stripping plans. We shall return to it in later chapters. In cases where Odette's obligation to the bank is secured by the U.S. corporation's obligation to Odette, the Revenue Service might well attack Odette's role in the venture as a mere "conduit" and seek to deny to the interest that flows through Odette to the bank the character of exempt portfolio interest. In this view the interest received by Odette subject to the obligation of turning it over to

---

[16]Note, however, that 1) foreign banks *can* receive exempt portfolio interest on bona fide passive investments such as corporate bonds and U.S. Treasury debt and 2) income tax treaties may shield some interest received by foreign banks that does not qualify as exempt portfolio interest.

the bank would be beneficially owned by the bank. Since 1993 a set of rules on "conduits," discussed more fully in chapter 24, have strengthened the Service's hand in this type of situation.

If, however, Odette had borrowed on her general credit only and had no other dealings with the bank, such an attack by the Service would likely fail. As a business matter, of course, such a transaction is implausible. A bank would almost certainly require that Odette's obligation to it be secured by the business corporation's obligation to her, unless Odette had sufficient unencumbered assets to cover the loan apart from the U.S. business venture. In that event Odette could have made the loan entirely from her own assets without having resort to a bank loan in the first place.

A variant of this back-to-back pattern is a loan from Marcel channeled through Odette on its way to the U.S. business, as follows:

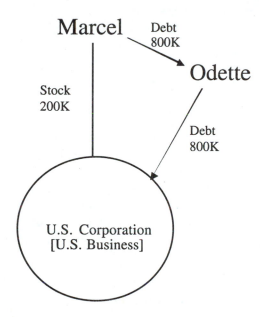

In principle, this is no different from the case involving a bank. The pattern does raise pointed questions of enforcement. How will the IRS find out about Marcel's loan to Odette? It is not obvious. Small private issues of debt to foreign persons that purport to generate exempt portfolio interest, however, are more likely to elicit probing questions from the IRS on the relation between debtholder and debtor than widely distributed bond issues.

Contingent Interest

Another exception, dating from the 1993 Act, removes several types of "contingent" interest from the class of exempt portfolio interest. Under section 871(h)(4)(A)(i), exempt portfolio interest does not include interest determined by reference to 1) the receipts, sales, or cash flow of the debtor, 2) the income or profits of the debtor, 3) a change in the value of appreciation or depreciation of property of the debtor, or 4) dividends or similar payments made by the debtor. These rules are designed to prevent direct participations by foreign persons in the profits of U.S. business operations from escaping U.S. taxation.

Dividends

U.S.-source dividends, like interest, are fixed or determinable income subject to flat rate tax. Unlike portfolio interest, they are entitled to no broad exemption from U.S. tax. It follows that dividends paid from earnings that have borne U.S. corporate income tax may suffer *two* layers of U.S. tax.[17] High-yielding U.S. equities are not, therefore, holdings of choice for foreign investors. Low yielding equities, on the other hand, given the absence of U.S. tax on most capital gains of foreign persons, are often ideal.

Under sections 871(i)(2)(B) and 881(d), dividends from an 80/20 company (a domestic corporation that has at least 80-percent active foreign business income) are exempt from flat rate taxation in the hands of foreign shareholders in the same proportion as the paying corporation's foreign source income bears to its total income. More simply put, the United States does not tax dividends attributable to the foreign source income of domestic corporations with predominantly foreign business operations.

Income from Intangible Property

The taxation of income derived from intangible property has evolved to deal with differences between the economic character of the income and the form of transaction from which it is derived. Royalties and other periodic consideration for the use of intangible property have always been regarded as "fixed or determinable" income, even though not explicitly so listed in the Code. Royalty income, you may remember from chapter 3, takes its source from the country where the property is

---

[17]Most income tax treaties reduce, but do not eliminate, the tax on dividends by the country of source.

used. Royalties for the use of intangible property in the United States (in a licensing arrangement, for example) are therefore taxable to foreign persons, at a flat rate if not derived from a U.S. trade or business. By contrast, lump sum gains from the *sale* of intangible property have their source in the place of residence of the seller,[18] and are free of U.S. tax unless related to a U.S. trade or business.[19]

Sale versus License

In this regime, both taxpayers and the IRS have paid close attention to the difference between sales and licenses of intangible property. The distinction can be elusive, however. The transfer of rights in intangible or intellectual property is often less clear cut than that of its tangible counterpart. Intangible property can often be used by several persons simultaneously. Sole possession being less critical, rights can be divided temporally, geographically, or by markets. There are certainties only at the extremes. A transfer of a copyright forever, lock, stock, and barrel, with no retained right of use, has always been a sale. The nonexclusive permission to use a secret process in exchange for a percentage of the resulting sales has never *not* been a license.

A case filling in the middle zone is Commissioner v. Wodehouse.[20] Wodehouse was an English author who had ostensibly "sold" the right to serialize a novel to an American magazine publisher for a lump sum price. The IRS insisted that the single payment was nonetheless "fixed or determinable" income (a royalty in effect) subject to flat rate tax. And despite the lump sum price the IRS won, on the ground that in the transfer of the serial rights Wodehouse retained so many other rights in the property that there had been no sale. Since *Wodehouse,* the difference between a sale and a license has turned not on the form of payment, but on the extent of the rights transferred in the underlying property.

Subsequent cases and rulings have fleshed out this boundary. In general, the transfer of *all* substantial rights in intangible property is a sale; and for many purposes so is the exclusive transfer of various lesser rights. The exclusive right to use a patent in a geographical area forever is a sale, for example, as is the exclusive right to exploit a copyrighted work in a medium of expression for the full life of the copyright.[21] Thus the exclusive and permanent transfer of all print rights in a work of

---

[18]§§865(a), (d).

[19]Remember that sales of property (other than U.S. realty) by foreign persons are generally untaxed if unrelated to a U.S. business.

[20]337 U.S. 369 (1949).

[21]See Rev. Rul. 60-226, 1960-1 Cum. Bull. 26.

fiction in the United States is a sale.[22] So is a similar transfer of the stage rights or the motion picture rights. Each transfer exhausts the U.S. rights within the medium of print, stage, or screen respectively.

There is a further question about the boundaries of a single medium of expression. For now, recognized separate media include print, stage, motion picture, and broadcast (radio and television). As cyberspace expands its power to transmit artistic and literary representations, it may come to be viewed as a separate medium of expression for this purpose.

Sales with Contingent Payments

The outcome of *Wodehouse* left opportunities for foreign taxpayers. As long as they transferred substantial and extensive U.S. rights in intangible property, their transactions were sales, even if they received a stream of payments contingent on the buyer's subsequent use of the property. A common form of transfer of rights in intangible property is the contingent sale, where the owner of a copyright or a patent transfers all rights in it for a percentage of the proceeds derived from its use by the transferee. In form the transaction is a sale, because the entire titular ownership in property has been transferred. In economic effect, however, it is a royalty arrangement in which the transferor retains a continuing economic interest in the intangible property.

To align taxation more closely with the economic character of contingent sales, section 871(a)(1)(D) imposes flat rate tax on U.S.-source "gains from the sale or exchange ... of patents, copyrights, secret processes and formulas, goodwill, trademarks, trade brands, franchises, and other like property, or of any interest in any such property, to the extent such gains are from payments which are contingent on the productivity, use or disposition of the property or interest sold or exchanged." As noted in chapter 3, the source of such contingent payments is determined as though the payments were royalties. Therefore, the place where intangible property is used, rather than the place of sale or the residence of the seller, governs the source of the gains. The effect of these provisions, roughly, is to treat contingent gains from the sale of intangible property as royalties.

Bear in mind that gain attributable to *fixed* payments is not subject to the tax of section 871(a)(1)(D), whether or not there are contingent payments in the overall transaction. It follows that a foreign seller of intangible property for use in the United States should hold out for a lump sum price rather than a contingent formula price predicated on events. It is, of course, much harder to come to agreement on a lump

---

[22]But not the transfer of the right of serial publication (at issue in *Wodehouse*), which does not exhaust the print medium.

sum price (because the buyer then bears the entire risk of poor results), and some contingent element will often be necessary as a business matter for an exchange to go forward. In that event, the tax planner should try to confine the contingent element to the smallest possible amount in the fewest taxable years, as far as can be done without undermining the economics of the transaction.

With section 871(a)(1)(D) in the Code, the distinction between sales and licenses is far less important for transactions in intangible property than in the days of *Wodehouse*: all contingent payments attributable to intangible property used in the United States are today subject to tax.

Chapter 6

The Meaning of a U.S. "Trade or Business"

The notion of a "trade or business" in the United States lies at the core of U.S. taxation of inbound transactions. As we saw in chapter 5, foreign persons' U.S.-source income from passive investment is taxed at a flat rate on a gross basis, or not at all. As we shall see in chapter 7, income "effectively connected" with a U.S. business is taxed on a net basis at graduated rates, much as the income of a U.S. person. Since a foreign person must have, or have had, a U.S. "trade or business" in ~~~~~~~~~~~~ "~~~~~~~~~~ ~~~~~~~~~~" ~~~~~ ~~ the existence of

determinable income and zero taxation of capital gains) by starting small restaurant in the United States or even giving a single lecture for money.[1] Today there are separate tax regimes for passive investment income and income derived from a U.S. business.

The Code offers no comprehensive definition of a "trade or business" for either domestic or foreign taxpayers. In various places, however, the concept is expressly qualified to specific ends. For foreign taxpayers in particular, the core notion of a trade or business is left largely to administrative or judicial determination, but the notion has also been overlaid with statutory rules governing specific activities and taxpayers. This chapter surveys the general scope of a "trade or business" and one or two special enclaves.

"Business" versus Passive Investing

The notion of a "trade or business" is best understood in contrast with what it is not: passive investment.[2] A "trade or business" suggests something active, perhaps even entrepreneurial. Passive investment entails little more than the commitment of capital and patient expecta-

---

[1]This regime was known as "force of attraction," because the U.S. trade or business appeared to "attract" all the U.S. income of foreign taxpayers.

[2]I am using the term "investment" not in the technical economic sense of creating a new income-producing capital asset, but in the colloquial sense of acquiring ownership rights in a passive income stream.

tion. Because there are near-infinite gradations of risk and involvement in the full range of economic activity, it turns out to be difficult if not impossible to articulate a universal test of a trade or business as opposed to passive investing. Rather, it is a factbound determination in which several elements—including most importantly the nature and extent of the taxpayer's activity—weigh in the scales.

A classic case on the distinction between a trade or business and pure passive investing is Higgins v. Commissioner.[3] Higgins lived (in Paris) from the income of his substantial holdings of real estate, bonds, and stock. He maintained an office in New York that generally watched over his securities. Higgins' employees did little trading, but deposited checks and kept records. Because Higgins had very substantial assets, this record-keeping and oversight entailed considerable activity. The Commissioner denied that the cost of managing the securities was an expense of carrying on a trade or business, and the Supreme Court agreed. The Court underscored the essentially factual boundary between pure passive investing and carrying on a trade or business, and concluded that even though the taxpayer's activities were extensive, merely keeping records and collecting income (albeit on a large scale) is not a trade or business. Significantly, though, the IRS conceded in the case—and the Court apparently agreed—that the taxpayer's ownership of rental real estate (and the attendant activity) *did* constitute a business. The difference was, one can infer, that Higgins' stocks and bonds were pure financial assets entitling him to an income stream only and giving him neither the right to participate actively in the operations of the underlying enterprises nor any liabilities beyond his commitment of capital. Higgins' ownership of buildings, by contrast, presumably gave him both the right and the obligation to deal with the property directly, as well as full liability for losses and other risks.[4]

An important inference from *Higgins* is that the existence of a trade or business depends at the outset on the nature of the interest in property from which gain is derived. Direct ownership, with the attendant responsibilities and risks, is an essential element of a trade or business, while pure financial assets that yield an income stream without involvement or liability are generally passive investments. The ownership of corporate shares therefore is not in itself a trade or business and the trade or business of a corporation is not imputed to its shareholders, or even to a single owner of all the shares.

---

[3]312 U.S. 212, *reh'g denied,* 312 U.S. 714 (1941).
[4]This implication of *Higgins* is confirmed in Investor's Mortgage Security Co. v. Commissioner, 4 T.C.M. 45 (1945), where a large foreign investor in U.S. financial assets was held also to have a U.S. business by virtue of its ownership of significant but lesser holdings of U.S. real property.

Direct ownership is necessary but not sufficient to constitute a trade or business. The right to a stream of royalties, for example, does not put its holder in a trade or business. A landowner who turns mineral rights over to a lessee who agrees to develop the property and pay back a percentage of production as a royalty does not thereby acquire a trade or business; nor does a landowner who receives a crop share from a tenant farmer. Owners of such passive royalty interests are not involved in the underlying activity.

Rental Real Estate and Natural Resources

Rental real estate in particular is a holding that constitute a trade or business for its owner. An ow day-to-day operation of the property is clearly engag who turns over the property entirely to independe tenants in net lease arrangements, may not be. The a somewhat shaky line between these possibilities.

In Pinchot v. Commissioner[5] a British citizen a several parcels of rental real estate in New York City. managed through an agent who leased them when they became idle, collected the rents, and paid the operating expenses, taxes, mortgage interest, and other necessary obligations. From time to time, properties were sold and others were bought. The court drew the inference from the scale of the holdings themselves that the transactions of the taxpayer in managing them "must have been considerable . . . as well as continuous and regular,"[6] assuming, in effect, that income cannot arise from properties of a certain size without some active massaging:

> What was done was more than the investment and reinvestment of funds in real estate. It was the management of the real estate itself for profit....It necessarily involved alterations and repairs commensurate with the value and number of buildings cared for, and such transactions as were necessary constitute a recognized form of business. The management of real estate on such a scale for income producing purposes required regular and continuous activity of the kind which is commonly concerned with the employment of labor; the purchase of materials; the making of contracts; and many other things which come within the definition of business ... within the commonly accepted meaning of that word.[7]

---

[5] 113 F.2d 718 (2d Cir. 1940.

[6] Id. at 719.

[7] Id. Other cases have followed the standard laid down in *Pinchot* and treat ownership and operation of real estate as a trade or business. E.g., Lewenhaupt v. Commissioner, 20 T.C. 151 (1953), *aff'd*, 221 F.2d 227 (9th Cir. 1955); de Amodio v. Commissioner, 34 T.C. 894 (1960), *aff'd*, 299 F.2d 623 (3d Cir. 1962).

Left open in *Pinchot* is whether smaller holdings of real estate allow the same inference of business activity and whether an owner of real property can escape a trade or business by surrendering all control to another. The decided cases involving rental real estate are not perfectly consistent on this score, but allow the inference that the ownership of even a small parcel of real estate may be a trade or business.[8] If, however, real property is subject to a long term net lease removing the owner from day-to-day involvement or control, ownership of the property by itself is not a trade or business.[9]

The IRS for its part has ruled[10] that a nonresident alien's ownership of real property subject to long-term leases shifting the burden of major expenses to the lessees does not amount to a business. Importantly, this ruling does not turn on the scale of the holdings. It seems therefore that a foreign person's ownership of the Empire State Building, if the property were subject to an appropriately stringent net lease, would not be a U.S. business.[11]

Interests in natural resources present similar possibilities. The owner of a pure royalty interest in U.S. mineral rights is not engaged a U.S. business. Nor even, in some circumstances, is the owner of a "working" interest, if the owner has turned over the day-to-day control and supervision to an independent operator.[12]

Other Activities

Most economic undertakings that engage the taxpayers' efforts, whether directly or through agents, add up to a trade or business. Some, however, such as lending money and certain kinds of buying and selling, may fall on the passive investment side of the line.

---

[8]Estate of Yerburgh v. Commissioner, 4 T.C.M. 1145 (1945) (a one-fifth interest in two small buildings managed by a commission agent constituted a U.S. business). Cf. Schwarcz v. Commissioner, 24 T.C. 733 (1955) (taxpayer who owned a single parcel of real property, but who was significantly engaged in operating it, *held* engaged in trade or business).

[9]Neill v. Commissioner, 46 B.T.A. 197 (1942); Herbert v. Commissioner, 30 T.C. 26 (1958).

[10]Revenue Ruling 73-522, 1973-2 Cum. Bull. 226.

[11]Foreign taxpayers preferring the graduated tax regime on net income (and they often would in such situations because their expenses are likely to amount to a significant percentage of gross rents) can *elect* to treat income from real property as though it were "effectively connected" to a trade or business. See §§871(d), 882(d).

[12]See Portanova v. United States, 690 F.2d 169 (Ct. Cl. 1982).

Services

Section 864(b)(1) expressly asserts the performance of personal services to be a trade or business. This treatment extends to the broadest array of "services," including artistic and athletic performances. A single prizefight or lecture in the United States, if compensated, constitutes engaging in a trade or business there.

Buying and Selling

There is little doubt that sales of property representing the last step of distribution or marketing operations, or the end point of production or manufacturing, are a form of doing business. When the property sold is "inventory," it is by definition being turned over in the normal course of a "business." Because selling property to customers as a habitual activity is so obviously a trade or business, the question that comes up more often, as discussed below, is where the business is carried out, rather than whether there is one in the first place.

Sales of pure investment assets, on the other hand, are not a trade or business, as the *Higgins* case and others abundantly establish. They are simply occasions for realizing gains and losses from passive commitments of capital. What makes sales of property a business, as a general matter, is some kind of added value resulting from the sale itself. A quart of milk sold by a grocer to a customer has moved a step further along its destiny of being consumed. A stock or bond, by contrast, is pretty much the same thing in the hands of successive owners, even if more or less valuable as such.[13]

There is a difficult line between inventory and investment assets. Sales of tangible property, with consumption value, are naturally more susceptible to being a business. Financial assets are most often sold anonymously on securities exchanges, not to "customers" in the colloquial sense. Such sales, unless made by a broker-dealer, rarely if ever amount to a trade or business, even if frequent. A one-time sale of a painting from a private collection will also hold up easily as the disposition of an investment. Sales of several paintings to different buyers, however, especially if coupled with purchases of paintings from different quarters, might well at some point become a business. But no bell rings at that point. It is undoubtedly possible, abstractly, to sell a number of tangible investment assets such as paintings in a relatively short period. As a foreign seller, however, I would go to some pains to negotiate the sales and have title pass outside the United States. That

---

[13]Note, however, that stocks and bonds generally do constitute inventory in the hands of a securities dealer, who, accordingly, *is* considered to be engaged in a trade or business.

would not be possible, of course, if the paintings were sold at auction in the United States, but the more anonymous character of art auctions, being assimilable in some respects to a securities exchange, provides considerable insulation to foreign sellers.

Lending Money

Holders of debt claims may be purely passive investors (as when they hold a portfolio of government bonds, for example) or may be lending money as a business (as does a bank in the course of its operations). There is, however, no self-evident line between purely passive loans, exemplified by debt securities held for investment, and loans made in the course of a lending business. Commonly, the professional moneylender is substantially involved in shaping the terms of a loan, while a pure investor typically buys (or abstains to buy) bonds or other debt securities ready-made. But this is not an unequivocal boundary between a lending business and passive investment. The single buyer of a large bond issue in a private placement may negotiate aggressively over the terms of the underlying loan. Does that make the loan a business? The available authority on point suggests not.[14] An element of recurrence, and possibly even dealing with *customers* (as opposed simply to borrowers) may be necessary thresholds of an actual business.

Within limits, a lender can perhaps influence the question by careful framing of the circumstances of loans. Call yourself a moneylender and you will be taxed as one. Call yourself an investor and that is what you may be. If you work in a storefront under a sign that says "Get Your Loans Here" you are in a business, even if you are unsuccessful and your actual transactions are sporadic. On the other hand, if you comb the financial press for opportunities to acquire privately placed debt for investment, and often follow through, you may nonetheless retain the tax status of investor.[15] Prescriptively, this means that a foreign lender who seeks to avoid being in a U.S. business (and thereby enjoy the exemption of U.S.-source portfolio interest) should try as much as possible to *look* like a passive investor.

---

[14]Consider Rev. Rul. 73-522, 1973-2 Cum. Bull. 226, discussed above, where a net lease of real property is not a trade or business even when the owner is directly involved in negotiating the lease.

[15]See Yaeger v. Commissioner, 889 F.2d 29 (2d Cir. 1989) (extensive investing during entire lifetime by individual for own account, including involvement in underlying businesses, *held* not a trade or business).

Manufacturing

Making things (i.e., manufacturing and production) is almost certainly a trade or business. It involves the commitment of capital and labor to the creation of added value and, in some form or other, almost invariably culminates in a sale or exchange of something. Surprisingly, no decided case expressly holds that manufacturing as such is a trade or business. There is, however, little doubt of this conclusion, notwithstanding some ancient cases and rulings that manufacturing is not by itself a trade or business.[16]

Business "in the United States"?

Once the existence of a trade or business is established, there is the further question whether the taxpayer is carrying on the trade or business *in the United States*. There are degrees of presence in the United States that, cumulatively, established a trade or business there. A resort hotel in Monaco clearly does not have a U.S. business simply by virtue of receiving American guests. Nor, one imagines, does a foreign mail order firm merely because some orders come to it from the United States. But what if these enterprises regularly run advertisements in The New York Times? As activities in support of foreign operations are imported into the United States, the threshold of a U.S. trade or business is eventually crossed.

In general, purely promotional activities do not rise to the level of a trade or business. Either of the foreign enterprises just described could therefore engage in advertising in the United States without crossing the line. Similarly, the mere purchase of goods in the United States for resale elsewhere does not amount to doing business.[17] On the other side of the line, any complete cycle of production and sale or purchase and sale conducted in the United States *is* a U.S. trade or business.[18]

Here again, sales of property pose the greatest difficulty. A sale of "inventory" implies the existence of a trade or business,[19] but where? Does passage of title to goods in the United States establish a trade or business there? Probably not. A foreign seller must engage in some

---

[16]See R.J. Dorn & Co. v. Commissioner, 12 B.T.A. 1102 (1928); 32 Op. Atty. Gen. 336 (1920). Cf. United States v. E.C. Knight Co., 156 U.S. 1, 12 (1895) (manufacture in itself not "commerce" within meaning of Sherman Antitrust Law).

[17]Cf. Consolidated Premium Iron Ores Ltd. v. United States, 28 T.C. 127 (1957) *(nonacq.)*.

[18]See United States v. Balanovski, 236 F.2d 298 (2d Cir. 1956), *cert. denied,* 352 U.S. 968 (1956).

[19]Inventory by its nature is property sold to customers in the normal course of business.

actual economic activity in the United States, at least by imputation. But how much and of what kind? What if the foreign seller also engages in promotion in the United States to generate orders, such as advertisements in U.S. publications or other media? Does this, coupled with the passage of title here, establish a U.S. business? Again, more likely not, but it is less clear.[20] As for sales through brokers, distributors, agents, and employees, they raise questions of the imputation of a business, which are discussed next.

The Imputation of a Trade of Business

It is entirely possible to be engaged in a trade or business without conducting the underlying activity with one's own hands. Someone can be in the coal business without ever wearing a miner's hat, and, as many readers of this book either know or suspect, it is possible to practice law as a senior partner without ever venturing into a law library. A taxpayer's "activities" can be the measure of a trade or business only if, across a broad spectrum of situations, the activities of some are imputed to others. Beyond one or two explicit statutory rules, however, principles of imputation can be derived only at some pains from cases and rulings that, on this score, are far from perfectly consistent.

Some imputation of a trade or business is statutory and automatic. There are two specific statutory rules of imputation. Under section 875, a trade or business is imputed 1) from a partnership to each partner,[21] and 2) from a trust or estate to each beneficiary.[22] Beyond that, it is all case by case.

A trade or business is generally imputed between agent and principal (especially between employee and employer) and between others who stand in relations of delegation and control. A senior partner who plays golf while an associate toils is nonetheless engaged in a trade or business. There is nothing talismanic about the agency relationship, however. An "agent," as that term is understood at common law, is subject to a high degree of control by the principal. It is this control, rather than the terms used to describe the relationship, that permits the activities of an agent to be regarded as those of the principal. This can be inferred from a number of decided cases, but is nowhere fully articulated. Relationships of lesser control—such as independent contractors or brokers—are generally not occasions for the imputation of a trade or business,

---

[20]There is no decisive authority on point, but Piedas Negras Broadcasting v. United States, 43 BTA 297 (1941), suggests this result.

[21]§875(1).

[22]§875(2).

although the sparseness of explicit authority on point makes it somewhat hazardous to bank on this conclusion.

Chapter 7

"Effectively Connected" Income

U.S. taxation of business profits of foreign persons is built on the notion of income "effectively connected" with a U.S. business. The "effectively connected" income of a foreign person is subject to U.S. tax, on a net basis, at regular graduated rates. This regime of graduated rates is the same net income tax regime to which U.S. persons are generally subject under the Code. As with U.S. persons, tax is payable by return.

The Basic statutory Scheme

Under section 871(b)(1), a nonresident alien individual is taxed "as provided in section 1 ... on his taxable income which is effectively connected with the conduct of a trade or business within the United States." The reference to section 1 and "taxable income" incorporates the essential rules of the U.S. income tax. Deductions are allowed for business expenses and specific personal itemized expenses. The same distinctions between business and personal expenses apply, as well as between current expenses and capital outlays. The relevant depreciation and amortization allowances are available. Foreign corporations are subject to a similar tax regime on their effectively connected income by virtue of the specific reference in section 882(a)(1) to the tax imposed on corporations by section 11. Oversimplifying slightly, foreign taxpayers are taxed on their "effectively connected" income as though they were U.S. residents with no other gains. The receipt of effectively connected income thus opens up for a foreign person the full intricacies of the Internal Revenue Code.

Effectively connected income is defined at some length in section 864(c). The main focus is on its relation to a U.S. trade or business. Only a foreign person who at some time has been engaged in a U.S. business can have effectively connected income.[1] The trade or business need not, however, exist in the same year as the income arises if there is a requisite economic or commercial relation between the income and the trade or business.

Once the existence of a U.S. trade or business is established, there are different tests of effectively connected income for income of different source and character. *U.S.-source* income is effectively connected according to rules contained in sections 864(c)(2) and

---

[1] §864(c)(1)(B).

864(c)(3). A small class of *foreign source* income is effectively connected under rules in section 864(c)(4). There is considerable further articulation within these categories.

Fixed or Determinable Income and Capital Gains

Fixed or determinable income and capital gains are effectively connected according to a two-pronged statutory test in section 864(c)(2):

> In determining whether [U.S.-source fixed or determinable income and capital gains and losses] is effectively connected with the conduct of a trade or business within the United States, the factors taken into account shall include whether—
>
> (A) the income, gain, or loss is derived from assets used or held for use in the conduct of such trade or business, or
>
> (B) the activities of such trade or business were a material factor in the realization of the income, gain, or loss.

These two standards are known as the "asset use" and "activities" tests respectively. These are intuitive tests, and in some degree overlapping. Regulations under section 864 fill in the broad-brush statement of section 864(c)(2).

Assets Used in the Business

The use of some assets constitutes a business in itself. Income from such use (which almost invariably is fixed or determinable) is therefore effectively connected. Rents from real estate or equipment leasing, for example, are effectively connected under the asset use test if the rental operations giving rise to them are a trade or business. Similarly, film rentals from movie distribution, if the distributor owns the films, are effectively connected (or not) according to the asset use test. If, however, the distributor has no proprietary interest in the films, the rentals might be viewed as flowing from an *activity*. The rentals might still be effectively connected, but under the activities test described below.

In some cases assets used in support of a business generate income that does not have the immediate look and feel of business profits. Some common items of fixed or determinable income (such as interest or dividends) received by the owner of a business, for example, have the same form as income derived from passive investments. These may nonetheless be effectively connected under the asset use test if they are derived from the working capital or inventory of a business. Instances of effectively connected interest and dividends include interest on bank balances held in support of the current operations of a business, interest derived from a business's accounts receivable, and interest or dividends on stock or bonds held as inventory by a securities dealer.

Activities

Income is effectively connected under the second prong of section 864(c)(2) if the "activities" of the business were a "material factor" in its realization.[2] Since the performance of services in the United States is usually a "trade or business," compensation for services is effectively connected under the activities test because the services are obviously a material factor in producing the income. Besides its immediate application to income from personal services, this standard also reaches royalties derived from active licensing operations, and gains from assets sold by traders whose activity has crossed the threshold of a business.

Some income—that derived from a restaurant, for example—results from a combination of sales of inventory and services. Since both elements are likely to be effectively connected to an underlying business conducted in the United States, albeit under different statutory tests, the exact breakdown of the income is not of crucial importance.

Other U.S.-Source Income

The reader may have noticed that the two tests of section 864(c)(2) do not reach the single most important class of business profits, namely, gains from the sale of inventory.[3] Gains from both manufacturing and merchandising most commonly take the form of profits from the sale of inventory to customers. Such gains are, however, neither fixed or determinable nor derived from the sale of capital assets, and therefore fall outside the reach of section 864(c)(2). Consider, for example, a foreign corporation that produces and sells automobiles in the United States. It is about as fully engaged in a trade or business as you can get. But it derives no fixed or determinable income from its operations, because gains from the sale of property, inventory or otherwise, are not fixed or determinable income.[4] The "asset use" and "activities" tests of section 864(c)(2) therefore have no bearing on whether this

---

[2]Reg. §1.864-4(c)(2)(ii).

[3]British readers should know that what is called "inventory" in American usage (materials and goods turned over in the normal course of a business) is generally called "stock" in Great Britain. In the United States (and in this book) the latter term refers to the shares of a corporation.

[4]For more on this score, see chapter 5.

corporation's gain is effectively connected. Common sense tells us that this corporation should derive taxable business profits from its U.S. operations. Section 864(c)(3) formalizes this intuition, along with some effects that are far less obvious.

Section 864(c)(3) casts as effectively connected to a U.S. trade or business all U.S.-source income *not* covered by section 864(c)(2). Accordingly, *any* U.S.-source income of a foreign person engaged in a U.S. business, other than fixed or determinable income or capital gain, is automatically treated as effectively connected to the U.S. business. Section 864(c)(3) is sometimes known as the "other income" clause.

Section 864(c)(3) is cast in the form of the old "force of attraction" principle: the entire residual class of U.S.-source gains is attributed to a U.S. trade or business. Since the overwhelming bulk of such gains are from sales of inventory in the United States, which have U.S. source by virtue of passage of title here, the results of this "attraction" are generally reasonable. An item cannot by definition be "inventory" without being part of a trade or business; its sale therefore produces a business profit. A large class of U.S.-source business profits, including all gains from the sale of goods and various income at the periphery (such as gains from the operation of a restaurant), are effectively connected by virtue of section 864(c)(3).

Often there is an economic connection between a U.S. business and "other" U.S.-source income made effectively connected by section 864(c)(3). If a foreign corporation opens a department store in the United States, section 864(c)(3) quite naturally makes the profits from U.S. sales effectively connected. A foreign dealer of objets d'art whose U.S. sales are frequent enough to constitute a trade or business would also derive effectively connected income under section 864(c)(3) unless the dealer had no U.S. office and title to the property sold passed legitimately outside the United States.

Section 864(c)(3), however, makes "other" U.S.-source income effectively connected *whether or not* it has an economic connection to a U.S. business. Its effect can be startling. A European mail order business, for example, might have a number of U.S. customers and significant U.S.-source income without being engaged in business in the United States. If the owner of the business were to perform personal services in the United States, even in the form of a lecture or two on a wholly unrelated subject, or if the business opened a small branch in the United States in some entirely different line, such as a restaurant, the entire U.S.-source income of the business (including the mail-order profit) would become effectively connected. This would result because section 864(c)(3) operates entirely by attraction rather than by requiring any actual connection between items of income and specific business activity. Thus, in the course of reaching inventory sold by U.S. businesses, section 864(c)(3) may reach much more.

This makes section 864(c)(3) a potential minefield, which can punish foot faults severely. A foreign artist selling paintings on consignment through an independent gallery in the United States more than likely does not have U.S. taxable income.[5] But if the artist gives a single lecture for a fee in the United States—sufficient by itself to constitute a U.S. business—section 864(c)(3) may swallow up all this hapless taxpayer's U.S.-source gains.

Foreign Source Income

A specific and quite narrow class of foreign-source income is attracted to a U.S. trade or business and treated as "effectively connected" under sections 864(c)(4) and 864(c)(5). These Code provisions, themselves quite elaborate, are backed up by extensive and detailed regulations, complete with numerous examples.[6]

At the outset, no such attraction can occur unless the foreign taxpayer has an office or other fixed place of business in the United States and the income is attributable to this office. Three types of foreign source income may then be effectively connected with the U.S. business:

> 1) Rents or royalties derived from the U.S. business for the use of intangible property outside the United States.
> 2) Financial gains (e.g., dividends, interest, gains from securities) resulting from a U.S. banking business or from the operations of an active securities investment company.
> 3) Gains from the sale "through" the U.S. office of inventory or like property, unless the property is sold for use outside the United States and a foreign office of the taxpayer participates materially in the sale.[7]

In determining the existence of a "U.S. office or other fixed place of business" (something of a term of art in this context), more than the physical space actually occupied by the taxpayer is taken into account. The office of an agent in the United States is imputed to the principal.[8] This imputation arises, however, only if the agent is a "dependent" agent. There is no imputation of the office of an independent agent

---

[5]The U.S.-source gains from the sale of the artist's "inventory" are not fixed or determinable and therefore escape U.S. taxation in the absence of a U.S. trade or business.

[6]Reg. §§1.864-5, 6, 7.

[7]§864(c)(4)(B).

[8]§864(c)(5)(A).

(such as a general commission agent or broker) acting in the ordinary course of business.

To get the flavor this type of foreign source effectively connected income, consider the following possibilities. 1) A foreign filmmaker distributes motion pictures all over North America through a sales and distribution office maintained in the United States. The rentals from film distribution in Canada (which have non-U.S. source) are effectively connected nonetheless. 2) A U.S. branch of a foreign bank makes a commercial loan to a customer in Mexico City; the loan is negotiated and cleared through the U.S. branch office. Interest on the loan (which has foreign source by virtue of the residence of the borrower/payor) is effectively connected to the U.S. branch business. 3) Our friend Marcel, in this incarnation a French wine merchant, opens a sales office in Detroit, Michigan, through which he sells wine to customers in Windsor, Ontario. If title to the goods passes in Canada, Marcel's gains have foreign source, but are effectively connected nonetheless.

Deferred Gains from a Trade or Business

There are, finally, provisions in section 864(c) that treat certain deferred income or gains as effectively connected. Sections 864(c)(6) and 864(c)(7) extend the scope of effectively connected income to include several types of income attributable to a U.S. business but arising in a year when the business no longer exists.

Section 864(c)(6) treats as effectively connected, in the year it is "taken into account," deferred income attributable to the performance of services, the sale of property, or any other "transaction" occurring in another year, if the income would have been effectively connected in the year of the actual sale, services, or transaction. Thus deferred compensation from U.S. services or installment payments from sales of business assets or inventory are taxed as effectively connected income at graduated rates. In the case of services these rules may well improve the tax regime of less affluent former U.S. residents who have returned to their countries of origin and who might otherwise suffer flat rate taxation of 30 percent (instead of tax at a 15-percent rate) on their low-bracket U.S.-source retirement income.

Under section 864(c)(7), when property once "used or held for use in connection with the conduct of a trade or business within the United States" is disposed of within 10 years of that use, the determination whether the resulting gain is taxable as "effectively connected" is made "as if" the disposition "occurred immediately before" the property ceased to be used in a U.S. trade or business. The effect of this "as if" determination is generally to treat the gains as effectively connected, because that is the usual fate of gains from property used in a U.S. business. Inventory or equipment from a U.S. business may thus bear the mark of that business, as a tax matter, for a decade.

Elective Effective Connection

As we saw in chapter 6, interests in U.S. real estate or natural resources can be held without creating a trade or business. In that case the current income of foreign persons from the property is not effectively connected and is therefore taxed at flat rates without deductions. This is highly disadvantageous in the common situation where the combined operating expenses, interest, and depreciation or depletion would, if available, significantly offset income taxable on a net basis. Rental real estate often produces tax losses when full account is taken of these deductions. A royalty interest in natural resources may also give rise to significant deductions for depletion and other costs if taxable on a net basis.

To pacify this problem there is an election for foreign taxpayers to treat income from real property in the United States as effectively connected with a trade or business regardless of its actual character.[9] The election extends to all income from real property, including income from natural resources.

---

[9] The election is codified in §§871(d) and 882(d).

Chapter 8

Gains from Sales of U.S. Real Property

Until 1980, sales by foreign persons of real property in the United States had essentially the same tax consequences as their sales of other property. If ownership of the property constituted a trade or business, or if the property was used in a trade or business, gain or loss from the sale was "effectively connected." If the taxpayer had no trade or business or if the real property was not connected to one, gain or loss upon a sale entailed no tax consequences.

The interplay of these and other rules created a favorable tax regime for U.S. real estate operations. A foreign person who owned and operated U.S. real estate as a trade or business could use the full range of deductions (interest, depreciation, etc.) to shelter the income from the property. The property could subsequently be sold on an installment basis with a small down payment in the year of sale. Most of the gain would ultimately be recognized in years in which the taxpayer was engaged in *no* U.S. trade or business, and would therefore escape U.S. tax altogether. Even better results could flow from the ownership of U.S. real estate through a corporation. Current income from the property would be offset by deductions within the corporation, whereas the gain from appreciation in value could be derived from the sale of the stock by the shareholders, a transaction usually attracting no U.S. tax. Section 897 brought an end to all that.

Section 897

Under section 897(a)(1), gains and losses of foreign taxpayers from the disposition of a "United States real property interest" are treated as "effectively connected" with a United States trade or business. Gains reached by section 897 are therefore taxed at graduated rates, as gains derived from business operations, regardless of their actual character. By virtue of being treated as effectively connected, the gains are brought essentially within the tax regime imposed on U.S. persons for gains of the same type. Section 897 makes the taxation of gains from U.S. real estate in the hands of foreign persons nearly unavoidable.[1]

---

[1]Tax can, however, be deferred for a time by using a foreign corporation to hold U.S. real property, as discussed further at the end of this chapter.

International Taxation

"United States Real Property Interests"

Numerous holdings are swept into the class of "United States real property interests," some obvious, some less so. A "United States real property interest" is defined in section 897(c)(1)(A) as

> (i) an interest in real property (including an interest in a mine, well, or other natural deposit) located in the United States or the Virgin Islands, and
>
> (ii) any interest (other than an interest solely as a creditor) in any domestic corporation unless the taxpayer establishes ... that such corporation was at no time a United States real property holding corporation during the shorter of—
>
> > (I) the period ... during which the taxpayer held such interest, or
> >
> > (II) the 5-year period ending on the date of the disposition of such interest.

Both direct holdings of real property located in the United States or the U.S. Virgin Islands and many types of shareholdings in domestic corporations owning U.S. real property are treated as United States real property interests within this definition. Among the numerous questions flowing from this provision are the nature of "real property" and the scope of an "interest" in real property.

Scope of "Real Property"

Under section 897, as elaborated in the Regulations, "real property" includes a broad range of holdings. Besides land, all mineral deposits and natural resources (including timber and agricultural crops) are treated as real property until they are actually extracted or severed from the land.[2] A royalty interest in minerals, for example, is an interest in real property. All "improvements," including buildings and other inherently permanent structures, are interests in real property.[3] Virtually any structure with walls constitutes a "building." "Inherently permanent structures" include parking lots, swimming pools, paved areas, wharves, docks, fences, billboards, outdoor lighting, oil rigs, silos, and much, much more.[4] Structural components (plumbing, heating, elevators, etc.) are also real property.[5]

"Real property" also includes "furnishings" and other "personal property associated with the use of the real property."[6] This category encompasses pipelines, railroad tracks, and other traditional fixtures, as well as power lines and transmission units. The Regulations extend the

---

[2]Reg. §1.897-1(b)(2).
[3]Reg. §1.897-1(b)(3).
[4]Reg. §1.897-1(b)(3)(iii).
[5]Reg. §1.897-1(b)(3)(ii).
[6]§897(c)(6)(B).

range of "associated" property to mining equipment, farm machinery, and even draft animals.[7] Construction equipment is also "associated" property if it is used by the landowner. All furniture and equipment used in lodgings held for rental (both permanent housing and hotels) and offices is included.

"Interests" in Real Property

The range of "interests" in real property reached by section 897 is as broad as the types of property. Besides fee ownership, co-ownerships, leaseholds, options, and all other possessory or beneficial interests in property are "interests" under section 897.[8]

Also included among U.S. real property interests—and this is a critical element—is an interest in any *domestic* corporation that has qualified as a "United States real property holding corporation" (hereafter "U.S. RPHC") at *any* time during the previous five years while owned by a foreign person.[9] A U.S. RPHC, in overview, is a corporation (domestic *or* foreign) the principal assets of which include United States real estate.

The terminology of section 897 is a little tricky and requires close attention. Only an interest in a *domestic* corporation can be a "U.S. real property interest," but *any* corporation holding U.S. real property can be a U.S. RPHC. In other words, a U.S. RPHC that is also a domestic corporation may be a United States real property interest.

The status of U.S. RPHC is defined by the degree of concentration of the entity's holdings of U.S. real property. More specifically, a U.S. RPHC is any corporation holding U.S. real property with a fair market value equal to 50 percent or more of the fair market value of its combined holdings of real property worldwide and assets used in the conduct of a trade or business.[10] In applying this 50-percent test, only real property (both U.S. and foreign) and active business assets are taken into account. Otherwise, portfolio holdings, passive investments, or interests in subsidiary corporations could routinely be used to dilute real property holdings and avoid section 897 altogether. Because of the five-year period established in section 897(c)(1)(A)(ii)(II), a domestic corporation, having once become a U.S. RPHC, may be treated as a U.S. real property interest for five years thereafter.

The test period for the status of U.S. real property interest is the shorter of five years or the taxpayer's holding period. Thus, while a U.S.

---

[7]Reg. §1.897-1(b)(4)(i)(A).
[8]§897(c)(6)(A).
[9]§897(c)(1)(A)(ii).
[10]§897(c)(2).

real property interest lasts five years after the dread RPHC ratios are established, the taint is removed by an ownership change and does not carry over to a purchaser. An *acquired* interest is not a U.S. real property interest unless the status of U.S. RPHC already exists at the time of acquisition.

Effects of Valuation

To the end of identifying gain attributable to the ownership of U.S. real estate, the definition of a U.S. RPHC is in fairly obvious ways both overinclusive and underinclusive. Being predicated entirely on *values,* the definition of a U.S. RPHC identifies *gains* attributable to U.S. real estate only accidentally, if at all. Suppose that more than half the assets of an entity consist of U.S. real estate that has declined in value, and the remainder of personal property that has gone up sharply. A foreign person's gain upon the sale of shares of the entity may be swept within section 897, even though 1) the gain is not attributable to U.S. real estate, and 2) gain from the sale of the same properties owned directly would escape U.S. tax altogether. For example, the sale of shares of a U.S. corporation holding land that has declined in value along with a portfolio of stocks that have increased enormously could attract the tax of section 897(a), even though the entire gain was attributable to the investment securities. If the investment portfolio does not constitute a trade or business, section 897 would apply even if the investments were worth considerably more than the land, because assets not used in a trade or business are not counted as part of the non-real-estate assets of a corporation in testing its status as a U.S. RPHC. Section 897 can thus make the ownership of certain U.S. corporate shares a veritable minefield for foreign persons.

As a result of changing valuations, a corporation could quite easily fall into the class of U.S. RPHCs without having been created for (or even significantly engaged in) investment in real estate. A business that owned its own land and buildings and was going through a period of poor profits and liquidity might readily become a U.S. RPHC. For example, Chrysler Corporation (now part of Daimler-Chrysler), though not widely perceived as a real estate investment company, might well have been a U.S. RPHC during the recession of 1981-83, when the value of its operating assets fell perilously close to zero and its real estate probably represented nearly the entire equity in the company. More obviously, virtually any oil company would be a U.S. RPHC, given the inclusion of natural resource holdings within the class of real property. This could have potentially surprising consequences to foreign portfolio investors on U.S. stock exchanges.

Publicly Traded Stock

To soften such untoward effects, and more generally to preserve the appeal of U.S. portfolio holdings for foreign investors, section 897(c)(3) provides an exception from the category of U.S. real property interest for holdings of stock regularly traded on an established securities exchange, if the holding constitutes less than *five* percent of its own class of stock. This exception largely removes concerns foreign investors might otherwise have over holdings of publicly traded U.S. equities.[11]

Foreign Corporations

A foreign corporation, even if loaded with U.S. real property (and hence a U.S. RPHC), is not a U.S. real property interest. This may seem to offer an easy escape to foreign persons from the tax of section 897. They need only hold U.S. real property through foreign corporations. Sales of the shares are not subject to U.S. tax. There is less here than meets the eye, however. The U.S. real estate remains a U.S. real property interest in the hands of the foreign corporation. If it has increased in value, it can't be sold (or otherwise disposed of) without triggering the tax of section 897 for the corporation. What guarantees this result is section 897(d), by which *any* disposition of U.S. real property by a foreign corporation is subject to tax. The use of a foreign corporation to hold U.S. real estate therefore offers at most deferral of U.S. taxation on appreciation in the property. While that may sometimes be worthwhile, the tax benefit may also be limited because the real estate cannot regain a fair market basis for depreciation without suffering the tax. Furthermore, if the property is a principal residence, the $250,000 exclusion of gain from income upon sale (granted by section 121) is available only if the property is owned directly by a foreign individual.

---

[11]It does not take care of all the problems, however. Renault S.A. (a French corporation) bought a large block (well over 5 percent) of American Motors stock in the 1980s, at a time when American Motors was quite possibly a U.S. RPHC by virtue of the depressed value of its operating assets. When Renault later sold its American Motors stock (to Chrysler), I am not sure anyone gave much thought to §897, which may well have applied. Of course if Renault sold its American Motors stock at a *loss* (eminently possible) the effect of §897 was salutary: the resulting effectively connected *loss* could have offset other U.S. business profits. (But did Renault have any?)

Closing Note on Section 897

An ironic sidelight on section 897 is that, initially, the Treasury did not want it. When it was adopted in late 1980, at the tail end of a period of oil crisis and inflation, foreign money was flowing into U.S. real estate at unprecedented levels. Section 897 was—and this is unusual for a tax measure—a grass roots provision from Congress reflecting concern that America's best assets were being sold to tax-beating "foreigners" who had caused the very inflation that put Heartland America beyond Americans' economic reach. From the Treasury's perspective, however, foreign investment in U.S. real estate was a way of righting the balance of payments by bringing Petrodollars back into the U.S. economy.

Only a few years later the situation had reversed. Oil price declines and recession kept foreign investors away from Heartland America in droves. Early proponents of section 897 now urged its repeal. But by then the Treasury had grown fond of it.

Chapter 9

The Branch Profits Tax

Overview

Until the adoption of the 1986 Act, the repatriation of U.S. earnings by a foreign corporation had no tax consequences in itself. Section 884 now imposes an additional 30-percent "branch profits tax" on earnings removed from the United States. The branch profits tax adds a second layer of U.S. income tax on earnings received by foreign corporations from U.S. business operations. The tax has, roughly, the effect of treating U.S. business operations of foreign corporations (commonly called "U.S. branch businesses") as though they were separately incorporated entities that make taxable dividend distributions to their foreign shareholders. The branch profits tax makes two-level taxation of foreign corporations' U.S. business operations more uniform than the regime that preceded it.

Why?

Before venturing into the mechanics of the branch profits tax (which are somewhat frightening) it may be helpful to review the problem that gave rise to it. Foreign corporations doing business in the United States can choose between three forms of organization of their venture. The simplest is a direct branch operation in the United States. A foreign corporation that does business in the United States directly, with assets that it owns as a proprietor, is said to have a U.S. "branch." A branch business is a direct presence of a foreign person in the United States. The other two possibilities entail the use of separately chartered subsidiary corporations to own and operate a U.S. business. The separate subsidiary can be domestic (that is, U.S.-chartered) or foreign (that is, chartered in a foreign country).

A problem, before the 1986 Act, was that a foreign corporation's direct branch business in the United States might be taxed differently from a separate subsidiary. The reason for the difference lay in source rules for dividends and in the range of application of the "second tax" on dividends that followed from the source rules. Consider, for example, a Fredonian corporation with widely dispersed foreign shareholders (A, B, C, and D) carrying out a U.S. business through a wholly-owned U.S. corporate subsidiary, as illustrated in the diagram on the following page.

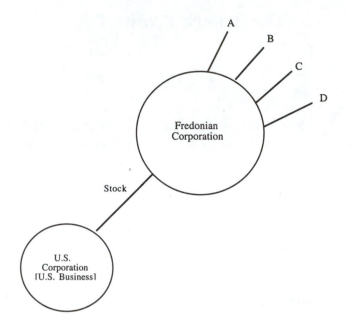

The business profits of the U.S. subsidiary are subject to U.S. corporate taxation. Dividends paid by the subsidiary to its foreign parent, being paid by a U.S. corporation, also have U.S. source and are subject to U.S. flat rate tax. This form of organization therefore entails two layers of U.S. tax on fully repatriated business profits of the Fredonian corporation,[1] which is the norm of U.S. corporate taxation. If the subsidiary conducting a U.S. business in this pattern was foreign-chartered, it made no difference before the 1986 Act.[2] Dividends paid by the foreign subsidiary to its parent, coming entirely from U.S. business profits, would also have U.S. source under the source rules (specifically the 25-percent rule[3] for dividends from a foreign corporation, which you may recall from chapter 3) and would be subject to the "second" U.S. tax on dividends.

Conducting the U.S. business as a direct branch, however, would eliminate the second tax if the U.S. business operations were small in relation to the worldwide operations of the foreign corporation. Suppose the Fredonian corporation derived 10-percent of its gross income from a U.S. branch business, as in the following diagram:

---

[1]Dividends from the Fredonian corporation to its individual shareholders (A, B, C, etc.) are free of U.S. tax, but two layers of U.S. tax have already been paid.

[2]It still doesn't, although the mechanics of taxation are somewhat different with the branch profits tax.

[3]Dividends from a foreign corporation with more than 25-percent "effectively connected" income have a proportional component of U.S.-source income. §861(a)(2).

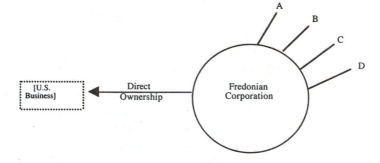

The U.S. business profits, then and now, would be taxed as effectively connected income. But before the branch profits tax, that would be the full extent of U.S. taxation. The repatriation of the profits to the Fredonian home office had no U.S. tax consequences. No part of any dividend distribution by the Fredonian corporation to its individual shareholders has U.S. source, and therefore no part suffered U.S. tax.[4] In this regime the taxation of a U.S. branch of a foreign corporation was often more advantageous than that of a separately chartered U.S. or foreign subsidiary.[5]

How?

The branch profits tax of section 884 replaces the "second tax" described above. The branch profits tax is similar in broad effect to a dividend tax, but is not triggered by a distribution from a corporation to its shareholders. Instead, the tax reaches business profits when they are withdrawn from a U.S. business. It is, in broad terms, a tax on remitted profits. Viewed at closer range, however, the branch profits tax is not literally a tax on the repatriation of U.S. business profits by foreign corporations, but a tax on the disinvestment of those profits from U.S. business assets. The tax brings all U.S. business operations of foreign corporations within the same tax regime, generally subjecting them to two layers of U.S. tax.

Mechanically the branch profits tax is distinctly complicated. It is triggered by a reduction in a foreign corporation's U.S. business assets, to the extent of any prior business profits. In effect the tax falls on

---

[4]The Fredonian corporation, remember, is below the 25-percent threshold of U.S. source in §861(a)(2).

[5]Technically, of course, a foreign subsidiary would have its own U.S. branch business—but one accounting for 100 percent of its gross income, which would impart U.S. source to its entire dividends under the 25-percent rule.

profits disinvested from a U.S. business. Think of it as a tax on a notional dividend from an imaginary separate subsidiary holding a U.S. branch business.

The "Dividend Equivalent Amount"

Section 884(a) imposes a tax of 30 percent of the "dividend equivalent amount" of a foreign corporation in each taxable year. The "dividend equivalent amount" is defined in section 884(b) as the corporation's "effectively connected earnings and profits" ("ECEP") "for the taxable year," adjusted up or down by decreases or increases respectively in the foreign corporation's "U.S. net equity."[6] Specifically, a foreign corporation's ECEP for the taxable year are 1) *reduced* by the excess of the foreign corporation's "U.S. net equity" at the end of the taxable year over its "U.S. net equity" at the beginning of the taxable year and 2) *increased* by the excess of the foreign corporation's U.S. net equity at the beginning of the taxable year over its U.S. net equity at the close of the year.[7] Mnemonically, think of ECEP as reduced by an increase in U.S. net equity and increased by a reduction.

The Taxable Event

If you ponder these provisions for a while, it may come to you that if a foreign corporation leaves its effectively connected earnings invested in a U.S. branch business the amount of its taxable ECEP will be just offset by the resulting *increase* in its U.S. business assets. Therefore, no branch profits tax. But if the foreign corporation pulls its profits out of the U.S. business, sending them to a bank account in its home country, for example, the corresponding decrease in its U.S. business assets will expose its taxable ECEP to the branch profits tax.

Note, further, that the branch profits tax can be triggered by any reduction of a foreign corporation's U.S. *business* assets, even if the amounts disinvested are not actually repatriated and remain in the United States. A simple shift of the accumulated business profits of a U.S. branch business into passive investments or even a *U.S.* bank account is sufficient. If a foreign corporation takes its U.S. business profits and parks them in U.S. Treasury bonds, for example, it will suffer the branch profits tax. The bonds, to be sure, may yield exempt portfolio interest, but the branch profits tax inflicts a heavy tax toll charge on a foreign corporation's purchase of the bonds with the profits of a U.S. business.

---

[6] §884(b); Reg. §§1.884-1(a)(2), (3). "U.S. net equity" is U.S. business assets.
[7] §884(b)(2)(A).

Relation to the Second Tax

Foreign corporations exposed to the branch profits tax have the partial consolation that dividends paid to their shareholders do not suffer the "second tax" on dividend distributions. Section 884(e)(3)(A) calls off the flat rate tax of sections 871 and 881 on dividends paid by a foreign corporation from its earnings for any taxable year in which it is subject to the branch profits tax.

A corollary of this effect is that the branch profits tax largely ended the differences in taxation of U.S. branches and separate subsidiaries of foreign corporations. Consider the Fredonian corporation in the diagrams above. Dividends from a foreign subsidiary are no longer subject to the second tax. Because distributions do reduce the earnings of the subsidiary's earnings invested in U.S. business assets, however, they are subject to the branch profits tax. The tax cost is the same (30 percent of the distributed amount).

The effect of the branch profits tax, in some instances, is somewhat different from that of the former second tax. When it applied, the second tax reached a portion of *all* dividends paid by a foreign corporation, regardless of their economic origin. The branch profits tax, in contrast, only reaches earnings withdrawn from U.S. business assets. Suppose, for example, that profits from the Fredonian corporation's U.S. branch business account for 50 percent of its gross income. With the second tax, half of any dividends of the corporation to its shareholders would have been subject to U.S. tax,[8] regardless of the location of the assets used to pay the dividends. With the branch profits tax, *all* amounts distributed to shareholders originating from U.S. business assets would be subject to additional U.S. tax, but none of any amounts distributed from assets already outside the U.S. economic environment. The Fredonian corporation can therefore distribute as dividends to its shareholders earnings attributable entirely to business activity outside the United States at no U.S. tax cost. Such a distribution will not trigger the branch profits tax because it entails no reduction of U.S. assets.

The Branch Interest Tax

Closely related to the branch profits tax is the tax of section 884(f) on interest paid by U.S. branch businesses of foreign corporations. It is considerably more complex than the branch profits tax (itself no slouch in that department) and I will attempt here to give only a fleeting

---

[8]Under the source rules, the dividends have a 50-percent component of U.S.-source income.

glimpse of this tax. The branch-level interest tax is triggered in some circumstances by the *payment* of interest by a U.S. branch business of a foreign corporation. The tax is imposed on a notional base to which no actual receipts may correspond. It is, furthermore, determined with reference to a class of *deductions* that are established only in regulations. From the face of the Code itself neither the object of the tax nor even its amount can be readily apprehended.

The branch interest tax is defined with reference to the rule of section 884(f)(1)(A) governing branch interest paid by foreign corporations and the expense allocation regulations applicable to foreign corporations. A feature of these regulations is that interest paid by a foreign corporation *outside* the United States may be allocated as a *deduction* to a U.S. branch business, and the corporation as a result may sometimes deduct more interest from its U.S. branch income than was actually paid by the branch. Mechanically, if the amount of interest allocated as a deduction to the effectively connected income of a foreign corporation exceeds the amount of interest that its U.S. branch business actually pays, the excess is subject to the branch interest tax.

Beyond these generalities, little of the branch interest tax is readily fathomable without recourse to the extensive regulations on branch interest issued under sections 882 and 884. Unless your future self is deeply, perhaps pathologically, involved with international taxation, you will get through life without any further concern for the branch interest tax.

III

Outbound U.S. Taxation

Chapter 10

Outbound Taxation in Overview

As elaborated in earlier chapters, the main concern of the U.S. tax system regarding *inbound* transactions is to define the thresholds of U.S. taxation for foreign persons investing or doing business in the United States. The key to tax planning for inbound transactions is hence to keep the economic presence of foreign persons in the United States below the relevant thresholds, where possible, in order to reduce or eliminate U.S. tax.

The essential structure of *outbound* U.S. taxation—the taxation of income derived by U.S. persons outside the United States—follows from two premises that are in basic respects at odds: the worldwide taxation by the United States of its citizens and residents and the status of corporations as separate taxable entities.

Double Taxation

One immediate corollary of worldwide U.S. taxation is possible double taxation. A U.S. person is at the outset fully subject to U.S. taxation on foreign income. Any tax imposed abroad therefore threatens to be a second layer. A pressing concern of a U.S. person pursuing foreign income is that any foreign taxes be imposed instead (rather than on top) of U.S. tax. Foreign tax advisers (viewing the question from their perspective as an inbound one) can help in creating a structure with the least exposure to foreign taxation. There are limits to what they can accomplish, especially when an outbound U.S. venture plays out in a high-tax environment, just as there are limits to the reduction of U.S. taxes that can be gained for foreign persons here. Nor can American enterprises afford simply to steer clear of high-tax foreign venues, because there, often, is where the money is. Countries with rich markets and developed commercial infrastructures that may reward investment by U.S. persons also tend to impose significant taxes.

Less than Single Taxation

Another possibility in outbound transactions, paradoxically, is low taxation of foreign income. Not all income beneficially owned by U.S. persons is subject to current U.S. taxation. This is a consequence of the separate identity of corporations and, more specifically, of the status of foreign corporations as foreign persons for U.S. tax purposes. As a

117

general rule, a foreign corporation is treated as a foreign person by the U.S. tax system and therefore is not exposed to U.S. taxation on foreign source income. This regime may apply even when the foreign corporation's shares are owned (and its assets are therefore beneficially owned) by U.S. persons.

The Tax System's Dual Response

The complexity of U.S. taxation of foreign income (which will become apparent in short order) reflects its attempts to deal with both of these possibilities. The system of outbound taxation aims at limiting double taxation *and* at containing possible avenues of escape from U.S. taxation.

To the former end the U.S. tax system allows a foreign tax credit, which is the centerpiece of U.S. taxation of foreign income. The credit is a mechanism to reduce U.S. taxes on foreign income by a full offset for foreign taxes up to the level of U.S. taxation. The foreign tax credit is discussed in chapters 11 through 14.

To the latter end the U.S. tax system has devices to reach the incomes of foreign corporations owned by U.S. persons—known as controlled foreign corporations—when they have been artificially deflected to low-tax environments for the purpose of tax avoidance.

Planning for outbound transactions consists either of making the fullest use of mechanisms that reduce double taxation, such as the foreign tax credit, or of changing the apparent status of a taxpayer to that of a *foreign* person not directly subject to U.S. taxation. In this regard the separate identity of corporations under U.S. law tax law plays an important part.

Foreign Corporations

For a number of reasons the most common form of organization of foreign business ventures conducted by U.S. persons is a separate corporate entity, rather than a direct branch of a domestic corporation or an individual proprietorship. Both U.S.-chartered and foreign chartered entities are used, but the latter predominate. In part, this is for business reasons. A locally chartered entity can make it easier to deal with foreign tax and regulatory authorities. Often, though, taxation is the main concern. A foreign corporation is, in form, a foreign person. If owned by U.S. shareholders, however, it embodies the economic interests of United States persons. Despite this manifest economic reality, foreign corporations are treated by the U.S. tax system across a broad range of situations as foreign taxpayers, and may receive foreign income beyond the reach of immediate U.S. taxation.

Controlled Foreign Corporations

In its treatment of foreign corporations, the U.S. tax system makes a central distinction between foreign corporations dominantly owned or controlled by United States persons and foreign corporations in which United States persons hold lesser interests. Foreign corporations actually controlled by U.S. shareholders are known as "controlled foreign corporations" (or "CFCs") and fall under a tax regime quite different from domestic corporations or wholly foreign corporations. Many of the foreign operations of CFCs are subject to current U.S. taxation. A narrowly defined type of passive income of foreign corporations that are *not* CFCs is also subject to current U.S. taxation.

The Entity Question

Because foreign operations conducted by a U.S. person through a separately chartered corporation may be taxed much differently from direct branch operations or partnership operations, an important threshold question is the characterization of entities, foreign and domestic, for tax purposes. Many readers have doubtless already encountered this question—known as entity classification—in other tax courses.

The Old Days

To compress a half-century of prior law into a paragraph, an organization, even if not possessed of an official corporate charter, was taxed as a corporation if it displayed a preponderance of corporate characteristics (the essential characteristics being limited liability, unlimited life, centralization of management, and free transferability of interests). Conversely, an organization or association (even if ostensibly a corporate entity) was treated as a "fiscally transparent" form of ownership[1] if it lacked a preponderance of corporate characteristics. Under this standard, virtually all regularly chartered corporations were taxed as such, while many limited partnerships, even though registered under state law, were acknowledged as flow-through entities.

---

[1] By a "fiscally transparent" entity I mean a form of direct ownership where the income and losses of the organization flow through to the owners, who may be direct proprietors or partners. Fiscal Transparency is sometimes called "flow-through" taxation.

This standard, while never easy, was especially hard to apply to foreign entities with features that do not line up perfectly with those of entities organized in the United States. In addition to the standard, full-bore corporation, there exist in many countries a variety of limited-liability organizations, including SARLs, GmBHs, and Limitadas, which have some but not all of the classical corporate characteristics. In the old regime, taxpayers and the Treasury doggedly scoured these forms of organization, one by one, to determine the balance of their corporate characteristics. The emergence of limited liability companies (LLCs) in the United States during the past two decades brought the problem home.

Check-the-Box

In 1996 the Treasury swept the tangle away in one enlightened stroke when it issued regulations permitting a "check-the-box" election of the tax character of a broad class of entities by their owners.[2] The "check-the-box" regulations have fundamentally changed the land-marks of entity classification.[3]

Actually, the determination of an entity's tax status entails slightly more than just checking a box. There is no unqualified election for all entities. In order to elect (or more colloquially "check the box") an entity must first establish its character as a separate entity,[4] and then it must fall within the group that are eligible to choose their own tax status. At several stages the rules differ somewhat for domestic and foreign-chartered entities.

Once identified as separate, a business entity with *two or more* owners is classified for tax purposes either as a "corporation" or a "partner-ship."[5] A separate entity with a *single* owner is either a corporation or is "disregarded" for tax purposes.[6] To be "disregarded" means to be "treated in the same manner as a sole proprietorship, branch, or division of the owner."[7] For several types of single-owner and multiple-owner entities, the classification at this stage is elective (which is what we mean by "checking the box").[8]

---

[2] These regulations are codified in Reg. §301.7701.

[3] It is important to bear in mind, however, that *publicly traded* partnerships are taxed across the board as corporations, without election, by virtue of §7704.

[4] Reg. §301.7701-1(a)(1).

[5] Reg. §301.7701-2(a).

[6] Id.

[7] Id.

[8] Reg. §301.7701-3(a).

Per Se Corporations

Several types of separate entity, however, are automatically classified as corporations, regardless of the number of owners. These include entities specifically denoted as "corporations," "joint-stock companies," "insurance companies," and "banks" chartered by the states or the United States.[9] Also included is a long list of foreign-chartered entities analogous to business corporations under U.S. law. These include the classic Inc.s (Corporation) S.A.s (Sociedad Anonima or Société Anonyme), A.G.s (Aktiengesellschaft), KKs (Kabushiki Kaisha), NVs (Naamloze Vennootschap), PLCs (Public Limited Company), Abls (Aktiebolag), and others that are the basic forms of state-chartered business corporations around the world.[10]

Elective Classification

An entity that escapes classification as a corporation under this per se rule "can elect its classification for federal tax purposes."[11] Eligible entities include partnerships, limited partnerships, joint ventures, LLCs, GmbHs, SARLs, Limitadas, and many more. An entity with at least two members can elect to be classified as either a corporation or a partnership. An entity with a single owner can elect to be classified as a corporation or to be disregarded as an entity altogether.[12] This is the election that we know and love as "check-the-box."

Default Rules

If an eligible entity fails to make any election, there are default rules. When a *domestic* business entity fails to elect its tax status, it is classified by default as a partnership if it has two more members and disregarded as an entity if it has a single owner.[13] An eligible *foreign* entity that fails to elect is treated 1) as a partnership if it has two or more members and any member has unlimited liability, 2) as a corporation if no member has unlimited liability, or 3) disregarded as an entity if it has a single owner with unlimited liability.[14]

---

[9]Reg. §§301.7701-2(b)(1)-(7).
[10]Reg. §301.7701-2(b)(8)(i).
[11]Reg. §301.7701-3(a).
[12]Id.
[13]Reg. §301.7701-3(b)(1).
[14]Reg. §301.7701-3(b)(2)(i).

Chapter 11

The Foreign Tax Credit:
Background and Overview

The heart of the system of U.S. outbound taxation is the foreign tax credit. Just as the United States taxes the U.S.-source income of foreign persons, other countries to which Americans are themselves foreigners tax income arising within them. U.S. persons pursuing foreign income can hardly avoid encountering national tax collectors asserting source-based tax claims. Coupled with the worldwide reach of U.S. taxation, these encounters would spell painful multiple layers of taxation if no concession was made by the U.S. Treasury. The central provision addressed to this problem in the U.S. tax system is the foreign tax credit. In broad outline, the credit prevents double taxation of the foreign income of United States persons by reducing the U.S. tax on that income by the amount of income tax paid to foreign governments.

The foreign tax credit is a unilateral measure adopted by the U.S. tax system. On the surface at least, the U.S. tax system asks nothing from foreign treasuries in return for the credit. In fact, the foreign tax credit is virtually a necessary concomitant of the U.S. system of taxing the worldwide incomes of citizens and residents. Countries that impose tax only territorially (that is, solely on income from sources within their boundaries) make a similar concession to the taxing power of other nations simply by not extending their own.

The foreign tax credit rests on a simple idea: income taxes paid to the U.S. Treasury are reduced (credited, in tax argot) by the amount of income taxes paid by U.S. persons to foreign governments.

Credit versus Deduction

If you have not yet mastered the difference between a tax credit and a deduction, now is the time to do so. A credit is a dollar-for-dollar reduction of U.S. income tax by the amount of foreign income tax. The tax saving from a credit is the exact amount of the credit itself. If, for example, the U.S. and foreign income tax rates were both 50 percent, there would be a foreign tax of 50 cents on a dollar of foreign source income. The U.S. tax on the foreign income, pre-credit, would also be 50 cents (U.S. tax is worldwide, remember), but would then be fully offset by a 50-cent credit for the foreign income tax. The tax ultimately paid to the U.S. Treasury on foreign source income would therefore be zero, and the taxpayer's overall effective tax rate would be 50 percent, the same as paid on income derived by a U.S. person entirely within the U.S. environment.

International Taxation

A deduction, in contrast, is a reduction of taxable income by the amount of a given expense, and reduces tax at the marginal rate of taxation otherwise applicable to the amount deducted. The tax saving from a deduction is the amount of tax that would otherwise have been imposed on the deducted amount. Deduction of the foreign tax in the example above would reduce taxable income by 50 cents, leaving 50 cents subject to U.S. taxation. After U.S. tax of 25 cents (at the 50 percent rate) the taxpayer would have 25 cents left over after payment of all taxes. When deducted (rather than credited) the payment of foreign income tax of 50 cents would reduce U.S. income tax by only 25 cents.[1] The taxpayer would end up paying tax (to two different countries) at an overall effective rate of 75 percent. For this reason it is almost invariably preferable to credit an amount against taxes than to deduct it.

Early History

Surprisingly, the earliest U.S. income tax laws provided no credit for foreign taxes. The only allowance for foreign income taxes in the 1913 Income Tax Law was a deduction for taxes paid to foreign governments as a cost of doing business. One reason for the oversight could have been that income tax rates were quite low in the 1913 Act—the income tax then was hardly more than a nuisance—and income taxes were not widespread outside the United States. If a U.S. enterprise subject to a 1% income tax under the 1913 law was also subject to a 1% income tax on its foreign income, the total income tax burden (after deduction of the foreign income tax from U.S. taxable income) was 1.99%. While this is a large *relative* increase in the tax cost of foreign international operations—it nearly doubles because at low rates a deduction from foreign taxes produces only a small U.S. tax saving—in absolute terms the total tax is not painfully high.

With the sharp increases in income tax rates (both in the United States and abroad) and rapid growth of U.S. foreign trade during World War I, the problem of foreign income taxes became more pressing. By 1918 the top marginal rate of U.S. tax on income was 60 percent, and rates were similarly high in Europe. A U.S. firm doing business in the U.K. might be exposed there to income taxation of 50 percent. If the U.S. rate was the same, all that remained from 100 of pre-tax U.K.-source income (after deduction of the U.K. tax from U.S. taxable

---

[1] At a 50-percent rate, a deduction of one dollar reduces income tax by fifty cents. At a 30-percent rate, by 30 cents, etc. Here, at a 50-percent rate, a deduction of 50 cents reduces income tax by 25 cents.

income) was 25.[2] The total combined income tax on foreign income was thus 75 percent, much higher than the tax imposed on the wholly domestic operations of a U.S. or U.K. firm.[3] While there is some U.S. tax benefit from the deduction of U.K. tax, there remains a far heavier tax burden on foreign income compared to domestic.

This overtaxation of foreign income was an obvious deterrent to foreign commerce, and was remedied in the Revenue Act of 1918, which allowed a "credit" against U.S. income taxes for "income ... taxes paid . . . to any foreign country."[4] From this modest kernel a truly stultifying set of rules has arisen framing the foreign tax credit.

In the simple formulation of the 1918 Act the amount of the credit was unlimited up to the amount of U.S. tax. Every dollar of foreign income tax paid could displace a dollar otherwise paid to the U.S. Treasury. When foreign income taxes were higher than U.S. taxes, the credit could therefore do more than offset U.S. tax on foreign income. The credit could reduce the U.S. Treasury's tax on *U.S.*-source income.

Suppose, for example, that in Year 1 the Fredonian income tax rate is 70 percent and the U.S. rate 50 percent. Suppose further that a U.S. person has 100 of Fredonian income and 100 of U.S.-source income. Income tax paid to Fredonia is 70. Year 1 is summarized below:

Chart I
(Year 1)

Country of source:	Fredonia	U.S.
Gain or (loss):	100	100
Foreign income tax:	70	—

U.S. income tax (before credit)	100	
Foreign income tax	70	
U.S. income tax (after credit)	30	

If credit is allowed against U.S. income tax for the full amount (70) paid to the Fredonian government (as was the case in the 1918 Act) the U.S. tax of 100 (pre-credit) is reduced to 30 by the foreign tax credit. The U.S. Treasury collects no tax on foreign source income and only 30

---

[2]Deduction of 50 of U.K. tax paid leaves 50 of taxable income subject to U.S. tax of 25 (at 50 percent), for a final after-tax income of 25.

[3]Note that in *relative* terms the double taxation is milder than in the example above with lower rates.

[4]Revenue Act of 1918, ch. 18, §222(a), 40 Stat. 1057.

percent of *U.S.-source* income, despite the basic 50-percent U.S. rate. Part of the U.S. tax otherwise payable on *U.S.*-source income has been displaced by the credit. In this situation the U.S. taxpayer is better off than under a regime of pure territorial taxation in which foreign source income and taxes are simply not taken into account.[5] In this regime the effective overall rate of taxation of worldwide income paid to all governments is the U.S. effective rate, regardless of the foreign tax rate.

The Credit Limitation

While this system is not necessarily bad as a matter of global efficiency, it was unsatisfactory to the U.S. Treasury. Congress responded in 1921 with a limitation on the foreign tax credit. In the 1921 Act the credit for foreign income taxes was limited to "the same proportion of the [U.S.] tax ... which the taxpayer's ... income ... from sources without the United States ... bears to his entire ... income."[6] This exact language survives in today's Code,[7] but embedded in a vastly more complex statutory architecture. The provision limits the credit to the amount of U.S. tax attributable to foreign source income. Mechanically, the limitation turns on a fraction—the ratio of foreign source income to total income—multiplied by the U.S. tax (determined initially without regard for the credit). The limitation on the foreign tax credit can therefore be expressed as a three-factor formula, consisting of the U.S. income tax (before credit) times the ratio of foreign source income to total worldwide income:

$$\frac{\text{Credit}}{\text{Limitation}} = \frac{\text{U.S. Income tax}}{\text{(pre-credit)}} \times \frac{\text{Foreign Source Income}}{\text{Total Income}}$$

Another way of expressing the limitation is that the foreign tax credit cannot exceed the U.S. effective rate of tax on foreign source income. This follows immediately from the formula. With the factors rearranged, the credit limitation can thus be stated as foreign source income multiplied by the ratio of U.S. tax to total taxable income, as follows:

$$\frac{\text{Credit}}{\text{Limitation}} = \frac{\text{Foreign Source}}{\text{Income}} \times \frac{\text{U.S. Income Tax}}{\text{Total Income}}$$

---

[5]If U.S. taxation were purely territorial, foreign income or loss would not enter into taxable income, and foreign income taxes would similarly be ignored. *U.S.-source* income would be taxed at the regular U.S. rates, no matter what the results of foreign operations or foreign income taxes.

[6]Revenue Act of 1921, ch. 136, §222(a)(5), 42 Stat. 227.

[7]§904(a)

On seeing the limitation formula for the first time (and realizing, or being told, that it limits the foreign tax credit to the U.S. effective rate of income tax on foreign source income) some wonder why the credit isn't simply limited to the U.S. effective rate of tax on foreign source income. Actually, the statutory formula sets out a necessary order of steps in determining the limitation. The problem with a different order stems from the graduated U.S. tax rates. With a graduated rate schedule there is no self-revealing effective U.S. rate. Since different rates apply to different segments of income, you don't know the effective rate of income tax until you have actually calculated the tax and stated it as a percentage of taxable income.

The first determination must therefore be the pre-credit U.S. income tax. The formula then gives you the amount of U.S. tax imposed on foreign source income. This implies a drill to follow in determining the credit limitation. First, compute the U.S. income tax on worldwide income without regard for the credit. Second, determine the ratio of foreign source income to worldwide income (the "limitation fraction"). Third, multiply the U.S. tax (pre-credit, remember) by the limitation fraction. The result is the limitation on the foreign tax credit. These steps are equivalent to determining the U.S. tax attributable to foreign source income (or applying the effective rate of U.S. tax to foreign source income.) Any other order, however, leaves greater room for error. When we get to the separate limitation baskets in chapter 13, things will get far more complicated, but these will remain the basic steps that you should follow in determining the credit limitation.[8]

Effect of the Limitation

The limitation is just that. It does not determine how much credit will be allowed, which depends initially on how much foreign tax is paid, but sets a ceiling that the credit cannot exceed. When the foreign income tax rate is lower than the U.S. rate, foreign income taxes can be credited in full, within the limitation, and the U.S. Treasury will collect a balance which is the excess of the U.S. rate over the foreign rate. The upshot of the credit coupled with the limitation is that the effective rate of tax on the foreign source income of a United States person is the higher of the U.S. or the foreign rate.

With the limitation, the situation in chart I, where foreign income taxes are higher than U.S. taxes, comes out differently. The limitation prevents any impairment of U.S. taxation of U.S.-source income, as shown in chart II:

---

[8]You will be doing so within separate categories of income, however.

Chart II
(Year 1 with credit limitation)

Country of source:	Fredonia	U.S.
Gain or (loss):	100	100
Foreign income tax:	70	—

U.S. income tax (before credit)	100
Foreign income tax	70
Limitation on the credit (100 X 1/2)	50
U.S. income tax (after credit)	50
Excess credit	20

Under the 1921 formula the limitation on the foreign tax credit is 50, determined as follows. U.S. tax pre-credit is 100 (50 percent of worldwide income of 200). The limitation fraction (the ration of foreign source income to worldwide income) is 100/200, or 1/2. The credit limitation is therefore: 100 X 1/2 = 50. Of the tax of 70 paid to Fredonia only 50 can be credited. The U.S. Treasury therefore collects 50. Now the burden of the higher foreign income taxes falls on the taxpayer rather the U.S. Treasury, which collects a tax equal to the full effective rate applied to U.S.-source income.

Excess Credits and Carryovers

The amount (20) by which the Fredonian income tax of 70 exceeds the credit limitation of 50 cannot be credited in the year paid, but is not permanently lost as a foreign tax credit. The amount of foreign income tax above the credit limitation paid in any given year (sometimes known as an "excess credit") can, under section 904(c), be carried back to the two previous taxable years and forward to the five following taxable years. An excess credit carried back or forward to a given year is treated as though it were a creditable tax paid or accrued in that year and can therefore offset U.S. tax imposed on foreign source income in that year.

The limitation on the foreign tax credit also applies in the carryover year, of course. If there is no room for any more credit within the limitation in that year, the excess credit will carry over to the following year, and so on until it is either credited or expires uselessly beyond the carryover period. There is in effect an 8-year window (the two carryback years, the year of payment, and the five carryforward years) within which a foreign income tax can be credited. If foreign income tax rates fluctuate, but are on average equal to or lower than U.S. rates over time, foreign income taxes may be credited in full within the limitation. Even with credit carryovers, however, if foreign income tax rates are persistently higher than U.S. rates, excess credits will pile up and eventually expire unused, having provided no U.S. tax benefit.

Returning to our Fredonian situation, suppose that in Year 2 the Fredonian income tax rate falls to 30 percent, while the taxpayer's income from all sources remains the same.

Chart III
(Year 2, with carryover)

Country of source:	Fredonia	U.S.
Gain or (loss) :	100	100
Foreign income tax:	30	—

U.S. income tax (before credit)	100
Foreign income tax	30
Limitation on the credit	50
Credit carryover from prior year	20
U.S. income tax (after credit)	50

The credit limitation in Year 2, as in Year 1, is 50 (100 of U.S. tax pre-credit multiplied by the limitation fraction of 1/2). The Fredonian income tax of 30 is well within the limitation and can be credited in full. If Year 2 were taxed in isolation, the U.S. Treasury would collect 70 (the pre-credit U.S. tax minus 30 of Fredonian income tax). The excess credit of 20 from Year 1 is carried forward, however, and treated as a foreign income tax paid in Year 2.[9] The 30 of Fredonian tax actually paid and the carryover of 20 from Year 1 add up to a foreign tax of 50 treated as paid in Year 2. This amount is just within the credit limitation and creditable in full. The U.S. Treasury collects 50. If we combine the two years as a single tax period, the average rate of Fredonian tax is 50 percent and all Fredonian income tax paid in the period is credited.[10]

---

[9]I have made the simplifying assumption that Year 1 is also the first year of operations, so that no credit carryback is available.

[10]If the Fredonian income tax rate fell only to 50 percent in Year 2, the credit carryover could not be credited in that year because the credit limitation would then just accommodate the Fredonian income tax of 50. The Year 1 excess credit would then carry over undiminished to Year 3. If the Fredonian income tax rate and the

The limitation-with-carryover system is roughly similar to combining a block of 8 years as a single period for allowing the foreign tax credit.

"Overall" and "Per-Country" Limitations

The limitation, which we shall revisit in chapter 13, is the central technical rule of the foreign tax credit. The basic mechanism of the 1921 limitation survives in the Code today (in section 904), still discernible through effusive statutory overlays. Its present form is a compromise of currents that have run through the foreign tax credit for over half a century. In the 1921 Act, the limitation was based on the taxpayer's overall foreign income, and that form of the limitation is hence known as the "overall" limitation. At other times the limitation has been computed separately on the basis of the income and the taxes arising in each foreign country. In that form it was called the "per-country" limitation and limited the credit for income taxes paid in *each* foreign country to the same proportion of U.S. tax (pre-credit) that the income from that country bore to total income. The fraction underlying the per-country limitation for each country is income from sources *within that country* over total income. In other words, the per-country limitation limited the credit for taxes paid to each country to the effective rate of U.S. tax on income from sources within that country. With the per-country limitation there were as many separately computed limitations as there were separate countries from which a U.S. taxpayer derived income.

Although the per-country limitation has been repealed and the original overall limitation modified almost beyond recognition, they warrant attention here in their basic form. It is difficult to understand the mechanics of the present limitation (which, it turns out, is a complex form of the overall limitation) without some sense of the different effects of the overall and per-country limitations. In the overall limitation the rest of the world is treated as a single taxing sovereign. All foreign results—gains and losses—are homogenized to arrive at a single limitation, by which credit for the aggregate of foreign income taxes is measured. The per-country limitation, by contrast, requires a discrete reckoning for each foreign country. Assume the following foreign and U.S. operations of a United States person and assume further (for arithmetic simplicity) that all three foreign countries impose a 50 percent income tax and that the U.S. effective income tax rate is 50 percent:

U.S. rate remain at 50 percent thereafter, the Year 1 excess credit will carry forward from year to year uncredited until it expires after Year 6.

Worldwide Operations of a U.S. Person

Country of source:	France	U.K.	Denmark	U.S.
Gain or (loss):	100	100	(100)	100
Foreign income tax:	50	50	–0–	—

Here the taxpayer has worldwide income of 200,[11] and has paid foreign income tax totaling 100 (50 each to France and the U.K.). The limitation determined under the "overall" formula of the 1921 Act is 50.[12] Therefore only 50 of the foreign tax of 100 paid can be credited against U.S. tax.[13]

Under the per-country limitation, there are separate limitations of 50 each for the United Kingdom and France,[14] while the limitation for Denmark is zero.[15] Foreign income taxes paid are thus creditable in full[16] and the U.S. Treasury collects nothing.[17]

You might conclude from this example that the per-country limitation, which preserves full credit for income foreign taxes, was more favorable to taxpayers. The particular combination of foreign income, losses, and taxes in this case seems plausible if not realistic. Consider, however, a different U.S. taxpayer with different foreign operations:

Worldwide Operations of Second U.S. Person

Country of source:	Kuwait	Bahamas	U.S.
Income or (loss):	100	100	100
Income tax rate:	90%	10%	50%
Foreign tax paid:	90	10	—

---

[11]This is the sum of gains of 100 each from the U.K., the U.S., and France (or 300) minus a loss of 100 from Denmark.

[12]The U.S. tax pre-credit is 100. Overall *foreign* source income adds up to 100 (gains of 100 each from the U.K. and France, minus a loss of 100 from Denmark). The limitation fraction is therefore 100/200 or 1/2.

[13]The additional 50 of foreign tax can be carried back or forward to other years, and possibly credited then.

[14]The separate limitation fraction for the U.K. is 1/2 (U.K. income of 100 over worldwide income of 200). The U.S. tax pre-credit (100) multiplied by this fraction gives a limitation of 50. The computation for France is the same.

[15]For Denmark the limitation is zero because Danish source income in the numerator of the limitation fraction is zero.

[16]Income taxes paid both to France (50) and the U.K. (50) are fully offset by a credit within the respective country limitation (50 in each case).

[17]The differences in the two forms of credit limitation reflect, among other things, the different effect of losses. Under the overall limitation, the loss in Denmark reduces total foreign source income and, therefore, the limitation and credit. Under the per-country limitation, U.K.-source and French source incomes are not reduced by Danish losses, which reduce total taxable income but not the credit for taxes paid to other countries.

131

Here a U.S. person pays an 90-percent income tax to Kuwait and a 10-percent income tax in the Bahamas. Under the overall limitation, the amount of foreign income tax paid (100 in total, consisting of 90 paid to Kuwait and 10 paid to the Bahamas) is credited in full.[18] Under the per-country limitation, only 60 of the foreign income tax paid can be credited. The separate limitations for Kuwait and the Bahamas would each be 50.[19] That allows full credit for the Bahamas tax with room to spare. Credit for Kuwait's tax of 90, however, would be limited to 50. The taxpayer will therefore pay income tax of 90 to the U.S. Treasury.[20] The uncredited 40 of Kuwaiti tax could be carried back and forward as an excess Kuwaiti tax, but will almost surely run into the separate limitation for Kuwait in other years, unless there is a drastic change in Kuwait's tax system. Meanwhile, the overabundant separate limitation for the Bahamas is useless as long as Bahamian income tax remains very low.

It is important to understand the difference between these two forms of the limitation. In the overall limitation all foreign income and foreign income taxes are lumped together. As a result, the taxpayer can credit the very high taxes paid to Kuwait against U.S. income tax attributable to low-taxed Bahamian income. This is known as "cross-crediting." Here, tax foreign imposed at higher-than-U.S. rates is cross-credited against U.S. income tax that would otherwise be imposed on low-taxed foreign source income. The possibility of cross-crediting mitigates the effect of the limitation, which was adopted, at least in part, to prevent full credits for higher-than-U.S. taxes. With the per-country limitation there is no cross-crediting between income taxes of different foreign countries. Low-taxed foreign income cannot soak up high income taxes paid to another foreign country by enlarging the available credit limitation.

The Stakes

The example with Kuwait and the Bahamas may seem to you somewhat contrived on first encounter. What kind of U.S. taxpayer has such farflung and disparate foreign operations? But it is in fact entirely

---

[18]U.S. tax pre-credit is 150 (50 percent of worldwide income of 300). The limitation fraction is 2/3 (200 of foreign source income over 300 of total income). The limitation is therefore 100 (150 X 2/3), which accommodates the entire foreign income tax paid.

[19]U.S. tax pre-credit is still 150. The ratio of Kuwait-source (and Bahamas-source) income to total income is 1/3 (100/300). The limitation for each country is therefore 150 X 1/3 = 50.

[20]There is a credit of 10 for Bahamas tax and 50 for Kuwaiti tax against the pre-credit U.S. tax of 150.

realistic, being a schematic representation of typical operations of a U.S. international oil company around 1975. This will be clearer if I fill in the types of income involved:

Second U.S. Person's Operations Unveiled

Type of income	Source	Amount	Tax rate
Oil Extraction	Kuwait	100	90%
Refining	Bahamas	100	10%
Marketing	U.S.	100	50%

What we have is an integrated international oil company that explores for oil and extracts it from the ground in the Persian Gulf, ships the crude oil by tanker to a refinery in the Bahamas, and sells the refined petroleum products (mainly gasoline) to motorists at gas stations in the United States. Such a company will encounter very high taxes in countries where oil is extracted from the ground (often OPEC countries), low taxes where oil is shipped and refined (the high seas and offshore locations of the taxpayer's choosing), and moderate-to-high taxes in countries where refined products are purchased and consumed. Before the systematic reworking of the foreign tax credit and the credit limitation in recent years, the use of shipping and refining operations in low-tax jurisdictions could offset the high taxes paid to oil-exporting countries within the large umbrella of the overall limitation. For reasons that will become apparent in later chapters, this particular pattern no longer results in significant tax advantage. Keep the possibility of cross-crediting in mind, however, because it survives, albeit in somewhat attenuated form, in today's foreign tax credit.

More broadly, under the overall limitation, taxes paid on foreign source income at rates higher than the U.S. rate can be credited in full nonetheless if there is also enough foreign source income taxed at lower rates to build up a sufficient limitation. Every dollar of low-taxed foreign income creates a larger limitation (by increasing the numerator of the limitation fraction), thereby creating more room to credit higher foreign taxes. This explains the perennial incentive of U.S. taxpayers with high-taxed foreign income to create or "find" enough low-taxed foreign source income to preserve credits for the foreign taxes through an enlarged limitation. The restructuring of the credit limitation in the 1986 Act brought severe, but not invariably fatal, restrictions on this possibility.

Before contending with the nuts and bolts of the foreign tax credit and limitation in their present form, we will first make a side trip in the next chapter through the question of creditable foreign income taxes.

Chapter 12

The Foreign Tax Credit: Creditable Foreign Taxes

The foreign tax credit is allowed for foreign "income ... taxes."[1] While the mechanics of the credit are piled high with statutory detail, on the question of creditable taxes the Code says little beyond those two words. We must look elsewhere to determine what is a "tax" and when it is imposed on "income." Although the former question is conceptually prior—something has to be a tax before it can be an income tax—it barely surfaced in case law and rulings until the 1970s. In the early years the dominant question on creditable taxes was whether a foreign tax was imposed on "income." To frame your thoughts on these questions, read the following story.

Your Vacation in Canada

Suppose you are taking a vacation by automobile in Canada. You come upon a sign that says "Maple Leaf Berry Farm. Pick Your Own Blueberries. $2 a Pound." You spend a few hours picking blueberries. As you leave the farm, your berries are weighed, and you pay the specified amount. A day or two later, you come upon a government-owned national park with a sign saying "Royal Canadian Berry Park. Pick Your Own Blueberries. Free." You drive in and pick up a storm. As you are leaving the park with your haul, a Canadian Mountie directs you to a sign that says "Income Tax Station. Weigh Your Berries Here." You say, "But the berries are free, why should I have to weigh them?" The Mountie answers, "Free they are, but we have to weigh them in order to value them and compute your Canadian income tax." The Mountie explains that the value of the berries is taxable income to you. The Canadian government seeks not to be paid for the blueberries you gathered from its land,[2] but to collect an income tax on your economic gain. You have expended your labor to create a tangible consumable product. Because you have no tax basis in your labor, the full return is taxable gain. On reflection you realize that, although the U.S. income tax does not typically reach self-gathered fruit, the Canadian government's claim is sound from first principles. You have derived from your labor an accretion to wealth, which is taxable compensation within an idealized

---

[1] §901(b)(1).

[2] The Mountie adds: "They are indeed beautiful berries, but I come to seize your berry, not to praise it.

income tax. The Canadian tax system is truer to the notion of income on this point than the U.S. system. So you pay the Canadian income tax and move on.

Embedded in this homely vignette are the essential questions concerning creditable foreign income taxes. These are 1) whether a payment made to a foreign government is indeed a "tax" and 2) if so, whether it is imposed on "income." The former, somewhat amplified, is the threshold question whether the relationship between the taxpayer and the foreign government is one that gives rise to a tax at all. When there is an extensive course of economic dealing between a taxpayer and a foreign government, ostensible taxes are hard to disentangle from an overall contractual relationship in which consideration for benefits received by the taxpayer, such as rent or royalties, changes hands. In order for your payment to be regarded as fully a "tax," the Canadian government must be deemed to have foregone any return from its ownership of berry-bearing lands. Conversely, if your payment is recast as some sort of proprietor's "rent" to the Canadian government, then Canada has abstained to exercise its taxing power. Judging by Canada's express assertion (the berries are "free," but it is imposing "tax") the former has occurred. But the situation ultimately is indeterminate.[3] If the return is satisfactory in amount to the Canadian government, to call it a proprietary crop share or a tax is a matter of indifference.

Essentially the same questions—with amounts at stake multiplied by ten billion or so—have arisen in connection with the operations of the U.S. international oil industry. In most oil-exporting countries (including all the OPEC countries) mineral resources are owned exclusively by the state. U.S. oil companies engaged in oil exploration and development in these countries therefore extract oil owned by the state. They are compensated, often, with a share of the oil that they recover from the ground, while the state keeps the balance. The companies are also subject to "income tax" in most oil-exporting countries. Determining which parts of the huge amounts that pass from U.S. oil companies to foreign governments are, respectively, owners' "royalties" and true income taxes has been *the* question on creditable taxes in the last 25 years.

---

[3]Suppose the sign outside the national park read: "Pick Your Own Blueberries. Tax Free. Pay Only the Posted Price." Suppose further that the posted price was a percentage of the value of the berries equal to the Canadian federal income tax on that amount of income.

Is a Foreign Tax an "Income" Tax?

As noted above, that was the dominant question on creditable taxes until the 1970s. The early case law, which involved small-scale transactions, was accommodating to taxpayers. In a pair of cases in the 1920s the Board of Tax Appeals (the predecessor of the Tax Court) took an expansive view of creditable foreign "income" taxes. In Keen v. Commissioner,[4] the Board allowed credit for a French tax imposed on an estimated tax base equal to a multiple of the rental value of a residence maintained in France by a U.S. citizen. In Burk Brothers v. Commissioner,[5] the Board found creditable a tax imposed by India on the export of animal hides based on the value of the hides and reduced by the relevant costs. In these cases, the Board of Tax Appeals required neither a tax base corresponding precisely to U.S. notions of net income nor an event of realization of the sort extolled in Eisner v. Macomber.[6]

Biddle *and* Bank of America

The Supreme Court gave the Service a potent counterweapon in Biddle v. Commissioner.[7] In *Biddle*, in the course of deciding whether a U.S. shareholder of a British corporation subject to an integrated British corporate tax could be treated as having "paid" the taxes imposed on the corporation, the Court threw in the following thought:

> 'Income taxes paid,' as used in our own revenue laws, has for most practical purposes a well understood meaning to be derived from an examination of the statutes which provide for the laying and collection of income taxes. It is that meaning which must be attributed to it.[8]

The Treasury embraced this language as scriptural.[9] Since *Biddle* the standard for a creditable tax has been an income tax within U.S. tax notions as epitomized by the Internal Revenue Code.

The Code being as it is, both vast and Byzantine, the contours of an "income tax" don't exactly jump off the page. With some exceptions,[10]

---

[4]15 B.T.A. 1243 (1929), *nonacq.*
[5]20 B.T.A. 657 (1930), *nonacq.*
[6]252 U.S. 189 (1920).
[7]302 U.S. 573 (1938).
[8]Id. at 579.
[9]For those of you who remember your law school course in the legal process, let me point out that the Court's statement is *dictum* on the question of creditable taxes. The Court was deciding whether the British tax had been *paid* within the meaning of U.S. tax laws, not whether the tax was imposed on "income."

however, the U.S. income tax is imposed on *realized net* gain. Accordingly, two questions run through the decided cases. Does the foreign tax at issue fall on "net" income (rather than gross) and is it triggered by an event of "realization"?

In Bank of America v. United States,[11] the Court of Claims offered a narrower formulation of the *Biddle* standard for creditable taxes. At issue in *Bank of America* was credit for foreign taxes imposed on the *gross* income of a U.S. bank: "[A] direct income tax is creditable, even though imposed on gross income, if it is very highly likely, or was reasonably intended, always to reach some net gain in the normal circumstances in which it applies." This standard, known as the *Bank of America* doctrine, gives taxpayers a little breathing space. A tax can reach "some net gain" in the normal circumstances in which it applies without being strictly based on net "taxable" income as defined in the Internal Revenue Code.[12] Most commentators, in this light, understand the *Bank of America* standard to allow credit for some foreign taxes similar to the Code's flat rate tax on the gross amount of U.S.-source fixed or determinable income of foreign persons.[13]

The Regulations on CreditableTaxes

The *Bank of America* test of an "income" tax is the basis of the Treasury Regulations on creditable foreign taxes, which were issued in the 1980s. The Regulations offer a more fully articulated statement of the *Biddle* and *Bank of America* principles. From *Biddle* they take the basic test that a tax is an income tax if its "predominant character ... is that of an income tax in the U.S. sense."[14] This standard is further broken down into requirements of realization, gross receipts, and net income. In keeping with *Bank of America* the Regulations allow some latitude on all three.

"Realization" in these regulations includes all realization events under U.S. tax principles, as well as subsequent events used as occasions for reckoning gain or loss.[15] Realization for this purpose also includes

---

[10]Consider, for example, the U.S. flat rate tax on the *gross* amount of U.S.-source fixed or determinable income.

[11]459 F.2d 513, 519-520 (Ct. Cl. 1972).

[12]Note, however, that all the taxes actually under review in *Bank of America* were held *not* to be creditable. These taxes were imposed on the gross income of enterprises engaged in active business. Because no deductions were allowed for the cost of producing the income, while the underlying business activity necessarily entailed expenses, the court concluded that the taxes would not predictably reach only net gain.

[13]See chapter 5.

[14]Reg. §1.901-2(a)(1)(ii).

[15]Reg. §1.901-2(b)(2)(i)(A).

a number of events *prior* to realization events in the U.S. sense, specifically: 1) the recovery or recapture of a previously allowed tax deduction or credit,[16] 2) increases or decreases in the value of property, and 3) the "physical transfer, processing, or export of readily marketable property" at any time.[17] This last rule accommodates foreign taxes triggered by the *export* of goods from the country of production.[18]

There is the further requirement that the foreign tax base be predicated on actual "gross receipts."[19] Here again the Regulations allow some latitude. If not imposed on actual "gross receipts," a foreign tax still passes muster if imposed on gross receipts computed under any method that is likely not to *overstate* them.[20]

The "net income" requirement gives effect to a standard of cost recovery. A foreign tax is treated as reaching net income if, judged on the basis of its predominant character, the tax allows 1) the recovery of significant costs and expenses (including capital outlays) attributable under reasonable principles to gross receipts, or 2) the recovery of costs and expenses computed under a method that approximates or exceeds the amount of actual costs and expenses.[21] These tests are alternatives. A tax that meets either one is treated as reaching net income.

These three requirements are further qualified by the "predominant character" standard. If, in its predominant character, a foreign tax is imposed on 1) realized 2) net gain derived from actual 3) gross receipts, the Regulations countenance departures from these requirements in some cases. In this light, the Regulations do not allow credit across the board for taxes imposed on gross receipts or gross income, but do accommodate tax on gross income "in the rare situation where that tax is almost certain to reach some net gain."[22] It follows that at least some flat rate taxes on fixed or determinable income, specifically on interest and dividends from passive investments, are creditable as income taxes.[23]

---

[16]Reg. §1.901-2(b)(2)(i)(B).

[17]Reg. §1.901-2(b)(2)(i)(C).

[18]Some countries tax gains from basic products (such as crude oil) when they physically leave the country. The alternative of waiting for a realization event in the U.S. sense (which in the case of a fully integrated oil company would be the sale of gasoline at the pump) is impractical.

[19]Reg. §1.901-2(b)(3)(i). This aims principally at the compulsory use of artificial "posted prices" as an income tax base in some oil-exporting countries.

[20]Id.

[21]Reg. §1.901-2(b)(4)(i).

[22]Id. This is an echo of *Bank of America*.

[23]Taxes on the gross amount of rents, royalties, and wages are on shakier ground by this standard, but at least some of them are creditable. See Reg. §1.901-2(b)(4)(iv) (Example 3) (40-percent tax on gross wages treated as reaching net income). Some taxes on gross income, furthermore, are creditable as "in lieu of" taxes, as discussed below.

Is the Foreign Payment a "Tax"?

In the *Bank of America* case the court seemed to think that it was putting the question of creditable foreign taxes to rest forever. The opinion reads like a doctrinal summation. What further developments soon revealed is that the question in *Bank of America* is not even the main event. The concern of recent rulings, regulations, and case law—with prodigious amounts at stake—is not whether payments to foreign governments are *income* taxes but whether they are *taxes* at all. This question came into sudden sharp focus in the mid-1970s, after the October 1973 War and ensuing oil embargo, in connection with payments by U.S. oil companies to governments of oil-exporting countries.

The Problem of Oil Payments

The problem had been simmering for a long while. U.S. oil companies have been engaged in exploration and production outside the United States since the 1920s. In that connection they have made huge payments to foreign governments. Everywhere in the world (except a few common law countries) the state owns all mineral resources. As such, it is in a position to act as an owner (and receive an economic rent from its property), as well as a tax collector (and demand a portion of an enterprise's profit). Being ultimately indifferent to the rubric covering the money it receives, a government that owns minerals can cast as a "tax" amounts received from mineral developers that would look much like a proprietor's royalties in dealings between purely private parties. If the characterization as a "tax" holds up, a U.S. taxpayer engaged in the extraction of minerals might derive, through the foreign tax credit, a full reduction of U.S. taxes for amounts that would otherwise, in purely private dealings, only be deductible from income as royalties.

Agreements between U.S. oil companies and foreign governments were structured in this light. By the mid-1970s income taxes on gains from oil exploration and development in some oil-exporting countries (that also owned the oil in the ground) were as high as 80 percent. In some instances, furthermore, there was no general income tax at all. If the formally designated royalty component of the arrangement was small (or nonexistent) in relation to a tax it was easy to infer that the ostensible "tax" contained an element of royalty, i.e. a consideration for a specific interest in the oil rather than a generalized payment in consideration of public goods. The foreign government could be understood to be acting more as an owner of minerals than as a tax-collecting sovereign. Part of the payment termed a "tax" could readily be considered the price of an interest in minerals resources purchased from the government. And you cannot reasonably expect a tax credit for goods or services purchased from a government any more than from a private person.

The question surfaced dramatically in a 1976 IRS ruling denying credits for ostensible payments of income taxes under production-sharing agreements between a U.S. oil company and the Indonesian government.[24] The Service's position in the ruling was that no "tax" was paid under the agreements, and that the total amount received by the Indonesian government was merely a royalty. The crucial vice of the arrangement, in the IRS's view, was the combination of 1) a guaranteed return for Indonesia, consisting of a single combined amount of ostensible "royalties" and "taxes," predicated on the quantity of oil extracted by the U.S. company and 2) the failure of the contract to allow for full cost recovery: "Thus, the effect of the [agreement] and the other prohibitions is to assure that the government will retain a fixed percentage of oil produced in any year regardless of whether [the taxpayer] has any net gain from such production. Such an assured share of production retained by the mineral owner is characteristic of a royalty and not of a tax within the United States concept of the terms."[25]

The problem was easier to state than to fix. The Treasury tried and ultimately rejected several different approaches. The first response of the Treasury was to require that the foreign government receive a reasonable and independent royalty before any payment from an oil developer could be treated as a tax. That approach proved unworkable, however, because there is no immediate touchstone of a "reasonable" royalty. Each area of exploration and development is unique. The royalty widely used in Texas, for example, would be far too small for most of Saudi Arabia, where the oil is far cheaper to extract.[26]

The next idea was more promising and became the standard of creditable income taxes in connection with natural resource payments. It occurred to the Treasury that while it may be hard, even impossible, to find an objective touchstone of a "reasonable" royalty, there is often a readily available test of a "reasonable" tax. At first this may seem surprising. The tax and the royalty are complementary components of a single amount received by a foreign government. When one is established, the other is the residual amount by default. Why should it be easier to establish a reasonable amount of income tax than a reasonable royalty? The answer lies in the available comparison with the amount of income tax paid by persons who have *no* course of dealing with the government. The "reasonable" income tax is the income tax borne by

---

[24]Rev. Rul. 76-215, 1976-1 Cum. Bull. 194.
[25]Id. at 197.
[26]If the oil is easily accessible, the landowner's royalty should be greater, because the developer incurs lower cost and risk.

persons who have no specific transactions with the government. It is, put anthropomorphically, the amount that the government "wants" to collect as a tax in its sole capacity as taxing sovereign. Therefore in regulations on creditable taxes issued in 1980 the Treasury required, as a condition of the foreign tax credit, that the amount termed an "income tax" be comparable in amount with the amount of tax paid by persons who did not deal with the government. This is known as the "comparability" requirement and has itself gone through a mutation or two.

In an early version of the regulations the comparability requirement was imposed in draconian fashion. If the amount termed a "tax" paid by an oil developer was very nearly the exact same amount as a general income tax paid by others, the oil tax was not "comparable" and *no* tax credit was allowed for *any* part of the payment to the foreign government. A near miss on comparability meant no foreign tax credit at all under these early regulations. U.S. taxpayers (mostly oil companies) objected that foreign governments could not be presumed to have foresworn their taxing power altogether simply because they also exacted royalties, and that the amounts paid to governments therefore necessarily had *some* component of tax, for which credit should be allowed. Initially, the Treasury countered that it was neither feasible nor even within its statutory power to break down ostensibly single foreign levies into separate components of creditable taxes and deductible royalties.

The difficulty, from the Treasury's perspective, is the following. Suppose that a foreign government owns all of the country's mineral resources and imposes a general income tax of 50 percent and a special oil tax of 75 percent on the profits of oil producers from oil concessions. There is a strong inference that part of this supernormal tax payment of 75 percent is a royalty, compensating the government's ownership of the oil in the ground. But what part? If the producer derives 125 of gross income from oil extraction at a production cost of 25, that leaves 100 of net extractive income, on which the tax at the special oil rate would be 75. Since the general income tax is 50 percent (which would entail a tax of 50 applied to this taxpayer's net income), it may seem that the royalty component of the total payment is the balance of 25, leaving an income tax of 50.

If this strikes you as the right tax, though, you're wrong. The problem with subtracting the difference in percentage points is that it doesn't take into account the *deductibility* of a royalty under a general income tax.[27] Let's assume that the royalty is 25 and the tax is 50. Then deduct the royalty of 25 from 100 of net income. That leaves 75 of net taxable income and 37.5 of tax, which is clearly wrong. You must consider that at a 50 percent income tax rate every dollar of royalty reduces taxable

---

[27]Income tax, by contrast, is not itself deductible from taxable income.

income by one dollar and tax by 50 cents. The correct approach is to work backward from the taxpayer's aftertax net income, in this case 25. To be left with 25 after paying a 50-percent income tax the taxpayer must have started with 50 of pretax income.[28] Therefore the *tax* component of the total payment of 75 is only 25, and the royalty must be 50. In short, you must allow for the deductibility of a royalty in dissecting the combined payment into its royalty and tax components.

Splitting Payments made by Dual Capacity Taxpayers

In a later version of the regulations (which are currently in force) the Treasury did allow single combined payments to foreign governments to be divided into separate components of deductible royalty and creditable income tax. The current regulations on creditable taxes sport a "splitting" formula for breaking down payments to foreign governments made by "dual capacity taxpayers."[29] When a "dual capacity taxpayer" is subject to a different type or level of taxation from other taxpayers, the element of pure income tax is broken out separately. The regulations are complicated, but their core is a "safe harbor formula" for separating tax and nontax components. This splitting formula reconstructs the amount that would have been paid under the foreign country's general income tax, and treats that amount as a creditable tax. The safe harbor formula takes into account the deductibility of the amount of any payment properly characterized as a royalty under a general income tax.

Mechanically, the qualifying amount of tax under the safe harbor formula is the following:[30]

$$(A - B - C) \times \frac{D}{(1 - D)}$$

A   is the amount of "gross receipts,"

B   is the amount of "costs and expenses,"

C   is the amount actually paid by the dual capacity taxpayer to the foreign government, and

D   is the applicable tax rate under the general income tax.

---

[28]If the tax rate is 50 percent, the amount of tax that you must pay to be left with 25 after tax is 25.

[29]These are the taxpayers that also transact business with the government.

[30]Reg. §1.901-2A(e)(1).

If we insert the numbers from the above example into the formula, we have gross receipts ("A") of 125, costs and expenses ("B") of 25, and the amount paid to the foreign government ("C") of 75. The term (A – B – C) is therefore (125 – 25 – 75), or 25. With the general income tax rate 50 percent (0.5), the factor D/(1 – D) is .5/(1– .5), or 1. The amount of tax paid is therefore 25 (25 X 1/1). It may seem like magic, but the formula is a more general form of the computation done above to work backward from aftertax to pretax income and from there to the tax paid. (A – B – C) is simply aftertax net income, the amount the taxpayer is free to take home after payment of all costs, royalties, and taxes. From that amount it is relatively easy to figure out the tax that was paid.[31]

Credit for "In Lieu of" Taxes

There is one more element of creditable taxes. Section 903 of the Code adds to the range of creditable taxes any foreign tax paid "in lieu of a tax on income … otherwise generally imposed by any foreign country." These are known as "in lieu of" taxes. An "in lieu of" tax is a substitute for an income tax that is otherwise generally imposed. Thus the foreign country must have in force a general income tax. A tax on gross income is not creditable, for example, if it is the only tax imposed by a foreign country. Flat rate withholding taxes are creditable as "in lieu of" taxes only if the foreign country also imposes a general income tax for which the flat rate tax is a substitute. Furthermore, a creditable "in lieu of" tax cannot be imposed *in addition to* a general income tax, but only *instead*. Excise taxes or value-added taxes, for example, paid by taxpayers that also pay income tax are not creditable. Because of these constraints, "in lieu of credits" are not widely available for foreign taxes that fail to qualify as full-blown income taxes.

---

[31]Easy, that is, when there is a single tax rate (here 50 percent). When foreign income tax rates are graduated, it is far more difficult. You have to plug different rates into the formula by trial and error until you find one that works.

Chapter 13

The Credit Limitation of Section 904

The "Overall" Limitation of 1921

The limitation on the foreign tax credit, as we saw in chapter 11, is designed to prevent high taxes on foreign income from offsetting U.S. tax on *U.S.*-source income. When we last looked in on the credit limitation, it was the 1921 version. This is an "overall" limitation that established a single limitation on the credit for all foreign income taxes on the basis of the ratio of foreign source income to worldwide income. While the credit overall could not exceed the U.S. effective rate of tax on foreign source income, some very high foreign income taxes could be credited in full if the taxpayer also had sufficient low-taxed foreign source income to build up the amount of the limitation.[1]

With the original overall limitation U.S. taxpayers subject to foreign income taxes higher than the U.S. rate had ready opportunities for "cross-crediting" by seeking out low-taxed foreign source income, which would enlarge the limitation on the credit and thereby permit the high foreign taxes to be credited in full. Low-taxed foreign income in this situation is a shelter of sorts for U.S. taxes, not because it is beyond the reach of U.S. taxation, but because it absorbs other foreign taxes that would otherwise exceed the credit limitation. In this regime U.S. taxpayers had non-economic incentives to shift income-producing operations offshore to low-tax environments.[2] An integrated oil company, for example, might move an oil refinery from the continental United States to the Bahamas.[3]

For years, the U.S. tax system took a benign view of such devices through its allowance of the unmodified overall limitation. Under this regime, all sorts of operations of U.S. taxpayers—from marketing offices to oil refineries—sprung up in tax-haven jurisdictions. One of the simplest ways to create low-taxed foreign source income is to make deposits in foreign banks, which yield interest often untaxed by the country of source.

---

[1]See the last three charts in chapter 11.

[2]Note that a wholly unlimited foreign tax credit (as in the 1918 Act) would eliminate this particular economic distortion. Such a suggestion, however, meets with a sullen reception from the U.S. Treasury.

[3]Reconsider the charts near the end of chapter 11 in this light.

International Taxation

The "Basket" System of the 1986 Act

The early form of the overall limitation survived more or less intact until the 1986 Act. The credit limitation was reworked and elaborated in 1986, however, to the point of being barely recognizable. The current form of the limitation on the credit divides foreign income into a number of separate categories or "baskets," for which a limitation is determined separately. Although the regime of separate limitation baskets is almost stultifyingly complex, it retains at the core some elements of the old "overall" limitation. It is impossible to expound here the separate basket limitation system in its gory detail, but I will try to convey the gist and a few highlights.

The basic statement of the limitation is in section 904(a): "the total amount of the credit . . . shall not exceed the same proportion of the tax against which such credit is taken which the taxpayer's taxable income from sources without the United States ... bears to his entire taxable income for the same taxable year." This statement of the limitation is essentially unchanged from the one introduced in 1921.

Section 904(d)

Section 904(a), however, states only the broadest framework of the limitation. The actual mechanics of the limitation are laid out in section 904(d), added to the Code in 1986, which provides that the limitation is determined separately for nine separate categories of income. Specifically, section 904(d)(1) provides that the limitation established in section 904(a)

> shall be applied separately with respect to each of the following items of income:
>   (A) passive income,
>   (B) high withholding tax interest,
>   (C) financial services income,
>   (D) shipping income,
>   (E) in the case of a corporation, dividends from each non-controlled section 902 corporation,
>   (F) dividends from a DISC or former DISC . . .
>   (G) taxable income attributable to foreign trade income . . .
>   (H) distributions from a FSC . . . and
>   (I) [all other income].

These nine categories are commonly known as the separate limitation "baskets."[4]

The Separate Baskets

In this regime a credit limitation is determined separately for foreign income taxes imposed on income in each separate limitation basket. The credit for foreign income taxes imposed on income within each basket is limited to the ratio of foreign source income *within that basket* to worldwide income.[5] In other words, the credit for foreign taxes on each of the nine types of income is limited to the U.S. effective rate of income tax on foreign source income of that type. If, for example, a U.S. person derives both foreign passive investment income and foreign shipping income subject to foreign income tax, the foreign tax credit is determined separately for the taxes on each type of income.

The following simple illustration summarizes two years' operations of a U.S. person receiving foreign source shipping income and passive income. Assume the U.S. income tax rate is 30 percent. The foreign income tax rate, on both shipping income and passive income, fluctuates from year to year.

	Foreign source shipping income	Foreign income tax on shipping income	Foreign source passive income	Foreign income tax on passive income	U.S.-source income
Year 1	50	20	50	10	100
Year 2	50	10	50	20	100

In Years 1 and 2 the separate limitation in both the shipping income basket and the passive income basket is 15.[6] The foreign income tax on passive income in Year 1 (10) is creditable in full. There is, however, an excess credit of 5 above the limitation in the shipping income basket, which carries forward to Year 2. The lower foreign tax on passive in-

---

[4]From now on I use the terms "separate limitation category" and "separate limitation basket" (or simply "basket") interchangeably.

[5]More precisely, the separate limitation for each basket in a taxable year is the same proportion of the total U.S. income tax (determined before the credit) as the amount of foreign source taxable income within the basket bears to the taxpayer's total taxable income. The numerator of the limitation fraction for each basket consists entirely of foreign source income within that basket.

[6]For the shipping income basket the limitation is U.S. tax pre-credit of 60 (30 percent of worldwide income of 200) times foreign source shipping income (50) over total income (200). [The limitation formula is $60 \times 50/200 = 60 \times 1/4 = 15$] In the passive income basket the computation is the same.

come in Year 1 has provided no tax benefit in the higher-taxed shipping income basket. In Year 2 the actual tax of 10 on shipping income plus the carryover of 5 from Year 1 in that basket are fully creditable. There is also in Year 2 an excess credit of 5 in the passive income basket, which can be carried back to Year 1 in that basket. The Year 1 tax return can therefore be amended to claim an additional foreign tax credit of 5 for the carryback of tax from Year 2 in the passive income basket. At the end of Year 2 foreign income taxes in both baskets have been fully credited, but without cross-crediting between the baskets.

In the system of separate limitation baskets a taxpayer, in order to cross-credit, has to generate low-taxed foreign source income *in the same basket*. Low-taxed foreign source interest or shipping income, for example, is useless to a taxpayer with high-taxed foreign manufacturing income.

The Point of it all

You might well be wondering exactly what section 904(d)(1) aims to accomplish. On first encounter, perhaps, no immediately obvious theme or reason runs through the baskets. But on further scrutiny a few things may come into focus.[7] The first four baskets ((A) through (D)) have something in common. All contain income from capital that is highly mobile. You can produce passive income (interest, dividends, and the like) anywhere in the world by shifting liquid capital there. Financial services income (from banking, insurance, and securities brokerage) rarely requires substantial fixed physical capital (like plant and equipment). That is why, for example, insurance operations controlled by U.S. firms have migrated to benign tax environments such as Bermuda. Shipping income is derived from capital assets that are *physically* mobile. The mobility of capital gives taxpayers considerable control over the *source* of the resulting income, and in turn over the numbers that go into the overall limitation formula.

These types of income also tend to be either untaxed or lightly taxed by foreign governments. Income from shipping on the high seas is rarely taxed by any government. Several types of passive income and financial services income (such as insurance income) are lightly taxed in much of the world.[8] Captive shipping operations of U.S. enterprises were a favorite method before the basket system for enlarging the credit limitation at no immediate tax cost. In fact, of the nine baskets of section

---

[7]Some of the terms ((E) through (H)) are so opaque to a casual reader as to be unfathomable. Forget about them for the moment.

[8]This may bring to mind the exemption of U.S.-source portfolio interest paid to foreign persons.

904(d) all but (E) and (I) contain income treated in some other part of the Code as tax haven income or as income enjoying a specially favored tax regime.

The General Limitation Basket

In the basket system the U.S. Treasury defers to the taxing power of foreign governments only within separate categories of income. Old-style cross-crediting is decidedly constrained, but survives within the ninth basket ((I)). The ninth basket ("other income") is a residual category that contains everything not enumerated in the others. Tax people often call it the "general limitation basket." In contrast with the other categories, the general limitation basket is large and diverse. It contains almost all income from manufacturing, marketing (including most importantly sales of inventory), and services,[9] or in other words your basic business profits. This type of income may be exposed to greatly varying degrees of foreign taxation in different environments, but all of it falls within the ninth basket.

Because of the breadth of the general limitation basket, the limitation on the foreign tax credit remains essentially an overall limitation, despite the apparent atomization of the baskets in section 904(d)(1). *Within* the ninth basket the full cross-crediting of foreign income taxes is still possible. Many large U.S. enterprises with foreign operations, if they have no finance or insurance subsidiaries or shipping operations, are largely unaffected by the basket system and continue to operate under a single overall limitation for their worldwide operations, even if these are far-flung, varied, and subject to highly different tax regimes. Many of the icons of U.S. multinational corporations (Microsoft, Procter & Gamble, and Ford Motors, among others) fall within this class.

Relevance of Source Rules

In this light, you may more readily understand the importance of the source rules that we explored earlier, particularly the 50-50 allocation formula for the source of income from combined production and sale of inventory property.[10] Suppose that a U.S. manufacturer has additional overseas operations in a high-tax environment such as Western Europe. If the manufacturer also has export sales of finished products in lower-tax environments, such as Latin America or parts of Asia, excess foreign tax credits can be accommodated in the general limitation basket. Manufacturing profits and gains from sales of the resulting output

---

[9]Other than financial services such as insurance and banking.
[10]See chapter 3.

both fall in the general limitation basket. By arranging for passage of title in export sales outside the United States, the manufacturer can make use of the 50-50 allocation formula under section 863(b) to impart *foreign* source to 50 percent of the combined gain from manufacturing products in the United States and selling them outside. If this foreign source gain is lightly taxed by foreign governments, then it builds up the limitation in the ninth basket to absorb higher foreign income taxes. The tax benefit for U.S. taxpayers of the 50-50 allocation formula, in other words, is that it serves to increase the limitation in the general limitation basket at little or no foreign tax cost. Low-taxed foreign income for a U.S. person with excess foreign tax credits really *is* low-taxed income, despite worldwide U.S. taxation.[11]

Further aspects of the basket system are discussed in the following chapter.

The Special Case of Oil and Gas

From the bare-bones summary of the basket system just expounded it would seem that the cross-crediting of high taxes on oil extraction income and low taxes on oil refining income, illustrated in chapter 11, would still be viable. Income from oil extraction and from oil refining both fall in the general limitation basket. So the low-taxed Bahamas refining income should build up a limitation in the ninth basket for the ultra-high Kuwait taxes on extraction income, right? Actually, no. There is a set of special rules codified in section 907 governing oil-extraction and oil-related income, above and beyond the basket system of section 904(d)(1). Section 907 is highly complex. Its effect is roughly equivalent to creating two additional separate limitation baskets, one for oil-extraction income and the other for "oil-related" income, the latter being income from oil and gas operations *other* than extraction (such as refining, shipping, and sale). The upshot of section 907 is to prevent cross-crediting of foreign taxes on oil and gas extraction and on other income derived from petroleum, both between each other and with the other nine baskets. Therefore the particular array of oil extraction, refining, and distribution illustrated in chapter 11 would leave the taxpayer with a substantial excess credit carryover and little prospect ever of offsetting it against U.S. income tax.

---

[11]Since the recent condemnation by the World Trade Organization (WTO) of the U.S. Foreign Sales Corporation (FSC) provisions as illegal export subsidies, the source rules may prove to be the last best surviving tax benefit for U.S. export sales. Incidentally, had the future of the FSC rules not been brought into doubt by the WTO, those rules would have been discussed in this book. Some readers may be thankful for the WTO's action.

Chapter 14

The Indirect Foreign Tax Credit

A more descriptive title for this chapter would be "The Foreign Tax Credit for Taxes Paid by Foreign Corporations." Double taxation is even more difficult to pacify, mechanically at least, when U.S. corporations engage in foreign operations through separately chartered foreign subsidiaries. If there were no special provision for taxes paid by foreign corporations, in fact, the foreign tax credit would be of no avail in such situations. To illustrate, suppose Odette, a U.S. citizen, owns the shares of a U.S. corporation, Uco, which in turn owns all the shares of Fco, a foreign corporation, as in the following diagram.

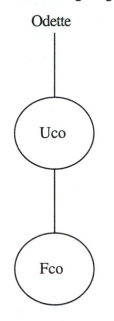

Fco is engaged in business outside the United States and is subject to foreign income tax. Fco itself has no claim to the foreign tax credit under section 901 because it is not a U.S. person and in any event pays no U.S. income tax. Fco's payment of foreign income tax therefore brings no immediate U.S. tax benefit. Distribution of Fco's earnings to Uco as a dividend, however, is subject to U.S. income tax. Section 901 by itself allows Uco no foreign tax credit for Fco's foreign income tax, because Uco did not pay them.[1] Uco has borne Fco's foreign taxes only indirectly as a diminution of distributable earnings. The income tax paid

---

[1]Bear in mind that we are considering here the effect of a tax imposed by Fco on Fco's earnings, not on its dividend distributions to Uco. A foreign withholding tax on Fco's distribution would be a tax paid by Uco and creditable as such.

by Uco is therefore a second layer of tax.[2] Upon ultimate distribution of Uco's earnings as a dividend to Odette, Odette is subject to shareholder-level income tax as an individual shareholder of Uco. Thus in the course of their journey from Fco to Odette, Fco's foreign earnings may be subject to three separate layers of income taxation, consisting of foreign and U.S. corporate income tax and U.S. individual income tax.

If Uco carried out its foreign business as a direct branch operation (i.e., without using a separately chartered foreign entity for its foreign operations) or through a U.S.-chartered subsidiary, there would be no problem. Foreign income tax would be offset (within the limitation, of course) by the foreign tax credit available to a U.S. person paying a foreign tax directly. There would be a single corporate-level tax (at the higher of the U.S. or foreign tax rate) and a shareholder-level tax for Odette upon her receipt of dividends. With no further adjustment, therefore, the taxation of separately incorporated foreign subsidiaries of U.S. corporations would be more severe than the taxation of their direct foreign branches or their domestic subsidiaries.

The problem was evident from the start, and as long as there has been a foreign tax credit there have been provisions extending it to foreign income taxes paid by foreign subsidiaries of U.S. corporations. The mechanical difficulty of this system mirrors that of the rest of the foreign tax credit. As with the limitation, I won't attempt here to scour every inch of the landscape.

The "Deemed Paid" System

An obvious occasion for an indirect foreign tax credit is a U.S. corporation's receipt of a dividend from a foreign subsidiary. In the 1918 Act (which also introduced the foreign tax credit), a U.S. corporation receiving dividends from a foreign subsidiary was "deemed to have paid" a proportional part of the foreign income taxes actually paid by a foreign subsidiary. This system, now codified in section 902, has become known as the "deemed paid" credit. Dividends from foreign subsidiaries in effect bring with them as a deemed paid tax some part of the foreign income taxes paid by the subsidiary.

---

[2]There is no dividends-received deduction here. If Fco were a domestically chartered corporation, Uco would be entitled to a 100 percent dividends-received deduction under §243, a provision which eliminates multiple corporate-level taxation of earnings within groups of related U.S. corporations.

The 1921 Act

To give effect to this basic idea, it is necessary to have some mechanism for connecting the dividends and taxes deemed paid with earnings and taxes actually paid by the foreign subsidiary. The early tax laws used a precisely layered matching system to this end. In the 1921 Act "[A] domestic corporation which owns ... the voting stock of a foreign corporation from which it receives dividends . . . shall be deemed to have paid the same proportion of any income . . . taxes paid by such foreign corporation to any foreign country ... upon or with respect to the accumulated profits of such foreign corporation from which such dividends were paid, which the amount of such dividends bears to the amount of such accumulated profits."[3] Taxes deemed paid under the 1921 Act could be stated as the following formula:

$$\frac{\text{Dividends received}}{\text{Accumulated profits}} \quad X \quad \begin{array}{l}\text{Taxes paid with}\\ \text{respect to}\\ \text{accumulated profits}\end{array}$$

We needn't dwell on the 1921 system, which has been superceded. It is enough to note here that it entailed a specific matching of dividends and deemed paid taxes with annual layers of the subsidiary's earnings and the taxes paid "with respect to" those earnings.[4]

American Chicle

A fundamental problem with the 1921 system was that it did not equalize the taxation of direct branch operations and foreign subsidiaries of U.S. corporations. Rather, it created a double tax benefit for foreign subsidiaries, in the form of a simultaneous deduction *and* credit of foreign income taxes paid by foreign subsidiaries. Foreign income taxes paid by the subsidiaries were excluded from the income of their U.S. parents as a simple consequence of not being distributable as dividends.[5] From the parent's perspective, this is functionally the same as with a *deduction* of the foreign taxes paid by the subsidiary.[6] If the

---

[3]Revenue Act of 1921, 67th Cong., 1st Sess., ch. 136, §238(e); 42 Stat. 227, 259.

[4]Readers who have studied corporate taxation know that dividend distributions are generally matched with vintage-dated annual layers of earnings in reverse chronological order. The early "deemed paid" system worked much the same way.

[5]Earnings of a subsidiary, once paid out as taxes, cannot be distributed as dividends to a parent corporation.

[6]If the full pre-tax earnings of the subsidiary had been included in the parent corporation's income (which would have occurred if a direct branch had been used instead

entire amount of the foreign income taxes paid by the subsidiary were in addition deemed paid upon distributions to the parent and were creditable in full, the parent would have in effect a deduction and a credit for the same foreign taxes.

The IRS attacked this double tax benefit, with partial success, in *American Chicle Co. v. United States.*[7] The IRS contended that the amount of tax deemed paid, and hence the foreign tax credit, should be *less* than the *total* foreign income tax paid by a foreign subsidiary, because some part of the tax had been paid *not* with respect to the earnings distributed as dividends but with respect to the very earnings paid over to the foreign government as tax. In other words, only part of the tax paid upon the entire pre-tax income of the subsidiary was attributable to the accumulated profits remaining after the tax itself was paid. It is easier to understand the competing contentions in *American Chicle* with some numbers.

Assume the foreign income tax rate is 25 percent. Tax of 25¢ would be paid to the foreign government on every dollar of the subsidiary's earnings, leaving 75¢ available for distribution. The taxpayer's position was that 25¢ of tax had been paid for each 75¢ of distributable profits, and that a 75¢ dividend should therefore bring 25¢ of tax deemed paid with it as the amount of tax paid "with respect to" the earnings. The IRS countered that when 25¢ of tax was paid "upon" a dollar of *pre*-tax earnings, only three-quarters of the tax (or 18.75¢) was paid "with respect to" *after*-tax profits, while 6.25¢ of tax was paid upon the 25¢ of earnings that subsequently left the company in the form of taxes paid to a foreign treasury. No matter how much was distributed as a dividend, therefore, some portion of the tax paid (specifically the amount of tax paid on earnings that left the company as tax payments to a foreign government) could not be brought along with a dividend as a tax deemed paid, and would therefore produce no credit.

The government prevailed in *American Chicle,* and foreign "taxes" deemed paid under the 1921 Act were understood to be less than the total tax paid by a foreign subsidiary. The case left the deemed paid system in something of a shambles. The foreign tax credit for taxes paid by foreign subsidiaries was scaled down somewhat, but the effective *deduction* of the foreign income tax remained. In the *American Chicle* regime foreign income taxes paid by foreign subsidiaries afforded their U.S. parents a one-and-a-half tax benefit consisting of a total deduction and a partial credit.

---

of a foreign subsidiary) and the parent had then deducted the foreign income tax, the result would be the same.
[7]316 U.S. 450 (1942).

"Gross-up"

This problem was fixed in 1962, with the addition to the Code of section 78. Now, the amount of any foreign income tax deemed paid by a domestic corporation under section 902(a) in any taxable year is included in the corporation's gross income *as a dividend* in that year. Amounts included in income under section 78 are treated as dividends for all income tax purposes. When a U.S. corporation is deemed to have paid a foreign tax upon receiving a dividend from a foreign corporation, its taxable income is the sum of the actual dividend received and the foreign tax deemed paid. This amount is usually the same as the pre-tax income of the foreign subsidiary from which the dividend was paid. The taxable income of the U.S. parent is in this manner "grossed up" to the pre-tax income of the subsidiary,[8] and there is in effect no deduction of foreign income taxes from the U.S. tax base. To this extent direct branch operations and foreign subsidiaries are taxed the same. Credit for the *full* amount of income tax paid by a foreign subsidiary when deemed paid now produces only a single tax benefit. The three regimes—the 1921 Act, *American Chicle*, and the current system of grossed-up dividends under section 78—are summarized and compared with direct branch operations in the chart on the following page.

Note that the total amount of income and foreign tax credit is the same under today's regime for direct branch operations and foreign subsidiaries. This does not mean, however, that the taxation of foreign branches and foreign subsidiaries is fully equalized in economic effect. A key difference is the timing of tax payments. With a subsidiary income tax is paid in stages, first the foreign tax, then the residual U.S. tax upon distribution of earnings.[9] Subsidiary operations therefore retain a potential advantage over branches. The accumulation of lower-taxed earnings in a foreign subsidiary permits a deferral of U.S. taxation until the ultimate distribution of those earnings to a U.S. parent, whereas branch operations attract full U.S. income tax immediately.

---

[8]Section 78 is often known as the "gross-up" provision.
[9]The chart reveals only the total tax imposed on foreign income, assuming all the earnings of a subsidiary are distributed currently and subject to U.S. taxation.

Comparison of Branch and Subsidiary Operations

	Foreign tax paid	Taxable distribution	U.S. tax (pre-credit)	Foreign tax "deemed paid"	U.S. tax obligation, after credit	Total tax paid
Branch (Direct Credit)	25	[n/a—foreign income taxed directly in U.S.]	50	[n/a—foreign tax actually paid by taxpayer]	25	50
1921 Act	25	75	37.50	25	12.50	37.50
American Chicle	25	75	37.50	18.75	18.75	43.75
"Gross Up" (Sections 902 and 78)	25	100 [75 + "gross up" of 25]	50	25	25	50

| U.S. Income Tax Rate: 50% | Foreign Income Tax Rate: 25% | Foreign Source Taxable Income: 100 |

The Current Pooling System

Another unsatisfactory aspect of the 1921 formula was the specific annual matching of dividends, earnings, and foreign taxes. This regime left open tactical possibilities for taxpayers to time distributions from foreign subsidiaries to coincide with periods of high foreign taxation.[10]

The 1986 Act replaced annual matching of dividends, taxes, and earnings with a system of pooling foreign earnings and taxes. Section 902 now treats dividends from foreign corporations as coming from a single cumulative pool of post-1986 earnings. In this regime, dividends from foreign corporations bring with them as taxes deemed paid a portion of all the foreign income taxes paid on the total earnings in the pool.

Section 902(a)

Under section 902(a) as revised in the 1986 Act a domestic corporation receiving dividends from a 10 percent or greater voting interest in a foreign corporation is "deemed to have paid the same proportion" of the foreign corporation's "post-1986 foreign income taxes" as the amount of the dividends (determined without regard to section 78) bears to the foreign corporation's "post-1986 undistributed earnings." To determine a tax deemed paid in this system it is necessary to maintain two cumulative accounts—that I call "pools"—of the earnings and foreign income tax payments respectively of a foreign corporation arising after 1986. The earnings and the income taxes of a foreign corporation arising after 1986 are each added to their own cumulative pool. A dividend distribution from the pool of post-1986 earnings brings with it a proportionate amount from the pool of post-1986 taxes. The amount of foreign tax deemed paid can be stated as the following formula:

$$
\begin{array}{c} \text{Foreign income} \\ \text{taxes deemed} \\ \text{paid by domestic} \\ \text{corporation} \end{array} = \begin{array}{c} \text{Post-1986 foreign} \\ \text{income taxes of} \\ \text{foreign corporation} \end{array} \times \dfrac{\begin{array}{c}\text{Dividend paid to} \\ \text{domestic corporation} \\ \text{by foreign corporation}\end{array}}{\begin{array}{c}\text{Post-1986 undistributed} \\ \text{earnings of foreign} \\ \text{corporation}\end{array}}
$$

The "post-1986 undistributed earnings" of a corporation are the earnings accumulated in years after 1986 through the close of any taxable

---

[10]Since a distribution brought with it the most recent taxes and earnings, distributions in high-taxed years entailed higher taxes deemed paid while low-taxed earnings (and low foreign taxes) were left behind in the foreign corporation.

year in which a dividend is distributed.[11] The "post-1986 foreign income taxes" of a foreign corporation distributing a dividend are the sum of the foreign income taxes "with respect to" the taxable year and the foreign income taxes "with respect to" prior taxable years after 1986.[12] Distributions from foreign corporations thus bring with them, as taxes deemed paid, a portion of the foreign income taxes from the year of the distribution itself along with earlier taxes.

There is Only One Foreign Tax Credit

On first encounter with the system of section 902 some students think that it establishes a second form of the foreign tax credit, known as the "indirect" or "deemed paid" credit. Not so. Let me underscore that there is *only one* foreign tax credit, allowed in section 901. All that section 902 does is to "deem" a U.S. corporation to have paid some part of the foreign income tax actually paid by a foreign subsidiary (hence the term "deemed paid" credit). The foreign tax deemed paid is entitled to credit only within the constraints of the foreign tax credit generally. It is subject to the limitation, which is applied by combining foreign taxes deemed paid and actually paid within each separate limitation basket, and so on. A foreign tax deemed paid by a U.S. corporation, in other words, is simply another amount that may give rise to the foreign tax credit.

Stock Ownership Requirements

Another element of the "deemed paid" system of section 902 is the stock ownership requirements. At the threshold, a foreign income tax paid by a foreign corporation can be deemed paid by a domestic corporation only if the latter "owns 10 percent or more of the voting stock of" the foreign corporation.[13] A U.S. corporation must therefore own at least 10 percent of the voting stock of a foreign corporation from which it receives dividends in order to be deemed to have paid a portion of the income taxes paid by the subsidiary.[14] The 10 percent requirement draws a line between substantial interests in foreign enterprises and smaller portfolio holdings.

---

[11] §902(c)(1).

[12] §902(c)(2).

[13] §902(a).

[14] I use the term "subsidiary" in this chapter very loosely to describe a foreign corporation in which a U.S. corporation has, through a chain of ownership, a stock interest exceeding the thresholds of §§902(a) and (b) (which may be no more than 5 percent). In this context, please note, I do *not* mean a majority-owned entity.

Lower-Tier Subsidiaries

There are additional ownership requirements for lower-tier foreign subsidiaries in section 902(b), which extends the indirect credit as far as the sixth tier. The requirements differ somewhat for second- and third-tier subsidiaries and for fourth-, fifth and sixth-tier subsidiaries. A foreign tax may be "deemed paid" by a U.S. corporation if it was originally paid 1) by a first-tier foreign corporation in which the U.S. corporation owns 10 percent or more of the voting stock *or* 2) by any lower-tier foreign corporations (above the seventh tier) connected to the U.S. corporation through a chain of foreign corporations in which each foreign corporation in the chain from the first tier down owns at least 10 percent of the voting stock of a lower-tier foreign corporation in the chain. In other words, the U.S. parent must own at least 10 percent of a first-tier foreign subsidiary, and at least 10 percent of each lower-tier subsidiary in a chain must be owned by a higher-tier subsidiary in the chain. There are further requirements for foreign corporations below the third tier. A tax paid by a foreign corporation in the fourth, fifth, or sixths tiers can be deemed paid by a U.S. corporation only if the foreign corporation is a "controlled foreign corporation" of which the U.S. corporation heading the chain of subsidiaries is a "United States shareholder."[15]

The system of deemed paid taxes does not extend to the seventh tier. It follows that no taxes paid by seventh- or lower-tier foreign subsidiaries can be deemed paid by intervening subsidiaries or a U.S. parent, regardless of the extent of their stock ownership.

5-Percent Minimum Beneficial Ownership

There is more. Standing alone, the requirement of 10 percent voting stock throughout a chain would allow U.S. corporations to claim the foreign tax credit for taxes paid by foreign corporations in which they held insignificantly small beneficial ownership. It would, for example, permit indirect credit for taxes paid by a third-tier foreign subsidiary in which a U.S. parent ultimately had only a one-tenth of one percent beneficial interest.[16] The stock ownership rules are further qualified, however, to prevent such a result. The total beneficial (i.e., indirect) ownership by a U.S. parent of voting stock in any lower-tier foreign subsidiary must be at least 5 percent. Specifically, the U.S. corporation at the head of a chain of foreign subsidiaries must itself own, in addition

---

[15]See §902(b)(2) (flush language). The definitions of a "controlled foreign corporation" and a "United States shareholder" are discussed further in chapter 15.
[16]10 percent of 10 percent of 10 percent is 1/10 of 1 percent.

to at least 10 percent directly of the first-tier foreign corporation in the chain, at least 5 percent *indirectly* (i.e. in beneficial ownership) of the voting stock of any member of the group.[17] Thus, if the U.S. parent has only 10 percent of the first-tier subsidiary, the first tier must hold at least 50 percent of the second tier, which in turn must own 100 percent of the third tier.[18] Of course, if the parent owns relatively more of the first-tier foreign subsidiary, smaller holdings of the lower-tier subsidiaries are permitted as long as the product of all percentages down the line is at least equal to 5 percent. Also, no holding at any level may be less than 10 percent, even though the overall 5 percent requirement would sometimes be met in such a case.[19]

Older Layers, Older Law

You may have wondered why I paid so much attention to the older system of matching dividends with layered profits and taxes. It was only in part to irritate you. The old system continues to apply in today's law to distributions from pre-1987 earnings of foreign corporations.[20] The older layers are reached when the post-1986 earnings pool is exhausted by distributions. In that event, distributions are matched with layered pre-1987 earnings, if any, in reverse chronological order, as under the pre-1987 version of section 902. Distributions from foreign corporations are therefore subject to two different regimes. If attributable to post-1986 earnings, they bring with them (as "deemed paid") foreign income taxes from the post-1986 pool. Distributions attributable to pre-1987 earnings are matched with all the annual rings of the pre-1987 tree.[21] Eventually the pools of post-1986 earnings will build up, and most distributions will be subject to the new rules of 902. Considering that some foreign subsidiaries of U.S. corporations have layered earnings reaching back to the 19th Century, however, the old matching system (including the *American Chicle* rule in the older layers) may never fade entirely from the scene.

---

[17]§902(b)(2)(B)(i).

[18]10 percent of 50 percent is 5 percent. No further reduction in interest being permitted, the second tier must own all of the third tier.

[19]Furthermore, since a foreign corporation below the third tier must be a controlled foreign corporation and the U.S. parent corporation its United States shareholder, the beneficial ownership requirements for corporations below the third tier are actually higher than for the second and third tiers.

[20]§902(c)(6)(A); §902(c)(3)(A).

[21]If all post-1961 earnings are distributed, a distribution from earlier earnings would actually be subject to the old *American Chicle* regime.

And it gets worse. Even some earnings of foreign corporations arising *after* 1986 will be subject to the old matching regime. For a newly acquired foreign corporation the pools begin, not in 1987, but at the time of acquisition by a U.S. corporation. "Post 1986 earnings" is a somewhat misleading term of art. The post-1986 earnings and post-1986 foreign income taxes of a foreign corporation include only those for the period beginning with the first taxable year in which the 10-percent ownership requirements of section 902(b) are met by a U.S. corporation.[22] Thus, if a U.S. corporation acquires all the shares of a previously unrelated foreign corporation in 2001, the pool of earnings and foreign taxes begins in 2001. If the foreign corporation has pre-2001 earnings, distributions will be matched with them, if there are no later earnings, under the system of pre-1987 law.

The survival of the pre-1987 regime will thus extend far beyond pre-1987 earnings in the literal sense. The acquisition by a U.S. corporation of a foreign corporation with a prior history of earnings may bring with it the old tracing rules for dividends well into the Third Millennium.

Grand Overview of Dividends from Foreign Corporations

We have now reached the point in our traversal of the foreign tax credit where we can consider in grand overview, with the help of the chart on the following page, the taxation of dividends from foreign corporations. This exercise (even though the chart is considerably over-simplified) will give you an idea of how massively complicated the system is.

Grand Chart

In the chart three U.S. corporations and one U.S. individual (Marcel) own voting stock in various foreign corporations or chains of foreign corporations. There are subsidiaries in the chart from the first to the seventh tier. Assume that all shares of stock not represented on the chart are owned by *foreign* persons. In the following pages we will work through the U.S. tax regime, particularly regarding the foreign tax credit, for dividends received by the four U.S. persons in the chart from their various holdings of foreign corporations' stock. The chart will also serve to expound some aspects of the credit and credit limitation that I have postponed until now.[23]

---

[22]§902(c)(3)(A).

[23]If you are trying to follow the chart and the discussion (which takes up a few pages) you might find it convenient to copy the chart and read the discussion with the chart in hand.

Grand Chart of Dividends
From Foreign Corporations

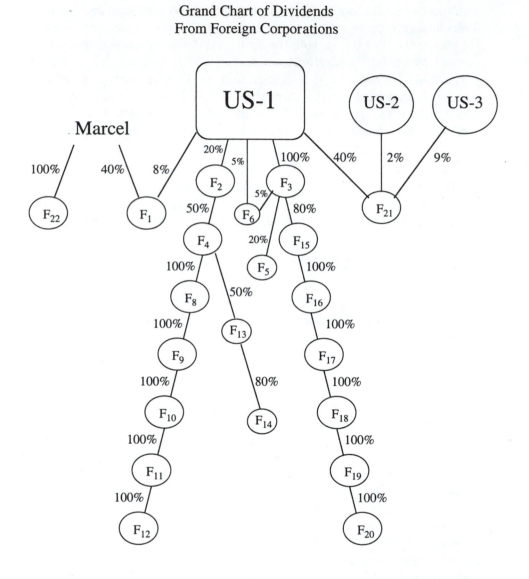

Let's start with dividends paid to the U.S. corporations.

Dividends from F_1 to US-1 bring with them no foreign income tax deemed paid and fall in the passive income basket. US-1's 8 percent stock holding is below the ownership threshold of section 902(a). The stock is simply a portfolio holding from which US-1 receives dividends.

Because US-1 owns 20 percent of the stock of F_2, dividends from F_2 to US-1 do bring with them, as a deemed paid foreign tax and as additional dividend income under section 78, some part of the foreign income tax actually paid by F_2.

10/50 Baskets This dividend income falls in a basket containing "dividends from each non-controlled section 902 corporation."[24] Quite possibly this term (from section 904(d)(1)(E)) made little impression on you when you first encountered it as a listed separate limitation basket in chapter 13. A "non-controlled section 902" corporation is a foreign corporation in which a U.S. corporation owns 10 percent or more of the voting stock (the ownership threshold of section 902), but which is *not* a controlled foreign corporation as defined in Subpart F (which for now you can think of as a foreign corporation in which U.S. persons own more than 50 percent of the stock).[25] The result is a separate limitation basket for dividends from *each* foreign corporation in which a U.S. corporation has a significant, but not controlling interest. [That's right, *each*.] Dividends from noncontrolled section 902 corporations may easily constitute several different baskets, because section 904(d)(1)(E) defines as its own separate limitation category the dividends from *each* noncontrolled section 902 corporation, regardless of the nature of that corporation's business.

These separate basket are known colloquially as "10/50" baskets and noncontrolled section 902 corporations as "10/50" corporations.[26] This separate limitation category is not a single pool; there are as many 10/50 baskets in the class as a U.S. corporation owns interests in different qualifying 10/50 corporations. There is no homogenization of income or foreign income taxes among different 10/50 baskets, and therefore *no* cross-crediting.[27] It may not be obvious just yet, but there are two more 10/50 baskets in the grand chart.

---

[24]§904(d)(1)(E).

[25]§904(d)(2)(E)(i). There is more on controlled foreign corporations in chapter 15.

[26]The threshold of stock ownership in §902(a) is 10 percent while the threshold of stock ownership of a controlled foreign corporation is 50 percent, hence the "10/50" sobriquet.

[27]The 1997 Act changed (and greatly simplified) the inner plumbing of the 10/50 baskets, but the change takes effect only in years *after* 2002.

In the chain of foreign corporations headed by F_2, dividends from F_4 to F_2 bring with them foreign income taxes paid by F_4.[28] Similarly dividends up the line from F_{11} to F_4 bring with them as deemed paid taxes foreign income taxes paid by those corporations.[29] Dividends up the line from F_{12} (a seventh-tier foreign subsidiary), however, bring no foreign income taxes with them, because there is no deemed paid tax below the sixth tier. Dividends from F_{13} to F_4 do bring foreign income tax with them,[30] but not dividends from F_{14} to F_{13}.[31]

Dividends from F_6 to US-1, like those from F1, bring no deemed paid foreign tax and fall in the passive income basket. Even though US-1 does have 10-percent *beneficial* ownership of F_6 (taking into account the 5 percent of F_6 shares owned by F_3), US-1 lacks 10-percent *direct* ownership of F_6 as required by section 902.

<u>Look-Through for Controlled Foreign Corporations</u> Dividends from F_3 (a 100-percent subsidiary) to US-1 do, of course, bring foreign income taxes with them as "deemed paid" taxes. Because F_3 is a controlled foreign corporation (and not a 10/50 corporation), the basket system applies to dividends paid from F_3 to US-1 in an entirely different manner. Under section 904(d)(3) dividends from F_3 to US-1 (which, remember, include deemed paid taxes by virtue of section 78) are subject to "look-through."[32] Specifically, dividends from a controlled foreign corporation to a "United States Shareholder" are treated as income in a separate basket in the same proportion as the foreign corporation's earnings in that basket bear to its total earnings.[33] More colloquially, dividends from a controlled foreign corporation fall in different baskets according to the character of the underlying earnings of the foreign corporation. When look-through applies, dividends received have the character of the earnings from which they were paid. The basket system applies in that event as though a U.S. corporation had received earnings directly from a foreign branch.

---

[28]There is greater than 10-percent direct ownership at both points in the chain, and US-1's beneficial ownership of F_4 is greater than 5 percent (because 20 percent of 50 percent is 10 percent).

[29]US-1's beneficial ownership of F_4 through F_{11} is 10 percent.

[30]There is 10-percent ownership at every point in the chain, and US-1's beneficial ownership of is 5 percent. (20 percent of 50 percent of 50 percent is 5 percent.)

[31]There is 10-percent ownership at every point in the chain, but US-1's beneficial ownership of F_{14} is only 4 percent. (20 percent of 50 percent of 50 percent of 80 percent is 4 percent.)

[32]The headings in §904(d)(3) actually use the term "look-thru." It is baffling to me that the Code, normally so profligate with words, here tries to save the space required for three letters (an "o," a "g," and an "h").

[33]§904(d)(3)(D). This assumes further that the dividends were paid from the earnings in question.

To illustrate, if F_3's income consists of equal amounts of financial services income and shipping income, 50 cents of a dollar dividend from F_3 to US-1 would fall in each of those baskets.

A controlled foreign corporation is a foreign corporation in which "United States shareholders" own more than 50 percent of the stock. A "United States shareholder" means not just any U.S. person owning shares, but a U.S. person owning 10 percent or more of the shares. From now on, when you read "United States shareholder" or "U.S. shareholder," think "U.S. person *and* 10 percent or greater shareholder."[34]

What about dividends from lower-tier foreign corporations (F_5, F_6, F_{15}, etc.) distributed up the line to US-1 through F_3? With look-through, they have the same character for US-1 as for F_3. Dividends from F_6 to F_3 are in the passive income basket and bring no deemed paid tax with them. Therefore, when distributed up to US-1 they are passive income as well and bring with them no foreign income tax. F_5 is a 10/50 corporation.[35] Dividends from F_5 to F_3 therefore bring with them foreign income taxes paid by F_5, fall in their own separate 10/50 basket (regardless of the nature of F_5's earnings), and retain that character when passed up to US-1. F_{15}, on the other hand, is a controlled foreign corporation (of which US-1 is a U.S. shareholder). Dividends from F_{15} to F_3 bring with them foreign income taxes, and retain their character for both F_3 and US-1. If, for example, F_{15}'s earnings come from manufacturing, they fall in the general limitation basket of section 904(d)(1)(I). They remain in the general limitation basket when passed up to F_3 and US-1.

All the foreign corporations below F_{15} in the chain (F_{16} through F_{20}) are controlled foreign corporations. Look-through therefore applies up the line. Dividends from F_{20}, however, bring with them no deemed paid foreign tax because F_{20} is below the sixth tier, which is the end of the line for deemed paid taxes.

Here is a more elaborate illustration of look-through. Suppose that in a given year F_3 earned 50 of shipping income and received a dividend of 50 from F_6, a dividend of 50 from F_5, and a dividend of 50 from F_{15} attributable entirely to manufacturing income, and F_3 distributed all its earnings (a total of 200) as a dividend to US-1. For US-1 this dividend would consist of i) 50 of shipping income (from F_3's earnings), ii) 50 of passive income (the dividend from F_6, which has the character of passive income for F_3 and hence for US-1), iii) 50 of income in the F_5 10/50 basket (because F_5 is a 10/50 corporation and the character of the dividend from F_5 to F_3 flows through to US-1), and iv) 50 of income in

---

[34]There is further discussion of controlled foreign corporations and United States shareholders in chapter 15.

[35]The direct and indirect ownership requirements of section 902 are met—US-1 beneficially owns 20 percent of F_5—but F_5 is not a controlled foreign corporation.

the general limitation basket (F_{15}'s manufacturing income, the character of which flows through F_3 to US-1).[36]

F$_{21}$ is a 10/50 corporation. Dividends from F_{21} to US-1 therefore fall in a separate 10/50 basket. Dividends from F_{21} to US-2 and US-3 are simply passive income, with no deemed paid tax attached. A small change in stock ownership, however, brings flow-through into play. In the chart, increase US-3's percentage of F_{21} stock to 11 percent (from 9 percent). Now F_{21} is a controlled foreign corporation and US-1 and US-3 are its "U.S. shareholders." Look-through under section 904(d)(3) now applies and the dividends from F_{21} to US-1 and US-3 fall in the baskets according to the character of the underlying earnings in F_{21}'s hands. US-2 continues to receive passive income.

Dividends from Foreign Corporations to Individuals Things are considerably simpler for an individual shareholder of a foreign corporation (Marcel in the grand chart), but generally less advantageous. No dividends received by Marcel (from F_1 or F_{22}) bring with them foreign income taxes deemed paid. The system of section 902 applies only to foreign shares held by U.S. *corporations*. The dividends from F_1 fall in the passive income basket.[37] Dividends to Marcel from F_{22}, a controlled foreign corporation, retain for Marcel the same character they had for F_{22}, by virtue of look-through.[38]

Helpful Similes?

To fix these patterns in your mind it may be helpful to classify them as follows. Dividends received by U.S. corporations from small (less than 10 percent) portfolio holdings in foreign corporations bring no creditable foreign tax and fall in the passive income basket. Because neither foreign tax nor the character of the income passes through, such small holdings of foreign stock can be thought of as *opaque*. Dividends received by U.S. corporations from substantial but noncontrolling interests in foreign corporations (10/50 corporations, in a nutshell) do bring with them foreign income taxes deemed paid, but the character of the underlying earnings (which now fall indiscriminately in separate 10/50 baskets) is obliterated. Such holdings of foreign stock can be thought of as *semi-opaque*. Dividends from a controlled foreign corporation to a U.S. corporation that itself is a 10-percent or greater share-

---

[36]Notice that I told you nothing about the character of F_5's and F_6's earnings in *their* hands. It does not matter, because in neither case does the character of the underlying income flow through.

[37]F_1 is not a controlled foreign corporation. Therefore, no look-through.

[38]Note that if US-1's holdings of F_1 stock were, say, 11 percent instead of 8 percent, F_1 would also be a controlled foreign corporation and dividends from it to Marcel would also be subject to look-through.

holder bring with them foreign income taxes deemed paid and retain their character in the U.S. parent's hands. Think of controlled foreign corporations as *transparent* to their U.S. corporate shareholders.[39]

For dividends received by individuals from foreign corporations, there are only two shades. A foreign tax cannot be "deemed paid" by an individual, and only a corporation can have a 10/50 basket. Dividends from noncontrolled foreign corporations bring no foreign income tax with them and fall in the passive income basket. Think of stock of such corporations as *opaque*. Dividends from controlled foreign corporations also bring no foreign income tax with them, but look-through applies in determining the basket in which they fall. A controlled foreign corporation can be thought of as *semi-transparent* for an individual shareholder.

---

[39]If you are "looking through" something, it must of course be transparent.

Chapter 15

Controlled Foreign Corporations

Foreign Corporations and Deferral

In the early years of the income tax, foreign corporations were widely used by U.S. persons to avoid U.S. taxation of foreign income, or at least to defer it indefinitely. The separate identity of corporations in the U.S. tax system means that a foreign corporation is not formally a U.S. person, even if owned by U.S. citizens or residents, and has no immediate U.S. income tax obligation on foreign source income.

A simple device to benefit from this accommodating regime was the "foreign personal holding company," a foreign corporation used as a sort of incorporated pocketbook beyond the reach of U.S. taxation. An individual would transfer income-producing assets (or assets ripe with unrealized gains) to a wholly-owned corporation chartered in a low-tax foreign jurisdiction.[1] Assets held in such entities would attract no current U.S. income tax if invested outside the United States. A more elaborate use of foreign corporations might consist of the performance of services outside the United States by a principal shareholder who was a U.S. person, but was acting on behalf of the corporation rather than individually. Under the source rules, the resulting compensation, formally received by a foreign entity, would have foreign source and would escape U.S. taxation.

Generically, this use of foreign corporations is known as "deferral," and often gained heightened effect from various forms of income-shifting. The latter consists of deflecting income originating as an economic matter in a high-tax environment to a foreign corporation basking in both a low-tax environment and deferral. Together, deferral and income-shifting are the main ingredients of almost all international tax shelters.

Deferral, it should be understood, is not permanent forgiveness of U.S. taxation. Some future event may expose income on which tax has been deferred to U.S. taxation. For example, a foreign subsidiary may distribute its previously untaxed earnings to a U.S. shareholder, who must treat them as a taxable dividend. Because of the undying fact of the time value of money, however, there is a benefit of deferral of U.S.

---

[1]The periphery of the United States, especially in and near the Caribbean basin, is dotted with such countries. The Bahamas, the Cayman Islands, Bermuda, Panama, and others have at times imposed no income taxes at all. Operations organized in such places are widely called "offshore," a term often applied (but not limited) to tax havens surrounded by water.

taxation in the difference between the U.S. income tax rate and the foreign rate on foreign earnings. Over a long enough period of time, postponement of taxation approaches the value of forgiveness.[2] What is more, deferral can be converted to total forgiveness of taxation through the mechanism of the restatement to fair market value of the basis of assets owned at death under section 1014. The heirs of owners of foreign corporations can sell the shares for their fair market value without realizing gain. The upshot of deferral, in short, is a more benign tax regime on foreign operations conducted in low-tax environments. Deferral results in taxation that approaches territorial taxation the longer it lasts and significantly undercuts the worldwide reach of the U.S. income tax.

Foreign Personal Holding Companies

The first breach in the wall of deferral came with the adoption in 1937 with the adoption of special rules for governing foreign personal holding companies (now codified in Code sections 551 through 558). Under these rules, the income of foreign personal holding companies is taxed directly to their U.S. shareholders, which eliminates the tax advantage of using foreign corporations.

A "foreign personal holding company" is defined in section 552 as a foreign corporation 1) in which more than 50 percent of the total combined voting power of all classes of stock or the total value of the stock is owned directly or indirectly, at any time during the taxable year, by five or fewer U.S. individuals[3] and 2) which derives at least 60 percent of its gross income in the form of "foreign personal holding company income." The latter item includes passive investment income, securities gains, gains from commodities transactions, income from estates and trusts, income from contracts to furnish personal services performed by 25 percent shareholders of the corporation, income from the use of corporate property by a 25 percent or greater shareholder, various rents, and more.[4]

Each U.S. shareholder of a foreign personal holding company must include in gross income, as a dividend, the amount that would have been received as a dividend if the corporation had in fact distributed its

---

[2]For example, at a discount rate of 10 percent the present cost of paying a dollar of tax in 36 years is little more than 3 cents. You should consider as well, however, that the owner of deferred income does not have the immediate enjoyment of it and that, as the deferred income grows through compounding, so does the amount of tax payable upon repatriation. Deferral is therefore more valuable if you want from the outset to reinvest while deferring consumption.

[3]A U.S. individual is a citizen or resident of the United States.

[4]Section 553(a).

taxable income.[5] This of course is the regime of current taxation that undoes the benefit of deferral.

Foreign Base Companies

The foreign personal holding company rules affected only a small class of U.S.-owned foreign corporations--those beneficially owned by five or fewer U.S. individuals. Until the 1960s the possibility of deferral of U.S. taxation through the use of more widely owned foreign corporations, including any and all foreign subsidiaries of publicly held U.S. corporations, still flourished. Entities falling outside the narrow definition of a foreign personal holding company could be set up for passive investment and financial operations such as insurance in low-tax foreign countries. For active business operations a simple avenue to benign taxation was to conduct them in a low-tax foreign country through a corporation chartered there. You might think that this tax benefit depended on the opportunities for gainful business operations in low-tax countries, which may be limited. But U.S. enterprises could and did set up elaborate structures for shifting taxable business income from high-tax environments to foreign corporations operating as "base companies" in low-tax environments.

A foreign "base company" is essentially a center of profit severed from its real economic moorings. A U.S. enterprise selling goods overseas, for example, might sell them in bulk at a low price to a foreign subsidiary in a tax-haven country (the base company), which would in turn sell them at a high price to a second subsidiary (possibly a lower-tier subsidiary of the same enterprise) engaged in selling the goods in their market of destination. The resale by the base company would be set at the highest possible price, resulting in a large profit in a tax-favored environment. The foreign corporation engaged in final distribution (and quite possibly operating in a high tax jurisdiction) would have a high cost basis in the goods and would rarely make substantial profit even if its marketing were successful. Overall, the pattern was a deflection of income from the place of manufacture and distribution to a tax-haven entity serving as a conduit. By the early 1960s foreign base companies were widely used for international production, marketing, and services of all kinds. The U.S. Treasury was not entirely helpless against foreign base companies in the days before Subpart F,[6] but none of the countermeasures available to it made a large dent in the regime of deferral.

---

[5] §551(b).

[6] For example, the transfer prices for goods and services between a U.S. enterprise and a foreign affiliate could be attacked under section 482, which in effect forces

Subpart F

The Revenue Act of 1962 substantially curtailed the use of foreign base companies, and deferral in general. A cluster of new Code sections extending from 951 through 964, widely known by their heading "Subpart F" imposed current U.S. taxation on many of the tax-haven operations of foreign corporations controlled by U.S. persons (known unsurprisingly as "controlled foreign corporations"). The original 1962 version of Subpart F left most active business operations, even if lightly taxed by foreign governments, unmolested. The provisions of Subpart F have been amended several times since 1962. Until the early 1990s all the changes extended the grip of current taxation relentlessly to several types of active businesses conducted in controlled foreign corporations. The most recent amendments of Subpart F have actually restored certain possibilities of deferral, especially in financial services. Overall, though, Subpart F today substantially limits deferral for controlled foreign corporations operating in conspicuously favorable tax environments.

Before venturing further into Subpart F, let me mention that it represents a pinnacle of statutory complexity. Its inner plumbing is thoroughly monstrous. Although I will try to spare you much of the lurid detail, there is no escaping it altogether.

The core of Subpart F is a single tightly coiled sentence in section 951(a)(1) imposing current U.S. tax on the "pro rata share" of a "United States shareholder" in various types of income of a "controlled foreign corporation."

The main building blocks of Subpart F are the definition of "control" that makes a foreign entity a "controlled foreign corporation," and the definition of the income of controlled foreign corporations that is currently taxable to their United States shareholders.

Controlled Foreign Corporation Defined

A "controlled foreign corporation" (hereafter "CFC") is defined in section 957(a) as "any foreign corporation if more than 50 percent of (1) the total voting power of all classes of stock ... entitled to vote, or (2) the total value of the stock, is owned ... by United States shareholders

---

U.S. taxpayers to recognize income properly attributable to their economic activity in the United States. See chapter 4.

on any day during the taxable year of such foreign corporation." Note that control is established *either* by voting power *or* by the value of stock.[7] Because *more* than 50 percent ownership or control is required, however, a foreign corporation owned exactly equally by foreign persons and United States shareholders (or even by United States shareholders and U.S. persons not qualifying as United States shareholders) is *not* a CFC.

"United States Shareholder"

"United States shareholder" is a term of art, defined in section 951(b) as "a United States person ... who owns ... 10 percent or more of the total combined voting power of all classes of stock entitled to vote of such foreign corporation."[8] A United States shareholder (hereafter sometimes referred to as a "U.S. shareholder") is thus not simply any U.S. person that owns shares of a foreign corporation, but one holding 10 percent or more of its voting power. If non-U.S. shareholders (and this includes U.S. persons who hold less than 10 percent of the voting power) own at least 50 percent of the value and voting power of a foreign corporation, then it is not a CFC.[9]

Indirect Ownership of CFCs and Attribution

A further element of the definition of control of a controlled foreign corporation is a set of rules of indirect ownership and attribution of stock ownership, under which a person is treated as owning shares of stock held indirectly through entities or owned by related persons, so that the status of United States shareholder cannot be avoided by creating long chains of lower-tier subsidiaries, or by spreading shares among family members or beneficially owned entities.[10]

---

[7]Before the 1986 Act, only voting power mattered in determining control.

[8]The elided portions of these two definitions refer to the different types of ownership--direct, indirect, and constructive under section 958--that satisfy the control requirement. This is discussed below.

[9]Although nonvoting ownership may be taken into account in determining control, only a U.S. shareholder of a CFC is subject to current taxation under Subpart F. Small portfolio shareholders and even large owners holders of nonvoting stock escape current taxation.

[10]§958.

Income Subject to Current Taxation under Subpart F

Current taxation of CFCs under Subpart F extends to what Congress considers to be "tax haven" income (a notion with a somewhat shifting content over the years) and not (with significant exceptions) to active business operations. What the tax writers understand as tax haven income includes passive income arising in a no-tax or low-tax environment and income artificially shifted to such an environment when it has no indigenous economic connection there. Thus income subject to current taxation under Subpart F is a mix of passive investment income, income from financial services operations (such as banking and insurance), income generated beyond the reach of any sovereign (such as international shipping and transportation income and some "oil-related" income), and income artificially deflected from high-tax to low-tax environments ("base company" income, the quintessential object of Subpart F).[11]

There is a strong family resemblance between currently taxable Subpart F income and income in the first four separate limitation baskets of section 904(d)(1).[12] Both consist of income derived from capital that is highly mobile and can easily be diverted from a high-tax to a low-tax environment. From this you can glean a common concern of Subpart F and the system of separate limitation baskets.

Foreign Base Company Income

Among the several items taxed currently under Subpart F, the most important is "foreign base company income," a category itself made up of several elements. A brief traversal of its composition may give you a somewhat clearer picture of the taxation of CFCs.

"Foreign base company income" occupies its own Code section.[13] The term describes several types of income—both passive and active in form. In the original form of Subpart F (1962) foreign base company income included only passive investment income and income from tax haven arrangements between related persons. No income from active business transactions with unrelated persons (even though conducted in low-tax jurisdictions) was included. Successive enlargements of foreign base company income brought foreign shipping income, foreign oil related income, and a broader range of financial income within the class. The various types of income reached by Subpart F now extend far

---

[11]§§952(a), 954(a).

[12]See chapter 13.

[13]§954. This is equivalent in statutory real estate to having your own Zip code.

beyond the combination of pure passive investment and tax haven income targeted by the 1962 Act. The common element of this income is that it is relatively easily shifted from a high-tax to a low-tax environment. One way to encapsulate Subpart F is as imposing current taxation on foreign operations in which relatively liquid or relatively mobile capital is a dominant factor.[14]

Foreign base company income, as defined in section 954(a), is made up of five different components:

1) Foreign personal holding company income,
2) Foreign base company sales income,
3) Foreign base company services income,
4) Foreign base company shipping income, and
5) Foreign base company oil related income.

Foreign Personal Holding Company Income

The first component of foreign base company income is "foreign personal holding company income" ("fphci"), itself defined in section 954(c)(1) as an assemblage of several components. The core element of fphci is the "portion of gross income which consists of … dividends, interest, royalties, rents, and annuities."[15] To this are added various gains and losses from transactions in property,[16] and more.[17] The components of fphci mostly have the form of income from passive investments, although several may arise in the course of an active business. Sometimes, however, a connection with a business shifts income from fphci to another category for the purposes of Subpart F.[18]

<u>Active Financial Services Income Excluded</u> An important exclusion from foreign personal holding company income, since 1997,[19] is income from active foreign banking and financing businesses conducted in CFCs. U.S. banks and other financial intermediaries can now do business outside the United States without current U.S. taxation, but not if they engage in systematic income-shifting to low-tax environments.[20] The legislative undergirding of this exception is formidable. Basically,

---

[14]Note, however, that the most recent change in Subpart F (1996) actually *removed* a significant class of financial services income—mainly from banking, securities brokerage, and insurance—from its reach.

[15]§954(c)(1)(A).

[16]§§954(c)(1)(B)-(D).

[17]§954(c)(1)(E).

[18]§954(c)(2).

[19]There were complications with the late line-item veto that kept these provisions from definitive effect until 1999.

[20]§954(h).

a qualifying CFC must have concentrated financial business operations within one or more specific countries and not engage in overly extensive or artfully manipulative cross-border maneuvers.

Rents and Royalties from an Active Business Excluded Foreign personal holding company income also does not include rents and royalties derived in an active business, unless received from a related person.[21] A number of rent-producing undertakings—such as the ownership and operation of rental real estate, equipment leasing, and film distribution—can thus be conducted through a CFC without triggering current U.S. taxation, as long as there is no obvious income-shifting among related persons.

Foreign Base Company Sales Income

Foreign base company sales income—perhaps the quintessential form of Subpart F income—is income that results from channeling sales of goods through a low-tax foreign entity that has no significant economic relation to the sales. Broadly, it is income derived from purchases and sales of property between related persons. Persons are "related" within Subpart F if one of them controls the other or if both are under common control.[22]

To be more specific, the following is a fairly close paraphase of the Code's definition of foreign base company sales income:

Foreign base company sales income is gain
1) from the purchase from a related person for resale to any person; 2) from the sale to any person on behalf of a related person; 3) from the purchase from any person for resale to a related person; or 4) from the purchase from any person on behalf of a related person of

any personal property manufactured, produced, grown, or extracted outside the country in which a CFC is organized, if the property is sold or purchased for use, consumption, or disposition outside that country.[23]

Added Value from Production Defers U.S. Tax The common thread running through foreign base company sales income is purchases and sales between related persons through entities organized in countries with no economic or commercial relation to the production, distribution, or consumption of the property sold. Section 954(d)(1) aims principally at income arising without economic activity in a CFC's country of

---

[21]§954(c)(2)(A).

[22]§954(d)(3).

[23]§954(d)(1). Foreign base company sales income includes commissions, fees, and other gains, along with the profits of sale from transactions of this type. Id.

incorporation. If there is substantial value added from production in the country of incorporation, the resulting income is not foreign base company sales income. If property is purchased for processing *and* resale, or is produced by a CFC from purchased components, section 954(d)(1) similarly does not bite. The production or processing must be substantial, however. Mere packaging or labeling, or even minor assembly, do not suffice for this purpose, while such activities as transforming wood pulp into paper, steel rods into nuts and bolts, live sardines into canned fish, and so on, *do* constitute sufficient processing operations.[24]

Foreign Base Company Services Income

Similar to foreign base company sales income is foreign base company services income, which includes income (of any kind) derived in connection with the performance of "technical, managerial, engineering, architectural, scientific, skilled, industrial, commercial, or like services" performed for or on behalf of any related person and performed outside the country of organization of a CFC.[25] This definition includes the type of services that are most easily shifted to a different country, such as architecture, engineering, much technical assistance, scientific research, and consulting.

Note, however, that Subpart F does not by itself entirely prevent the use of tax havens to perform services. An engineering firm can create a subsidiary in Bermuda, move personnel there, and carry out actual engineering work beyond the reach of current U.S. taxation.[26]

Foreign base company services income does not include income from services directly related to the sale of property produced by a CFC. Displaying shoes to a potential customer does not produce Subpart F income; nor does installation services or essential training to enable the use of property by its buyer.

Foreign Base Company Shipping Income

Foreign base company shipping income includes income from the use of any aircraft or vessel in foreign commerce or derived from

---

[24]The facts of each case are ultimately controlling, but the Regulations provide a safe harbor, acknowledging activity as bona fide manufacturing if production costs (direct labor plus factory costs) account for 20 percent or more of the total cost of goods sold. Reg. §1.954-3(a)(4)(iii).

[25]§954(e)(1).

[26]That is because, in this case, the services would be performed in the place of the CFC's incorporation. Note further, though, that if the firm is very small (fewer than 6 shareholder/employees), the foreign personal holding company rules may come into play as well.

"space or ocean activity."[27] The category also includes much related income, such as income from leasing vessels or from services relating to the use of vessels; gains from the disposition of aircraft or vessels; income from joint ventures in shipping; dividends and interest attributable to the shipping income of subsidiary corporations; and gains from the sale of stock if attributable to the shipping income of the entity sold.

This provision is aimed at captive foreign shipping operations of U.S. corporations. Shipping conducted in the benign tax environment of the high seas is rarely heavily taxed. Entities engaged in shipping on behalf of affiliated members of the same multinational enterprise therefore served in olden days as vessels for the accumulation of untaxed income. An obvious example (and probably the prime target of the shipping provisions) was the transportation of oil products by integrated oil enterprises. Shipping subsidiaries of oil firms could build up profits taxed more favorably overseas than those from the extraction, refining, or marketing of minerals, especially if their intra-family pricing arrangements survived challenge under section 482.[28] The captive shipping firm is, in this respect, similar to a captive insurer.

Foreign Base Company Oil Related Income

The final item of base company income is "oil related income," which is income derived from the processing, transportation, or marketing of oil and gas and related products.[29] Also included are income from various related services and gains from the sale of assets used in oil related activity. In essence, oil related income is all income connected with oil and gas other than income from their extraction. Oil related income does not, however, include income with its source in the country of extraction of the oil and gas or in the country in which the oil products are sold for ultimate use or consumption.[30]

Here as elsewhere, Subpart F aims at income (from activity such as refining or transporting oil products) that has been shifted to a tax environment separate from the place of original production or ultimate use. The obvious targets of this provision are foreign subsidiaries owning tanker fleets or oil refineries in tax haven venues. The provision does not apply to wholly independent refiners, however.[31] Thus an enterprise engaged solely in refining oil can operate offshore and still enjoy the regime of deferral.

---

[27]§954(f).
[28]See ch. 4.
[29]§§954(g), 907(c).
[30]§954(g)(1).
[31]§954(g)(2).

Let me point out before closing this chapter and (mercifully) moving on that I have presented here only the broadest outline of Subpart F, ruthlessly suppressing entire segments and mountains of detail.

Chapter 16

Passive Foreign Investment Companies (PFICs)

A further exception to the regime of deferral for foreign corporations is the taxation of Passive Foreign Investment Companies (or PFICs). A PFIC[1] is a foreign corporation that receives predominately passive foreign source income. U.S. persons owning shares of PFICs are generally subject to current U.S. taxation or the equivalent. As with Subpart F, the PFIC tax regime is exceedingly complex in its full detail. This chapter sketches only the big pficture, and even then omits a number of landmarks.

Background and Overview

Until the 1986 Act current U.S. taxation of foreign corporations was strictly tied to control of the corporation held by U.S. persons. Minority and portfolio interests in foreign corporations owned by U.S. persons were not to any extent subject to look-through taxation. The PFIC regime, introduced in the 1986 Act, considerably enlarged current taxation of foreign passive investments of United States persons through foreign corporations. PFIC taxation applies without regard to the extent of U.S. ownership.

The taxation of PFICs is built on the idea of denying to United States persons (and hence capturing for the U.S. Treasury) the value of deferral of U.S. taxation on *all* passive investments channeled through foreign entities. The rules achieve this end either in the obvious way—current taxation of U.S. investors in PFICs—or in the indirect way of imposing an interest charge on the deferred distributions and gains of those investors. Among the notable features of PFIC taxation is that it does not depend on any threshold of ownership or control by U.S. persons.

The central elements in the taxation of PFICs are 1) the definition of a PFIC, and 2) the tax regime imposed on U.S. owners of shares. Noteworthy in the former is that *any* foreign entity holding passive investments may be a PFIC, regardless of the extent of U.S. ownership or control. The unique feature of the latter is an interest charge (equivalent to the value of deferred U.S. taxes) imposed on the realized gains of U.S. shareholders, unless the U.S. shareholders make an election that results in current taxation.

---

[1]"PFIC" is usually pronounced as a semi-acronym ("pee-fick") rather than a full acronym (which would be "pfick").

PFIC Defined

A "passive foreign investment company" (PFIC) is *any* foreign corporation if "(1) 75 percent or more of the gross income of such corporation for the taxable year is passive income, or (2) the average percentage of assets ... held by such corporation during the taxable year which produce passive income or which are held for the production of passive income is at least 50 percent."[2] A PFIC is thus an entity that receives mainly passive investment income or holds mainly passive investment assets.

Taxation of PFICs

The U.S. shareholders of a PFIC are subject to a special (indeed unique) income tax regime. The specifics depend on whether the shareholders of the PFIC have elected to be taxed as shareholders of a "qualified electing fund," or whether the "pure" PFIC tax regime of section 1291 applies.

The PFIC Regime of Section 1291

Under section 1291, amounts received by a U.S. person from a PFIC (whether as a distribution or the proceeds of a sale of shares) are first allocated "ratably" to all the separate years of the taxpayer's holding period of the PFIC stock.[3] Amounts allocated to earlier years are included in income and subject to U.S. tax *plus* a "deferred tax amount,"[4] which is an increase in tax determined by adding an interest element reflecting and offsetting the prior deferral of U.S. taxation.[5]

The system of section 1291, very roughly, negates the tax benefit of deferral. If you bear in mind that the economic value of deferral of U.S. taxation is the time of value of the deferral itself, you will understand how PFIC taxation, by taking back the time value of deferral through the deferred tax amount, undoes the advantage.

There is an admirably clear summary of the workings of section 1291 in, of all places, the preamble of the Treasury Regulations on PFICs:

---

[2]§1297(a).
[3]§1291(a)(1)(A).
[4]§1291(a)(1)(C).
[5]§1291(c)(2).

Pursuant to section 1291, a U.S. person that is a shareholder of a section 1291 fund pays tax and an interest charge on receipt of certain distributions and upon disposition of stock of the section 1291 fund. Under this rule, gain from a disposition or the portion of any distribution that is an excess distribution (defined in section 1291(b)) is treated as ordinary income earned ratably over the shareholder's holding period of the stock of the section 1291 fund. The portion allocated to the current year, and to years when the corporation was not a PFIC, are included in the shareholder's gross income for the year of the distribution; the remainder is not included in gross income, but the shareholder must pay a deferred tax amount (defined in section 1291(c)) with respect to that portion. The deferred tax amount is, in general, the amount of tax that would have been owed if the allocated amount had been included in income in the earlier year, plus interest.

The QEF Election

As an alternative to this complex and generally severe tax regime, U.S. shareholders of PFICs can elect *current* U.S. taxation of their share of the earnings of a "qualified electing fund" ("QEF"). An election by a U.S. person brings the allocable earnings of a QEF within a tax regime[6] similar (but not identical) to that of Subpart F, which you may remember from the preceding chapter.

The Mark-to-Market Election

The most recent feature of the landscape is the election of section 1296, designed to mitigate the complexities of PFIC taxation for U.S. investors in foreign mutual funds. Small[7] U.S. holders of foreign mutual funds, many of which are PFICs in the hands of U.S. shareholders, would often find it difficult to comply either with the pure PFIC tax regime of section 1291 or to make a QEF election.[8]

To ease the plight of such U.S. investors, the "mark-to-market" election of section 1296 allows shareholders of PFICs, if their stock is marketable, to recognize unrealized gain or loss in the shares annually instead of undergoing the PFIC tax system.[9] Specifically, a U.S. person who owns "marketable stock" in a PFIC may elect to include in income (as ordinary income) the excess of the fair market value of the stock at the close of the taxable year over its adjusted basis or to deduct (as an ordinary loss) the excess of its adjusted basis over the year-end fair

---

[6]See §1293(c) for the details.

[7]Note that I mean "small" in the financial sense, not the Lilliputian sense.

[8]The difficulty of the latter is getting enough information about the earnings of the fund from its managers, given different requirements of reporting outside the United States.

[9]Annual recognition of unrealized gain or loss is known as "marking to market." It is a regime that also applies to many traded commodities contracts. See §1256.

market value.[10] The shareholder's basis is adjusted up or down to reflect amounts included or deducted pursuant to this election.[11] PFIC stock that has been marked to market takes a *carryover* basis (instead of the usual fair market value basis) at the death of its owner.[12]

Needless to say, a taxpayer who has made a mark-to-market election under section 1296 is not subject to the pure PFIC tax regime of section 1291.[13]

It also goes without saying that only "marketable" stock can be marked to market. PFIC stock is "marketable" for this purpose if it is regularly traded on a suitably regulated securities exchange or if it is a foreign open-end or closed-end mutual fund that makes periodic reports of net asset values.[14]

---

[10]§1296(a).
[11]§1296(b)(1).
[12]§1296(i).
[13]§1291(d)(1).
[14]§1296(e).

Chapter 17

International Corporate Reorganizations

The Different Corporate Tax Environments

Subpart F, which is summarized in chapter 15, creates a separate tax regime for controlled foreign corporations ("CFCs") and their U.S. shareholders. The rules governing passive foreign investment companies (PFICs) similarly create a separate tax regime for PFICs and their U.S. owners. There are as a result several distinct corporate income tax environments within the U.S. tax system. There is the domestic corporate environment, combining full current taxation of worldwide corporate income with separate taxation of shareholders. There is the CFC environment—a mix of current taxation and deferral, with eventual taxation of foreign earnings upon repatriation as dividends to U.S. persons. There is the PFIC environment, consisting of current taxation of passive investment income or the equivalent, backed up by deferred interest charges. And there is the wholly foreign (or non-CFC) environment, in which full deferral of U.S. taxation is generally possible.

Income and assets move around among these tax environments. Foreign corporations receive capital from domestic corporations, distribute dividends back, merge, divide, liquidate, and so on. The U.S. international tax system must therefore follow and coordinate transition between various tax regimes. In the wholly domestic setting, the Code contains an extensive set of rules—known as Subchapter C to its aficionados—governing the movement of assets into, out of, and within corporate solution. A key element of Subchapter C is the transfer of assets into and within the corporate environment without recognition of gain. Contributions of assets to corporations by their controlling shareholders, most distributions between affiliated corporations (including liquidations), and mergers and divisions are often either partly or wholly free of immediate tax. Assets and shares involved in these nonrecognition transactions generally retain their tax attributes, including basis, intact.

An unstated premise of the corporate nonrecognition rules is that an appropriate amount of gain should be preserved for future taxation. Earnings and profits shifted from one entity to another in a nonrecognition transaction will produce dividends upon ultimate distribution to shareholders. Unrealized appreciation is preserved when the basis of assets is carried over to a new entity and survives there as a tax attribute. If there were no qualification of the nonrecognition rules in international transactions, however, the movement of assets from a taxable to a nontaxable environment could mean forgiveness rather than deferral of taxation, given the different tax regimes applicable to different classes of domestic and foreign corporations. The nonrecognition rules are therefore considerably modified in international corporate transactions. The provision carrying the freight in this area is section 367.

Section 367

Section 367 applies differently to different patterns of corporate transactions, which include outbound, inbound, and wholly foreign transfers and exchanges Section 367 itself contains relatively little detail. It consists largely of a mandate to the Treasury to issue regulations on different types of international corporate reorganizations, coupled with some broadly sketched guidelines. The regulations under section 367, in provisions of numbing complexity, severely limit nonrecognition of gain in international corporate transactions according to a somewhat elusive notion of tax avoidance.

The regulations work by imposing conditions—known colloquially as "toll charges"—on international reorganizations. Sometimes the condition is partial or complete immediate recognition of gain; in other cases it is the preservation of certain tax attributes and prescribed adjustments to others.

Despite the overwhelming clutter and obscurity of the regulations under section 367 the basic idea of section 367 is nearly fathomable. It aims to preserve for U.S. taxation all gains that originally arose within the reach of U.S. taxation. This entails limiting the transfer of unrealized appreciation from the United States to a foreign corporate environment and preventing the earnings of CFCs (to the extent not currently taxed to U.S. shareholders) from slipping into wholly foreign corporate solution or domestic corporate solution without recognition of gain. The regulations under section 367 can be understood only in light of these objectives.

Outbound Transfers Under Section 367(a)

Section 367(a)(1) generally requires recognition of gain on transfers of property to a foreign corporation by a U.S. person, overriding in this regard the nonrecognition provisions of Subchapter C. There are exceptions—restoring *non*recogntion—for selected outbound transfers.[1]

Active Business Exception The main exception to the rule of section 367(a)(1) (and hence allowing possible nonrecognition) is for "property transferred to a foreign corporation for use by such foreign corporation in the active conduct of a trade or business outside the United

---

[1] §§367(a)(2)-(4).

States."[2] This is consistent with the pattern of Subpart F, which, you may remember, generally does not treat active businesses and as tax haven operations.

In an exception to this exception, recognition of gain *is* required, even when active business assets are transferred, when the assets of a foreign branch business with previously deducted losses are transferred to a foreign corporation.[3] You can understand this as an extension of the tax benefit principle (recovery of prior deductions as taxable income) in the international setting.

Transfers of Stock   By far the most complex aspect of section 367(a) is outbound transfers of shares of stock. These are generally taxable under section 367(a)(1), but section 367(a)(2) allows exceptions (pursuant to regulations, naturally) for certain transfers of stock pursuant to a valid tax-free reorganization. The regulations spell out this possibility in considerable detail. In broad outline, the regulations permit nonrecognition in outbound transfers of stock of domestic corporations (such as a stock-for-stock "B" reorganization) if U.S. transferors of stock of a domestic corporation hold no more than 50 percent of the stock of a transferee foreign corporation.[4] There must, in other words, be some dilution of U.S. ownership in a combination of a domestic corporation with a foreign entity.

There are further wrinkles. If U.S. ownership of the stock of the transferee foreign corporation is widely dispersed in small holdings after the transfer, there are no other requirements. U.S. persons who own 5 percent or more of the stock of the foreign corporation, however, must enter into specific gain recognition agreements with the IRS, whereby upon certain subsequent events within 5 years (such as a disposition by the *foreign* corporation of the transferred domestic stock) gain initially deferred is recognized in full.[5]

Nonrecognition is possible in outbound transfers of a *foreign* corporation's stock if *either* the U.S. transferor owns less than 5 percent of the transferee foreign corporation after the after *or* the U.S. transferor enters into a five-year gain recognition agreement with respect to the transferred stock as described above.[6] Therefore a transferor that ends up with less than 5 percent of the transferee foreign corporation escapes recognition of gain without taking any action, while holders of 5 percent

---

[2]§367(a)(3)(A).
[3]§367(a)(3)(C).
[4]Reg. §1.367(a)-3(c)(1).
[5]Reg. §1.367(a)-8(e).
[6]Reg. 1.367(a)-3(b)(1).

or more of the transferee foreign corporation must either recognize gain immediately or enter into a five-year gain recognition agreement.

Inbound and Wholly-Foreign transfers Under Section 367(b)

The regime in regulations under section 367(b) for inbound and wholly foreign transfers is even more complex. It is enough to say here that the regulations are concerned primarily with assets held by controlled foreign corporations (CFCs). If the assets of a CFC remain in a CFC in the course of a corporate adjustment—a frequent but not invariable consequence of a wholly foreign reorganization—current U.S. taxation is generally not imposed under section 367(b). Certain tax attributes are identified and preserved, however, to prevent erosion of the U.S. tax base later. When assets move from a CFC to a foreign corporation that is not a CFC, current U.S. taxation *is* generally imposed on the accumulated earnings that are now leaving the CFC environment. The reason for this is the greater possibility of subsequent escape by those earnings from full U.S. taxation. Finally, when assets move from a CFC to a domestic corporation (often by a liquidation that would normally be tax-free under section 332) a "toll charge" is imposed on foreign earnings (in the form of a constructive dividend).

Taken together, these patterns ensure that all earnings arising in CFCs will eventually be subject to U.S. tax at ordinary rates. To this end, toll charges are imposed when earnings slip out of controlled foreign corporate solution or are repatriated, and the earnings are reckoned and preserved for future taxation when adjustments occur within the controlled foreign corporate environment.

Enough Said

There is little point in trying to fathom the universe of section 367 in greater detail. The ruthlessly simplified sketch I have offered here should serve mainly to give you a very rough sense of the tax constraints imposed on international corporate reorganizations.

Chapter 18

U.S. Citizens Abroad

Americans living and working abroad experience a somewhat different income tax environment from the rest of us. They are allowed under section 911 an annual exemption from income tax for up to $80,000 of foreign source earned income. Several explanations, of which some may have merit, have been offered for this apparent windfall. Among them are that 1) Americans living abroad do not derive the full benefit of public expenditures financed by taxation in the United States; 2) the cost of living overseas is higher, particularly for U.S.-style amenities; 3) the U.S. foreign tax credit provides no offset for foreign taxes when foreign governments rely heavily (as they often do) on indirect taxes (which can neither be credited nor deducted); 4) tax incentives are necessary to induce Americans to suffer the discomforts of living and working in less developed areas.

Section 911

Section 911 provides an income tax exclusion and a "housing allowance" for Americans abroad. Under section 911(a), a "qualified individual" may elect to exclude "foreign earned income" from income and exempt the "housing cost amount" from taxation for any taxable year.[1] The rest of section 911 fleshes out such matters as who can claim the exclusion, how much, with respect to what income, and in what years.

Qualified Foreign Residents

To qualify for the exclusion, a U.S. citizen must 1) have a "tax home" in a foreign country and 2) *either* be a "bona fide resident" of one or more foreign countries for at least one entire taxable year *or* have spent at least 330 full days in foreign countries during a period of 12 consecutive months.[2] The notion of a "tax home" has already come up in chapter 2, in connection with the definition of a resident alien in section 7701(b). It is much the same in section 911, except that it has a more specifically residential character. The central element of a tax

---

[1] The dollar amount of the earned income exclusion and the housing cost exemption are specified in sections 911(b) and 911(c).

[2] §911(d)(1). The exclusion is also available to individual alien residents of the United States who have the requisite foreign "tax home" and spend the minimum of 330 days abroad.

home under section 911(d)(3) is an individual's "abode." As for "bona fide" foreign residence under section 911, it is essentially the same as "residence" for all individuals under the older common-law standard of residence that preceded section 7701(b).[3]

Foreign Earned Income

Excludable "foreign earned income" is earned income from sources within a foreign country attributable to services performed by an individual during the period of qualifying overseas presence.[4] It includes wages, salaries, and other amounts received as compensation for personal services actually rendered.[5]

Excluded Amount

The amount of the exclusion under section 911 will increase from year to year until 2002. For taxable years beginning in 1997 and earlier, the exclusion amount was $70,000.[6] It will increase to $80,000 in increments of $2,000 per year for taxable years beginning in 1998 and later.[7] Therefore in 2002 and beyond, the exclusion amount will be $80,000.[8]

Allowance for Housing Costs

A separate allowance for overseas Americans is the "housing cost amount." A qualifying foreign resident can elect to exclude from income the "housing cost amount" for any taxable year. This allowance for housing costs is designed to offset the frequently heavy expense of obtaining American-style housing overseas. Reflecting this cost, the terms of employment for overseas Americans commonly include either free housing or a separate housing allowance. Section 911(c) accommodates either pattern.

---

[3]See chapter 2 for further discussion.
[4]§911(b)(1)(A).
[5]§§911(b)(1)(A), 911(d)(2).
[6]§911(b)(2)(D)(i).
[7]Id.
[8]Starting in 2008 the exclusion will be indexed for inflation. §911(b)(2)(D)(ii).

The "housing cost amount" is, in fact, the excess of actual housing costs over a basic norm measured by an average middle-class housing cost in the United States.[9]

When housing is provided entirely by the employer, the housing cost amount is simply excluded from income. Overseas Americans who pay for their own housing can *deduct* a portion of their housing expenses corresponding to the housing cost amount.[10]

---

[9]§911(c)(2).
[10]§911(c).

Income Tax Treaties

Chapter 19

Income Tax Treaties in Overview

The only true "international" element of international taxation arises in tax treaties. An income tax treaty is, literally, an act of law "between nations." An income tax treaty frames a tax regime for economic activity connected with the treaty countries that may differ in important respects both from the wholly domestic taxation of either country and any treaty regime between other countries.

Mutual Character of Tax Treaties

Income tax treaties provide for adjustments between the income tax systems of different countries. So also, as we have seen, does the foreign tax credit. The difference lies in the mutual character of income tax treaties. While the foreign tax credit is available to all comers, with little regard to similar measures adopted by other countries,[1] an income tax treaty is typically composed of a set of negotiated adjustments and concessions between the tax laws and treasuries of two countries. While the foreign tax credit is both unilateral and multilateral, income tax treaties are strictly bilateral.

Tax Treaties and Double Taxation

The central concern of income tax treaties, as with the foreign tax credit, is double taxation. Treaties generally limit the extent of taxation imposed by each of the treaty countries on transactions that touch on both. The provisions of a typical income treaty include an enumeration of specific abatement or exemption of taxation for residents of one country on certain types of income from the other. Items commonly shielded from full taxation in the treaty country of their source are interest, dividends, royalties, and business profits. On first encounter you might conclude that an income tax treaty was designed to confer tax advantage on certain taxpayers. Although tax treaties may occasionally have that effect, however, that is not what they are mainly about. Rather, they are principally concerned with the apportionment of tax revenues between the treasuries of the treaty countries.

---

[1]By this I mean that the foreign tax credit does not depend on similar allowances under foreign law. It *does* depend on the nature of the foreign taxes imposed. But it is a unilateral concession by the United States in that a bona fide income tax imposed by almost any country may be credited, without regard for any specific agreement with the United States.

Allocating Function of Tax Treaties

Reduced rates or exemption for income derived from one treaty country by a resident of the other country usually imply a larger share of tax for the latter. Most countries allow their residents some form of foreign tax credit for income taxes paid on foreign income. If the foreign tax is abated or eliminated, the foreign tax credit falls away as well. Therefore when a treaty provides, for example, that a resident of one country is not taxed on interest income derived from another, the interest income is not entirely tax-exempt as a result. The country of residence will now tax the income, and at a rate undiminished by any credit it might otherwise have allowed under its own tax laws for taxes imposed by the other country. In this event the effect of the treaty provision for interest income is simply to shift tax revenues from the treasury of one treaty country to another's. Treaties, in short, serve to allocate tax revenue between countries rather than to exempt income altogether.

Given this basic function, income tax treaties most commonly arise between relatively high-tax countries. An out-and-out tax haven has little to offer by way of concessions in an income tax treaty with an industrial or commercial country, and treaties between such disparate partners are relatively rare.

It does not follow, however, that income tax treaties make no difference in the taxation of individuals and enterprises. If income tax rates were always exactly the same in countries entering into treaties, treaties would indeed affect only the treasuries of the two countries and not taxpayers. Because rates differ, the practical effect of treaties often is to create a more favorable tax regime than would otherwise be available. If income tax rates in the country of source are *higher* than in a taxpayer's country of residence, exemption from tax in the country of source under a treaty improves the tax regime of the taxpayer in the other country. At the extreme, if one country does not tax foreign source income at all, and the country of source also does not tax the income by virtue of an income tax treaty, income derived in one country by a resident of another escapes taxation altogether. This is rarely the intended result of an income tax treaty, to be sure, and countries generally avoid entering into treaties with this effect. It is not unknown, however, for treaties to create avenues of complete exemption for certain income. Once uncovered, these avenues are pursued to the hilt by tax-averse international investors until their eventual restraint or elimination by the nations involved.

National Treaty Policies

In entering into treaties countries generally seek to protect the interests of their own treasuries, taking into account the patterns of their habitual economic relations with specific other countries. For example, countries that are importers of technology and capital can be expected to pursue terms in treaties that leave the taxation of royalties and license fees in the country of source. Exporters of capital and technology can be expected to press for exemption in the country of source and taxation by the country of residence of the owner of the capital or technology. The position of the United States in treaty negotiations, for example, has consistently been that the country of source should defer to the country of residence in taxing rentals and royalties from intellectual property. In contrast, developing countries, which are almost invariably importers of capital and technical assistance, commonly seek to leave primary taxation of royalties and license fees with the country of source.

Countries may well prefer one pattern in their treaties with some countries and a different one in others, depending on the flow of investment between them. If the flow of capital and income between two countries were exactly equal, any rule would have the same effect in the end. Any concession to foreign residents made by the country of source would be offset by an equal increase in its taxation of its own residents deriving income from the other treaty country. This is not a common situation, however, even in the very long run.

Advancement of Trade

Besides allocating revenue, tax treaties aim at facilitating business transactions and other economic exchanges between the treaty countries that might otherwise be inhibited by intrusive national taxation. Beyond the cost of actual tax payments, the mere fact of exposure to the tax system of another country imposes significant transactional burdens on enterprises venturing beyond their national boundaries. Dealings between tax authorities and taxpayers in connection with the collection of an income tax can be protracted and difficult. This is one of the concerns underlying the provisions of income tax treaties for allocating the taxation of business profits between the treaty countries. The central element to this end in treaties is the threshold of taxation known as a "permanent establishment."[2]

---

[2]Generally, the business profits of an enterprise of one country are not taxable in the other unless derived from business conducted through a permanent establishment. See chapter 21.

International Taxation

The Treaty Network of the United States

There were few income tax treaties in force before the Second World War. The first income tax treaties of the United States were, not surprisingly, with Canada and Great Britain. As the post-war economies developed, the treaty network of the United States grew to include virtually all the industrial and commercial countries, to which have been added in the last 20 years a fair number of developing and Third World countries as well.[3] The extension of income tax treaties probably received some impetus from the development of international organizations such as the General Agreement on Tariffs and Trade (that recently molted into the World Trade Organization) and the Organization for Economic Cooperation and Development (OECD).

There is no single mold of income tax treaties. Each treaty is separately negotiated with a foreign country and may reflect a particular set of economic relations. As discussed above income tax treaties between economically developed countries function principally to allocate tax revenue between national treasuries. Between developed and developing countries tax treaties may impound subsidies and economic aid in the guise of particular tax concessions.

Model Treaties

The OECD Model Treaty

Although each treaty may differ from all others in some respect, treaties between economically similar countries bear a family resemblance. In the interest of international commerce, the Organization for Economic Cooperation and Development (OECD) has issued (and periodically revised) a Model Income Tax Treaty, which exerts a strong influence on the form and content of income tax treaties among developed countries.

The U.S. Model Treaty

To set the framework of its treaty negotiations the U.S. Treasury has drafted and issued over the years successive versions of a U.S. Model Income Tax Treaty. The U.S. Model Treaty is similar in many respects to the OECD Model Treaty, but also reflects unique concerns of the United States, particularly regarding tax-haven operations. The U.S. Model Treaty establishes the official profile of U.S. treaty policy, consisting of a compendium of the baseline positions the United States

---

[3]The United States recently signed an income tax treaty with Mexico.

puts on the table in negotiating income tax treaties. The following chapters on income tax treaties are based on the current (1996) version of the U.S. Model Treaty. You should bear in mind, though, that no U.S. income tax treaty actually in force is exactly congruent with the U.S. Model Treaty. But many provisions that first surfaced in one or another version of the U.S. Model Treaty have become staple elements of the recent income tax treaties between the United States and other countries.

Chapter 20

Residence in Income Tax Treaties

Income tax treaties involve the taxation of persons who are normally subject to the taxing power of one or both of the treaty countries. The basic pattern is forbearance by the country of source to tax some income (that it would otherwise tax by reason of source) of a "resident" of the other treaty country. Residence, being the status on which treaty benefits are most commonly predicated, is more important in this regard than citizenship. Even a citizen of one country, who does not reside there, may not be able to claim benefits accorded in a tax treaty to "residents" of that country. By the same token, a resident of one country, even though not a citizen, can often claim the benefit of the income tax treaties between that country and others.

Treaty "Residence"

The notion of "residence" has its own special flavor in income tax treaties, having absorbed some aspects of citizenship. It is rarely congruent with the notion of residence established by the national tax laws of any treaty country. Broadly speaking, a "resident" of a country in an income tax treaty is a person within the class that can invoke the benefits of the treaty. In the U.S. Model Treaty, a

> "resident of a Contracting State" means any person who, under the laws of that State, is liable to tax therein by reason of his domicile, residence, citizenship, place of management, place of incorporation, or any other criterion of a similar nature.[1]

Under the Model Treaty, therefore, all persons whose status exposes them to worldwide taxation by the United States are U.S. residents. Thus U.S. citizens along with "residents" can invoke the benefits of the Model Treaty. A corporation is a U.S. resident within this definition by virtue of being chartered in the United States, which of itself implies worldwide U.S. taxation.[2] As so defined, the idea of "residence" is

---

[1]U.S. Model Treaty, art. 4(1).

[2]Other countries determine corporate residence according to an entity's principal place of business or seat of management. The U.S. Model Treaty accommodates this standard, to an extent, by providing that a corporation is a resident of a treaty country if it is liable to tax there by reason of its "place of management." Art. 4(1). By this standard, a corporation chartered in a third country would be a resident of a treaty country if it had connections with the treaty country sufficient to make it a resident corporation under that country's own tax laws.

perhaps better conceived as a form of "fiscal domicile." That is, "residence" is the degree of presence in a country that triggers taxation there. The concept includes citizenship to the extent that citizenship is itself a basis for taxation under the laws of a given country—which in the United States, of course, it is.

Individuals and corporations subject to worldwide taxation under U.S. tax laws are thus residents of the United States under the general terms of the Model Treaty. These include foreign nationals who are U.S. residents under section 7701(b) (that is, individuals who either have the requisite immigration status or meet the "substantial presence" test) and all corporations incorporated in the United States. This definition of a resident works best (and perhaps only) in treaties between countries that tax incomes on a worldwide basis. Countries with more territorial tax systems have no reason to grant to U.S. citizens residing in third countries tax concessions that ultimately benefit the U.S. Treasury, when similar concessions made by the U.S. Treasury to their own citizens are of different effect. Thus, for example, the income tax treaty between the United States and Italy (a country with a relatively territorial income tax system) defines a resident of a State as "any person who, under the laws of that State, is liable to tax therein by reason of his domicile, residence, place of management, place of incorporation, or any other criterion of a similar nature."[3] In this treaty individual *citizens* of either country are not, as such, treated as residents.

The definition of a "resident" in the U.S. Model Treaty is followed by the immediate qualification that a resident of a Contracting State "does not include any person who is liable to tax in that State in respect only of income from sources in that State or of profits attributable to a permanent establishment in that State."[4] As a result, foreign individuals and corporations do not become U.S. residents merely by receiving U.S.-source income that is subject to U.S. tax.

Resolving Dual Residence

Within the Model Treaty's definition of residence it is entirely possible for individuals and corporations to be residents of more than one country. For example, another country tying residence to a specific duration of physical presence could claim as a resident a person also claimed by the United States under the extended form of its "substantial presence" test. The Model Treaty therefore contains, along with its definition of residence, a set of tie-breaking rules to establish a single

---

[3]Treaty with Italy, art. 4(1).
[4]U.S. Model Treaty, art. 4(1)(a).

country of residence under the Treaty, largely eliminating the possibility of dual residence. These are layered, in Article 4(2), in a sequence of clauses, each one of which comes into play when the previous one has failed to settle an overlap of residence. First, "an individual ... resident of both Contracting States ... shall be deemed to be a resident of the State in which he has a permanent home available to him."[5] For individuals who have only one home, there is no problem. Further, this provision offers those who have some wealth and a degree of flexibility in their lifestyles much control over their "residence" under income tax treaties. Someone who owns a dwelling in one country and always stays in hotels (or similarly transient quarters) in other countries can assert exclusive residence in the country of the permanent dwelling.[6]

The constraint of staying in hotels is one that many who divide their time between two countries may not find appealing, however, which leads to the next rule. An individual who "has a permanent home available to him in both States ... shall be deemed to be a resident of the State with which his personal and economic relations are closer," a place also known in the Model Treaty as the "center of vital interests."[7] This test has a flavor similar to the U.S. standard of residence applied to foreign individuals before 1984, which was predicated on a weighing of essential connections between an individual and a place.

If there is a permanent home in both States, the Model Treaty continues: "[i]f the State in which [an individual] has his center of vital interests cannot be determined, or if he does not have a permanent home available to him in either State, he shall be deemed to be a resident of the State in which he has an habitual abode."[8] Which leaves us to determine exactly what is an "habitual abode." An apartment, even a pied-à-terre, certainly qualifies. What about the abode of a special friend with whom the taxpayer is very very close? What if the taxpayer always stays at the same hotel? In the same room? To be safe, individuals seeking to avoid U.S. residence might do well to spread their sojourns in the United States among different hotels and their attentions among different special friends.

Moving on, an individual who has an habitual abode in both countries (or neither) is treated as a resident of the country of his nationality.[9] Finally, the residence of an individual who has dual nationality (or none) is a matter for determination by the "competent authorities" of the

---

[5]U.S. Model Treaty, art. 4(2)(a).
[6]Holding a dwelling under a long-term lease is probably the equivalent of ownership in this situation.
[7]U.S. Model Treaty, art. 4(2)(a).
[8]U.S. Model Treaty, art. 4(2)(b).
[9]U.S. Model Treaty, art. 4(2)(c).

treaty countries.[10] The "competent authorities" (who surface ubiquitously in income tax treaties) are the tax authorities of the respective treaty countries. In effect, the IRS gets together with its foreign counterpart to thrash out the taxpayer's residence when none of the tie-breaking rules resolves a case of dual residence.

"Saving" Clauses

If you picked up the U.S. Model Treaty and quickly read a few provisions conferring tax benefits on foreign "residents," you might conclude that the United States accords treaty benefits to its own citizens who reside in treaty countries. Not so. The United States (like most other countries) reserves in its treaties its taxing power over its own citizens and residents who happen to reside in another country. All U.S. income tax treaties contain some form of a provision reserving to each of the treaty countries the right to tax its own residents and citizens as though the treaty were not in force. In such provisions—known as "saving" clauses —each treaty country "saves" its taxing power over its own constituents. In the U.S. Model Treaty the saving clause is conspicuously asserted near the beginning, in Article 1(4): "Notwithstanding any provision of the Convention ... a Contracting State may tax its residents ... and by reason of citizenship may tax its citizens, as if the Convention had not come into effect." In other treaties, especially older ones, the saving clause may be buried deep in the text, sometimes in provisions that seem purely administrative.[11]

Saving clauses are rarely absolute. Treaty countries extend some treaty benefits even to their own citizens and residents. In the U.S. Model Treaty, for example, social security benefits are taxable only by the country paying them and child support payments are not taxable at all under the treaty, even if paid to a resident or citizen of the United States.[12] In other treaties of the United States the foreign tax credit

---

[10]U.S. Model Treaty, art. 4(2)(d).

[11]I must admit to having concluded once, as a beginning lawyer, that a U.S. citizen residing and working in a foreign country was not subject to U.S. taxation on his salary because of an apparently unequivocal provision in the relevant treaty exempting the salaries of "residents" of each country from taxation in the other. Of course I had missed the saving clause (which was disguised under a somewhat obscure heading). The lesson here is: when giving an opinion on a treaty, always read more than the few lines that seem on point.

[12]U.S. Model Treaty, art. 1(5)(a).

is extended, for the benefit of U.S. persons, to a broader range of foreign taxes than would normally be creditable.[13]

---

[13]Note that in this case the foreign treasury benefits as well, in being able to offer an advantageous tax regime to U.S. investors (in the form of fully creditable local taxes) without loss of revenue.

Chapter 21

Business Profits—Permanent Establishments

The main event in most income tax treaties is a provision concerning the taxation of active business operations of an enterprise of one treaty country in the other. Generally the business profits of an enterprise of one treaty country are not taxable in the other treaty country unless they are attributable to a "permanent establishment." There is some such provision—with different shadings—in all income tax treaties. In the U.S. Model Treaty the provision governing business profits—and it is entirely typical—is the following:

> The business profits of an enterprise of a Contracting State shall be taxable only in that State unless the enterprise carries on business in the other Contracting State through a permanent establishment situated therein. If the enterprise carries on business as aforesaid, the business profits of the enterprise may be taxed in the other State but only so much of them as is attributable to that permanent establishment.[1]

A permanent establishment is both a threshold of taxation of business profits and a limitation. Only if a foreign enterprise has a permanent establishment may the country of source tax its business profits, and then only those "attributable" to the permanent establishment. The key questions, then, are the exact contours of a "permanent establishment" in a given treaty and the range of business profits attributable to it.

Before pursuing those questions, however, we first consider the reasons underlying the taxation of business profits in income tax treaties.

Marcel's Wine Business

It may be easier to understand the idea underlying the taxation of permanent establishments through an example. Consider again our friend Marcel, now a citizen and resident of France engaged in the production and sale of French regional wine. Marcel wants to expand his sales outside France. He need not look far. There are a number of contiguous or nearby countries[2] (and the United States just a boat trip away) that offer promising markets for French wine. Entering these markets will involve at some point warehousing goods, wholesale distribution, and

---

[1]Art. 7(1). The sparse punctuation is original.
[2]Belgium, Luxembourg, Germany, Austria, Holland, the U.K., Switzerland, Denmark, and Sweden are affluent countries that import wine.

retail sales. But Marcel, at least initially, probably will not want to do these things himself. In virtually every commercial country, a class of independent distributors, agents, wholesalers, and others has arisen to facilitate the acquisitive undertakings of those (inside or outside the country) for whom it would not be feasible to provide such support for themselves. Marcel is therefore likely to enter markets in Europe and the United States with the help of such intermediaries, who, in the normal course of their business, also serve as intermediaries for other enterprises. By acting through a pre-existing network of independent distributors and agents a producer like Marcel might easily sell wine in a score of different countries, in none of which he could afford to create his own commercial infrastructure.

What about the taxation of these operations? If Marcel's foreign sales conducted through independent intermediaries were exposed to unmodified taxation in the countries of destination, Marcel might find himself subject to a battery of different tax obligations. By virtue of regular sales of inventory in the normal course of business Marcel could be considered—at least within a technical meaning often followed in national tax laws—to be "doing business" in many countries. That would be so, most likely, in the United States, with the further consequence that Marcel would have "effectively connected" income there as a matter of U.S. law. To the extent national tax systems tax something like effectively connected income of foreign persons (and most do) Marcel might find himself with taxable business profits under *many* national tax laws.

This would be a dreadful result for Marcel, not because of the tax cost per se—France would allow him a foreign tax credit for the non-French taxes—but because of the burden of dealing with all the national tax authorities. The mechanics of taxation of business profits are not easy. Income taxation, generally based on filed returns, entails extended dealings with national tax authorities. For each separate foreign operation you have to measure the income of relevant source and the allocable deductions under different national tax laws. This would add up to a significant hurdle to Marcel's foreign operations.

Enter income tax treaties with "permanent establishment" clauses. All the countries in this scenario are connected by such treaties. With the existence of a permanent establishment as a threshold of taxation of business profits by the country of source, the farflung sales of an enterprise can be carried out within the regime of a single country's national tax laws (in Marcel's case France). Merchants like Marcel can extend their operations into other countries through independent agents without multiplying the burdens of tax compliance.

The shield of business profits from taxation offered by treaties extends, however, only to foreign undertakings pursued *below* a specific level of sustained activity or investment. Suppose that Marcel found a particularly favorable reception for his products in Holland. He might also find it convenient, in order to pursue his Dutch business more efficiently, to open his own sales office there and to rent or buy warehouse space for his own exclusive use. These steps would create for Marcel a permanent establishment in Holland, and expose him to Dutch income taxation on his business profits earned there. But, having a more extensive presence in Holland, Marcel would also be in a better position to deal with the accounting and administrative incidents of Dutch income taxation. After establishing a substantial and protracted presence in Holland, Marcel can be deemed to have accepted the same terms of participation in the Dutch economy as those burdening home-grown Dutch enterprises.

Business Profits

"Business profits" are defined in the U.S. Model Treaty as "income from any trade or business, including income derived by an enterprise from the performance of personal services, and from the rental of tangible personal property."[3] This statement is a broad description, not an exhaustive enumeration. "Business profits" are pretty much what they sound like: income from business operations. The treaty notion of "business profits" has no exact counterpart in the U.S. domestic tax laws. There is a family resemblance, to be sure, between business profits and income "effectively connected with a trade or business" under the Code, but there are differences as well. "Effectively connected" income is composed of several different elements bound together in a complex definition, while business profits partake of a more broadly drawn, but unified, economic character.

A common provision in income tax treaties (which pacifies what would otherwise be difficult questions of characterization) is that business profits do not include items of income dealt with separately in other provisions of the treaty.[4] This does not mean, however, that the other income escapes full taxation: items of income set apart from business

---

[3] Art. 7(7).

[4] In older treaties lacking such a provision the respective spheres of the provisions governing business profits, rentals, natural resource royalties, and other items of income can be difficult to unravel. The U.S. Model Treaty contains a variant of this provision to the effect that where business profits overlap with income dealt with in other provisions of the treaty, the other provisions are not affected by the provisions for business profits. Art. 7(6).

profits, including interest, compensation for services, and royalties, are nonetheless taxed as though they were business profits when similarly derived from a permanent establishment.[5]

"Permanent Establishment"

A "permanent establishment" is the major threshold of taxation, for business undertakings, between the tax regimes of treaty countries. There is, however, no single universal notion of a "permanent establishment," good for all treaties. The elements of permanent establishments vary from treaty to treaty, reflecting the agreement between the treaty countries over their respective spheres of taxation. The threshold for the taxation of business profits in the U.S. Model Treaty is fairly high because the United States, as a matter of policy, has always leaned toward taxation by the country of residence rather than the country of source. Many other countries, and particularly developing countries, countries that import capital, and countries with economies built on basic industries, take a different view and seek in their treaties to set fairly low thresholds of taxation by the country of source for the business profits of foreign enterprises.

Exporters of capital or goods, in contrast, and highly commercial countries usually prefer the threshold of taxation to be high for the foreign operations of their own enterprises in treaty countries. Often a significant presence is required for a permanent establishment in treaties between developed economies, while a far lesser presence will suffice under treaties among developing countries or between countries of different levels of development.[6]

---

[5]This regime of full taxation is generally prescribed in the separate provisions governing the taxation of these types of income. See, e.g., U.S. Model Treaty, Article 12(3) (royalties derived through a permanent establishment taxed as business profits).

[6]The exact definition of a permanent establishment sometimes reflects narrowly parochial concerns of the treaty countries. A former treaty between the United States and Canada, for example, included the use of "substantial equipment or machinery" (such as construction equipment or harvesting combines) in a treaty country as a permanent establishment there. 1942 Treaty with Canada, Protocol 3(f). The point was to bring the seasonal operations of builders and agricultural harvesters, who frequently cross the U.S.-Canada border, within the tax reach of the country where the activity was conducted. Most likely this provision, which in any event is no longer in the current U.S. treaty with Canada, was for the benefit of the Canadian treasury, because of greater U.S. ownership of construction equipment or harvesting combines used in Canada than vice versa.

Definition in the U.S. Model Treaty

The definition of a permanent establishment in the U.S. Model Treaty is typical of treaties between developed countries:

> 1. For the purposes of this Convention, the term "permanent establishment" means a fixed place of business through which the business of an enterprise is wholly or partly carried on.

> 2. The term "permanent establishment" includes especially:
>   (a)   a place of management;
>   (b)   a branch;
>   (c)   an office;
>   (d)   a factory;
>   (e)   a workshop; and
>   (f)   a mine, an oil or gas well, a quarry, or any other place of extraction of natural resources.[7]

Like most income tax treaties the U.S. Model Treaty also contains an enumeration of elements (even though fixed and relatively permanent) that *do not* constitute a permanent establishment in a treaty country:

> 4. [T]he term "permanent establishment" shall be deemed not to include:
>   (a) the use of facilities solely for the purpose of storage, display, or delivery of goods or merchandise belonging to the enterprise;
>   (b) the maintenance of a stock of goods or merchandise belonging to the enterprise solely for the purpose of storage, display, or delivery;
>   (c) the maintenance of a stock of goods or merchandise belonging to the enterprise solely for the purpose of processing by another enterprise;
>   (d) the maintenance of a fixed place of business solely for the purpose of purchasing goods or merchandise, or of collecting information, for the enterprise;
>   (e) the maintenance of a fixed place of business solely for the purpose of carrying on, for the enterprise, any other activity of a preparatory or auxiliary character;
>   (f) the maintenance of a fixed place of business solely for any combination of the activities mentioned in subparagraphs (a) to (e).[8]

These excluded elements bear a family resemblance. While they all betoken a presence in a country that is less than a complete industrial or commercial cycle (consisting of the manufacture or the combined purchase and sale of goods), they do permit a significant level of economic

---

[7]Art. 5. The U.S. Model Treaty also includes construction projects lasting more than 12 months among permanent establishments, while expressly excluding shorter ones. Art. 5(3)

[8]Art. 5(4).

activity without engaging the full tax regime of the host country. Not surprisingly, an enterprise of one treaty country can be a customer for goods and services in another without tax consequences there.

Permanent Establishments through Agents

Dependent Agents Besides resulting from a substantial physical presence, a permanent establishment can arise by imputation from an agent. Under Article 5(5) of the Model Treaty, for example, "[n]otwithstanding [the requirement of a fixed place of business] where a person ... is acting on behalf of an enterprise and has and habitually exercises in a Contracting State an authority to conclude contracts in the name of the enterprise, that enterprise shall be deemed to have a permanent establishment in that State." An enterprise thus need not have its own presence in a country as a condition of having a permanent establishment there. The presence of an agent with the authority to enter into binding contracts may be imputed to the principal as a permanent establishment. This arises when enterprises repeatedly send executives or other officers to a country to negotiate and enter into contracts. Even if they are careful to maintain no fixed place of business (by operating, for example, from hotels), their activity, if "habitual," may create a permanent establishment. The possibility is especially pervasive in industries (such as entertainment) where much business takes the form of deals concluded by the owners, managers, and agents of an enterprise.

An agent whose activities are limited to those exempted from the category of permanent establishments (as enumerated in Article 7(4) of the Model Treaty quoted above) does not, however, create a permanent establishment for the principal.[9] Thus an agent can habitually enter into binding contracts for the display of goods, the purchase of goods, advertising, or various combinations of these activities without thrusting a permanent establishment upon the principal. Concluding contracts of sale, however, or engaging in most forms of production are generally steps of no return.

Independent Agents There is a further, vitally important, qualification of the imputation of a permanent establishment from an agent to a principal: it does not extend to most *independent* agents. Under Article 5(6) of the U.S. Model Treaty, an enterprise does not have a permanent establishment in a country if it carries on business there solely "through a broker, general commission agent, or any other agent of an independent status, providing that such persons are acting in the ordinary course of their business."

---

[9]U.S. Model Treaty, art. 5(5).

This is the provision that permits Marcel to extend distribution and sales of French wine to Europe and the United States without becoming a taxpayer all over the place. It removes from permanent establishments virtually the entire class of commission agents, brokers, and independent distributors through which one can do business in foreign markets, along with many other intermediaries of independent status. This remains so even if the independent agents have the authority to conclude contracts. The requirement of "independent" status, however, implies that an agent or intermediary can be neither an employee nor even under the day-to-day control of the principal. It is perhaps necessary as well for the agent to have at least one other client, if not several.

<u>Which is Which</u>? An immediate practical problem is determining who are dependent and independent agents, a distinction not always visible to the naked eye. A case on the question is Handfield v. Commissioner,[10] where a Canadian citizen sold postcards in the United States under an arrangement with a U.S. distributor. The taxpayer contended that the U.S. distributor bought the cards and sold them in the course of its own business. The Revenue Service countered successfully that the U.S. distributor was an agent in a contract for consignment sales. As such, the distributor was filling orders for customers in the United States from a stock of merchandise, and thereby created a permanent establishment for the Canadian taxpayer under the income tax treaty with Canada in force at the time. Although its facts are somewhat uncertain, *Handfield* is the most widely cited case on the matter of permanent establishments, for the simple reason, no doubt, that it is one of the very few.

Profits "Attributable" to a Permanent Establishment

Another question concerning business profits is: how are they properly allocated to a permanent establishment? Or more simply, how do we determine the taxable income of a permanent establishment? In the Code, there are elaborate rules for determining the income "effectively connected" with a U.S. trade or business and even more elaborate regulations governing allocable expenses. Treaty provisions on business profits "attributable" to a permanent establishment are, by contrast, broadly drawn.

In determining the business profits attributable to a permanent establishment, most treaties require an "arm's length" standard. In Article 7(2) of the U.S. Model Treaty "there shall in each Contracting State be attributed to [a] permanent establishment the business profits which it might be expected to make if it were a distinct and independent

---

[10]23 T.C. 633 (1955).

enterprise engaged in the same or similar activities under the same or similar conditions." This provision empowers the tax authorities of the treaty countries to allocate business profits to and among permanent establishments from related persons as though they had dealt with each other on an arm's length basis, as unrelated persons would have done.

Article 7(2) also implies that a permanent establishment is treated as a separate and distinct enterprise in its dealings with its own home office. Therefore, instead of allocating income and expense between a permanent establishment and its home office as items arising within a single entity (which in titular effect they are), Article 7(2) of the Model Treaty invites computation of the permanent establishment's income according to a notional course of dealing between the permanent establishment and its home office as though it were a separately chartered subsidiary dealing at arm's length with its parent. Suppose, for example, that the home entity produced inventory and shipped it to a U.S. permanent establishment for sale to customers. Article 7(2) implies that income from the sale would be reckoned and attributed to the permanent establishment as though the home entity had sold the inventory to the permanent establishment at an arm's length price (to be determined under transfer pricing principles such as those of section 482), and not as gain from a foreign person's U.S. sale through a U.S. office. On this basis a considerable part of the gain would be attributed to the home office, beyond the reach of U.S. taxation. The computation of income under the Code (and specifically section 865(e)(2)) would be different.[11]

Most treaties require an actual connection between a permanent establishment and "attributable" business profits. The U.S. Model Treaty, for example, specifically limits the business profits to be attributed to a permanent establishment to those derived from the assets or activities of the permanent establishment.[12] This suggests a standard analogous to the "asset use" and "activities" tests for effectively connected income under the Code. Article 7(2) would not countenance a "force of attraction" mechanism like the one in Code in section 864(c)(3), which treats all residual U.S.-source income as effectively connected.[13] Enterprises therefore need not fear that economically unrelated business profits or other income will be attributed out of the blue to a permanent establishment under the Model Treaty.

Article 7(8) of the U.S. Model Treaty does, however, specifically provide for business profits generated by a permanent establishment and deferred to a later year to be "attributed" to the permanent establish-

---

[11]The entire gain would have U.S. source and would be subject to U.S. taxation as effectively connected income. See chapters 3 and 7.

[12]U.S. Model Treaty, art. 7(2).

[13]See chapter 7.

ment: "[A]ny income or gain attributable to a permanent establishment or fixed base during its existence is taxable in the Contracting State where such permanent establishment or fixed base is situated even if the payments are deferred until such permanent establishment or fixed base has ceased to exist." This provision deals with deferred business profits in much the same way as the Code.[14]

---

[14]See chapter 7.

Chapter 22

Compensation for Personal Services

In addition to business profits, most income tax treaties deal with more specific types of income similar to business profits. Of particular concern to individuals working or plying a trade in foreign lands are the provisions for personal services.

Compensation for Personal Services

The treaty regime for compensation for personal services is similar to the one imposed on business profits. Treaties aim to make it easier for residents of one country to work in the other, and to this end establish thresholds of taxation for income from personal services in the country of source that allow considerable services to be performed there without local taxation. The result, generally, is that business travelers and other mobile workers are taxed only in their country of residence or citizenship.

Although the exact terminology varies, most treaties divide services into two classes: 1) "independent services," which generally means services performed as an independent contractor or in self-employment, including most professional services such as legal advice or medical treatment, and 2) "dependent services," which means services performed as an employee under the close direction of an employer. In addition, treaties commonly make special provision for the compensation of performing artists and athletes, as well as the incomes of students, teachers, and scholars.

Independent Personal Services

In the U.S. Model Treaty, an individual resident of one treaty country performing services "in an independent capacity" is taxed only in the country of residence, unless the services are performed in the other treaty country *and* the income is attributable to a "fixed base regularly available to the individual" for the purpose of performing services.[1] The term "fixed base" is not defined in the Model Treaty, but it bears an evident similarity to a permanent establishment.

The regime for independent personal services is accommodating. It covers lawyers, doctors, consultants, and piano tuners who ply their trades outside their countries of residence in treaty countries where they

---

[1]U.S. Model Treaty, art. 14.

have no office or fixed place of business. A lawyer can thus travel to another country to advise a client without being taxed there, as long as the lawyer's firm maintains no office there. If it does, the treaty provisions on independent personal services offer no protection. A fixed base need only be "regularly available," furthermore, to expose the services to taxation in the country where they are performed. There is nothing to be gained by steering clear of the office or other premises of the firm while working for it in a treaty country.

In many treaties, the "fixed base" rule is combined with a limitation, usually 183 days, on the period in which income from independent personal services is exempt from tax in the country of source. Under the treaty with the United Kingdom, for example, independent services performed in one treaty country by a resident of the other can be taxed in the former country *either* if the individual performing them has a "fixed base regularly available" in that country, *or* if the individual spends more than 183 days in that country within a taxable year.[2] This dual threshold of taxation of independent personal services is the closest thing to a norm in income tax treaties, and appears in the treaties between the United States and Australia, Belgium, China, Cyprus, Finland, France, Germany, Hungary, Iceland, Italy, Japan, New Zealand, Norway, Poland, Romania, and the United Kingdom.

Some treaties impose more restrictive rules, reducing the period of exempt presence to 90 days, in some instances with a dollar limitation as well.[3]

I caution the reader that this skeletal summary does not capture a number of specific features of individual treaties. Some impose time *and* dollar limitations; others impose them in the alternative. When you are faced with an actual question of compensation, there is no substitute for recourse to the exact terms of the currently applicable treaty.

Dependent Personal Services

Tax treaties are generally less accommodating to income from employment (or what are called "dependent personal services" in treaty patois). The U.S. Model Treaty adopts a nearly universal pattern, known as the "183-day rule." At the baseline income from employment is taxable in the country in which the services are performed.[4] But—and these are key qualifications—income from services performed in a treaty country by a resident of the other treaty country is *not* taxed in the country where they are performed if 1) the employee is present

---

[2]Treaty with United Kingdom, art. 14.
[3]E.g., Barbados, Denmark, Egypt, Malta, and the Philippines.
[4]U.S. Model Treaty, art. 15(1).

there for 183 days or less during the taxable year, 2) the compensation is paid by an employer who is not a resident of the country of performance, and 3) the compensation "is not borne by a permanent establishment or a fixed base which the employer has" in that country.[5] In short, an employee of an employer in one treaty country can spend up to 183 days annually in the other treaty country without being taxed there. Employees of enterprises in countries with a broad treaty network can therefore move quite freely within the treaty countries, while remaining subject to income tax only in their country of residence.[6]

Johansson *and "Loan-out" Companies*

The treaty regime for personal services is of great practical importance because it permits movement of people between countries that would otherwise be constrained by tax barriers. It often influences the patterns of business travel between treaty countries. Not surprisingly, various acquisitive undertakings have been shoehorned into forms designed to benefit from the 183-day rule. Residents of third countries, for example, are frequently tempted to set up residence and employment in a treaty country in order to invoke the 183-day rule. A widely noted case in this regard is Johansson v. United States.[7] In *Johansson* a professional boxer (and citizen of Sweden) sought to claim the benefits of the income tax treaty between the United States and Switzerland. Johansson established "residence" in Switzerland and created a Swiss corporation, Scanart S.A., which ostensibly employed him to engage in championship prize fights in the United States against Floyd Patterson. Johansson was thus attempting to fight in the United States in the guise of an employee of a Swiss corporation. Literally, Scanart S.A. undertook to provide an opponent for Floyd Patterson in the person of its employee Johansson. Scanart paid Johansson its entire receipts for his services of administering and receiving beatings (he did some of both), minus amounts contributed to a pension fund for Johansson, who was Scanart's sole employee (and most likely its sole shareholder as well). Since Johansson spent fewer than 183 days in the United States in the years in which he fought Floyd Patterson, he claimed exemption from U.S. taxation on his compensation from Scanart (a Swiss entity) under the income tax treaty

---

[5]U.S. Model Treaty, art. 15(2).

[6]Bear in mind that what is involved here is the taxation of the salary income of the employee, *not* the employer's business profits derived from the employee's activity, which may well be subject to tax in the country of source.

[7]336 F.2d 809 (5th Cir. 1964).

then in effect between the United States and Switzerland (which contained a variant of the 183-day rule).[8]

Under attack from the Revenue Service, the arrangement failed in court. The court found that Scanart had no independent identity and accordingly that Johansson was in effect fighting on his own behalf. Scanart had come on the scene late and had done little that was visible to the naked eye. The court essentially refused to take Scanart seriously as an entity and concluded that Johansson's pugilistic endeavors were more nearly those of an independent contractor than of an employee.

The *Johansson* case has thrown a long shadow. The structure attempted unsuccessfully there is known as a "loan-out" company and has been widely used by performers and athletes. The tax objectives of such arrangements include income-splitting, deferral of taxable gain, and the advantageous use of income tax treaties. Although the taxpayer lost, *Johansson* does not systematically foreclose these possibilities. Rather, it suggests a road map to success by avoiding its pitfalls. If Scanart had employed several boxers, had had real economic activity in Switzerland, and had taken on other indicia of reality, the arrangement could have succeeded.[9]

"Artistes and Athletes" Clauses

More broadly, performers and athletes have often been able to gain advantage from the standard treaty provisions on compensation for services. They move around a lot and derive income from many countries. As residents of a country connected to others through a useful network of treaties, and not itself given to fierce taxation, performers and athletes could enjoy virtual exemption from taxation under standard treaty provisions governing the performance of services. Under a treaty that exempts "independent" personal services from taxation in the country of source (as does the U.S. Model Treaty), a performer could fairly easily arrange to work as an independent contractor and avoid creating a "fixed base" in the country of performance. Even under a treaty that has only the standard 183-day rule for "dependent" personal services, a performer can seek shelter by arranging to be employed by

---

[8]Scanart itself, to be sure, was probably subject to U.S. taxation because it was doubtless engaged in business in the United States and might well have had a U.S. permanent establishment to boot; but Scanart's taxable income would in any event have been fully offset by deductions for compensation paid to Johansson personally and amounts paid into his pension fund.

[9]See, e.g., P. R. Bass v. Commissioner, 50 T.C. 595 (1968) (Swiss corporation owning U.S. oil interests entitled to treaty benefits by virtue of its significant business activity).

a "loan-out" company (ultimately under his control) incorporated in a well-chosen treaty jurisdiction.

For that reason most recent treaties, and the U.S. Model Treaty, have special provisions for performers and athletes limiting the tax benefits available for their compensation and explicitly undercutting the use of loan-out companies. The typical "artistes and athletes" clause strengthens the taxing hand of the country of source.[10] In Article 17(1) of the U.S. Model Treaty, for example, "income derived by a resident of a Contracting State as an entertainer, such as a theater, motion picture, radio, or television artiste, or a musician, or as a sportsman, from his personal activities as such exercised in the other Contracting State ... may be taxed in that other State, except where the amount of the gross receipts derived by such entertainer or sportsman, including expenses reimbursed to him or borne on his behalf from such activities does not exceed twenty thousand United States dollars ($20,000) or its equivalent in the taxable year concerned."[11] This is an explicit exception to the Model Treaty's taxation of personal services generally. With the $20,000 floor (which leaves the second stringers and members of the chorus mostly unaffected) the provision aims squarely at top athletes and headliners. Article 17(2) extends this regime to income paid to "loan-out" companies on account of the services of performers and athletes.

Students and Scholars

Another group widely favored in income tax treaties is students, with whom scholars are often (but not always) associated. In the U.S. Model Treaty:

> Payments received by a student, apprentice, or business trainee who is, or was immediately before visiting a Contracting State, a resident of the other Contracting State, and who is present in the first-mentioned State for the purpose of his full-time education at an accredited educational institution, or for his full-time training, shall not be taxed in that State, provided that such payments arise outside that State, and are for the purpose of his maintenance, education or training.[12]

---

[10]Note that the term often used in treaties is not "artist" but "art*iste*." "Artiste" is an old-fashioned word for a performing artist (a singer, for example) and does not describe a painter or sculptor.

[11]U.S. Model Treaty, art. 17(1).

[12]U.S. Model Treaty, art. 20. In the case of an apprentice or business trainee the exemption from tax lasts only one year. Id. Some treaties, including those with France and Germany, offer students even greater protection from taxation during overseas study.

Under this provision, the financial support of foreign students and trainees is not taxed by the country in which they study, when it "arises" outside that country. The reasons for these terms, one imagines, is to prevent the largesse of governments and other institutions toward students of their own country from being diverted into the treasuries of the foreign countries where the students pursue their studies. Since the Internal Revenue Code unilaterally grants foreign students much the same protection as the Model Treaty,[13] the provision may serve in some instances mainly to improve the position of American students studying outside the United States.

Somewhat less widespread than protection for students and trainees are treaty benefits for teachers and scholars. The U.S. Model Treaty, for example, does nothing for them. Some older treaties, however, accord visiting professors from one country a two-year period of tax exemption in the other.[14]

---

[13]See §872(b)(3).
[14]E.g., Treaty with Japan, art. 19.

Chapter 23

Interest, Dividends, Royalties, Rents, and Other Gains

Passive investment in a foreign country commonly generates interest, dividends, and royalties, in various combinations. Interest and royalties (but rarely dividends) also arise from active business operations such as banking and software development. Recall that in the Code U.S.-Source passive investment income paid to foreign persons is subject to a flat 30 percent tax on the gross amount. Since most countries welcome passive foreign investment—which adds to the capital available to an economy without bringing indigenous business activity under direct foreign control—most income tax treaties offer significant concessions by the country of source in taxing passive investment income paid to residents of the other treaty country. A widespread pattern, epitomized in the U.S. Model Treaty, is exemption for interest and royalties in the country of source and reduced rates of tax for dividends.

Interest

In the U.S. Model Treaty "interest derived and beneficially owned by a resident of a Contracting State shall be taxable only in that State."[1] With this, interest is exempt in the country of its source in the hands of a resident of the other treaty country. The Model Treaty defines interest broadly as "income from debt claims of every kind."[2] The exemption of interest income in the U.S. Model Treaty does not extend to interest "determined with reference to receipts, sales, income, profits or other cash flow of the debtor."[3] This provision, which mirrors the exclusion of contingent interest from exempt portfolio interest in the Code, aims at the use of equity-flavored debt instruments, which were once great favorites of foreign investors in the United States.

Unlike the Code's exemption of U.S.-source "portfolio" interest, the broader exemption of interest income in the U.S. Model Treaty applies to interest paid to 10-percent (and greater) shareholders and other owners, and is available to foreign banks for interest on loans not made through a permanent establishment in the United States.[4]

---

[1]U.S. Model Treaty, art. 11(1).
[2]Art. 11(2).
[3]Art. 11(5). Contingent interest of this type is treated as though a dividend. Id.
[4]Section 881(c)(3), in contrast, denies to most U.S.-source interest paid to foreign banks the character of exempt portfolio interest. See chapter 5.

We will revisit the treaty exemption of interest in the next chapter, where it appears as the active ingredient in many treaty-based international tax shelters.

Dividends

Treaties rarely exempt dividends, unlike interest, from taxation entirely in the country of source. Dividends received from one treaty country by residents of another are generally subject to reduced rates of tax by the country of source. In the U.S. Model Treaty, the tax imposed on dividends by the country of source is reduced to 15 percent for the bulk of dividends, and to 5 percent if the recipient is a corporation owning at least 10 percent of the voting stock of the corporation paying the dividend.[5] Some such two-tiered reduction of the normal national rates is the standard tax regime for dividends in treaties.

The U.S. Model Treaty also provides that one country may not tax dividends paid by a corporation chartered in the other treaty country except in specific narrow situations.[6] This clause eliminates what is known as the "second tax" imposed under the U.S. tax laws on certain dividends paid *by* foreign corporations.[7] Most other treaties make similar provision for the second tax on dividends.

Treaties and the Branch Profits Tax

The branch profits tax is a second level U.S. tax on business profits of foreign corporations similar in effect, but not form, to a tax on dividends. The branch profits tax is not literally imposed on a dividend payment, but is imposed directly on the earnings of a foreign corporation that are repatriated from the United States. Treaty provisions concerning dividends paid by foreign corporations therefore provide no literal protection from the branch profits tax, whether they apply to the baseline U.S. tax on dividends received from U.S. sources by foreign taxpayers or to the "second" tax on dividends.

The U.S. Model Treaty expressly allows the imposition of a branch profits (or similar) tax on the business profits of a foreign corporation attributable to a permanent establishment, along with other gains treated

---

[5]U.S. Model Treaty, art. 10(2). Recall that in the Code the baseline tax imposed on dividends received by foreign taxpayers is 30 percent.

[6]U.S. Model Treaty, art. 10(7).

[7]This provision is largely redundant in practical effect because §884(e) also calls off the second tax on dividends paid by foreign corporations subject to the branch profits tax, which is nearly all of them.

as effectively connected income in U.S. taxation.[8] The branch profits tax is limited, however, to the 5-percent rate imposed on dividends paid by domestic corporations to 10-percent corporate shareholders.[9] The branch profits tax, far more than the second tax on dividends, is now where the question of corporate double taxation is played out.

The treaties entered into by the United States since 1986 (when the branch profits tax was adopted) allow the imposition of a branch profits tax on the profits of a corporation chartered in one treaty country derived from business operations in the other, but with limitations that make the branch profits tax essentially equivalent to the taxation of dividends under the treaty. The typical provision limits the branch tax to after-tax profits attributable to a permanent establishment and to the rate of tax imposed on dividends from related corporations, often 5 percent.[10]

Section 884(e)

Older treaties rarely make explicit provision for the branch profits tax. Section 884 and the associated regulations, however, coordinate the branch profits tax and the taxation of dividends under treaties that are silent on the matter. Specifically, section 884(e)(2) limits the rate of the branch profits tax (normally 30 percent) imposed on a corporation of a treaty country to the maximum rate of U.S. withholding tax provided under the relevant treaty for dividends from a wholly-owned U.S. subsidiary of a foreign corporation.

There is more fine print in section 884(e) of the Code. A reduced rate of branch profits tax in a treaty applies only to "qualified" foreign corporations, which are corporations of treaty countries, of which at least 50 percent of the stock is owned by individual residents of the treaty country or by individual citizens or residents of the United States.[11]

Possible Conflicts with Treaties—Questions of Precedence

You may have noticed (and several foreign governments have forcefully pointed out) that the Code's section 884(e) is inconsistent with (and may well limit in practice) some of the treaty provisions mentioned above. That is true, and that's life. In the U.S. legal system there is no

---

[8]Art. 10(8).
[9]Art. 10(9).
[10]See, e.g., the Treaty with the Netherlands, art. 11.
[11]§884(e)(4)(A). Also "qualified" are publicly traded corporations primarily traded on securities markets of their country of incorporation, as well as their wholly-owned subsidiaries. §884(e)(4)(B).

absolute precedence between statutes and treaties. Each may contradict or displace the other.

This element of U.S. law is formalized in section 7852(d)(1): "For purposes of detemining the relationship between a provision of a treaty and any law of the United States affecting revenue, neither the treaty nor the law shall have preferential status by reason of its being a treaty or a law." The baseline rule of precedence in resolving conflicts is that the later enacted prevails over the earlier. Absent more specific provision or inference, therefore, statutes displace prior inconsistent treaties, and treaties displace prior inconsistent statutes.[12] That means in practice that a provision buried in section 884(e) of the Code can and does modify rights ostensibly established by valid treaties.

To mitigate the severity of conflicts (and the pain of surprise), Code section 894(a) provides a general balm: "The provisions of [the Code] shall be applied to any taxpayer with due regard to any treaty obligation of the United States which applies to such taxpayer." The broad terms of this language, however, are not entirely reassuring. The relation between statutes and treaties in taxation is difficult, and it is hard to get specific. Let me try to tide you over with the following. To the extent that treaty benefits are accorded with reference to baseline U.S. taxation, they prevail. For example a treaty exemption for royalties is effective notwithstanding the U.S. tax that would otherwise be imposed. Were it not so, what would be the point of treaties? But provisions in the Code, such as section 884(e), that expressly purport to *limit* treaty benefits also prevail, even over equally explicit treaty provisions.

Royalties

In the U.S. Model Treaty royalties received by a resident of a treaty country are taxable only in that country.[13] This is taxation on the basis of the residence of the recipient and implies exemption from tax in the country of source. A similar treatment of royalties is found in a number of treaties between the United States and developed countries.[14] An equally common pattern is taxation at a reduced rate by the country of source of royalties received by residents of the other treaty country.[15]

This is generally a simple tax regime. More difficult is determining the boundary of "royalties." In the U.S. Model Treaty, "royalties" are

---

[12]See Whitney v. Robertson, 124 U.S. 190, 194 (1888).

[13]U.S. Model Treaty, art. 12(1).

[14]E.g., the treaties with Belgium, Germany, the Netherlands, the United Kingdom, and several of the former Soviet Republics.

[15]E.g., Canada (10 percent), France (5 percent), and Japan (10 percent).

defined as income from the use of a broad range of intangible property, as well as certain contingent gains from the sale of such property:

> The term "royalties" as used in this Convention means:
>
> (a) any consideration for the use of, or the right to use, any copyright of literary, artistic, scientific or other work (including computer software, cinematographic films, audio or video tapes or disks, and other means of image or sound reproduction), any patent, trademark, design or model, plan, secret formula or process, or other like right or property, or for information concerning industrial, commercial, or scientific experience; and
>
> (b) gain derived from the alienation of any property described in [(a)], provided that such gain is contingent on the productivity, use or disposition of the property.[16]

A notable feature of this definition is the specific inclusion of income from computer software and motion pictures among royalties (and hence the tax-favored group). A number of treaties differ on this score. The characterization of royalties under treaty provisions raises the same kinds of questions that arise in nontreaty cases. In Boulez v. Commissioner,[17] for example, involving a recording contract of a foreign orchestra conductor, the Service characterized the income received as compensation for services rather than royalties, as in Ingram v. Bowers,[18] under both the Code and U.S. treaty with Germany, and prevailed on both fronts.

The inclusion among royalties of contingent gains from the sale of intangible property is true to their economic character.[19] In some treaties the assimilation of contingent gains to royalties prevents royalty arrangements from being disguised as sales to garner a more favorable tax regime. In the U.S. Model Treaty the provision generally matters little, because gains from sales of intangible property and explicit royalties are both taxed benignly.

Royalties Attributable to a Permanent Establishment

The provisions governing royalties in the U.S. Model Treaty do not apply to royalties from active business operations. If the royalties are attributable to a business conducted in a treaty country through a permanent establishment, they are subject to tax in that country as business profits.[20] Roughly speaking, therefore, the property producing the

---

[16]U.S. Model Treaty, art. 12(2).
[17]83 T.C. 584 (1984).
[18]See chapter 3.
[19]See also chapter 5.
[20]U.S. Model Treaty, art. 12(3).

royalties must be an investment asset in the hands of its owner at the time the royalties are received if they are to be exempt under the Model Treaty. That does not mean that the asset may not have originated from the operations of an active business, only that the posture of the recipient of royalties must be, or have become, relatively passive. The writer of a book, therefore, cannot also publish and actively distribute it in a treaty country without losing, in all likelihood, the protection of the royalties under the treaty.

Rentals from Tangible Property

In contrast with royalties, most income tax treaties make no explicit provision for rentals derived from tangible personal property. The U.S. Model Treaty, for example, has no article directly governing rents of this type. One could easily conclude that rentals from tangible property were simply subject to the baseline tax of the country of source, which in the United States would be a flat rate tax of 30 percent. As it turns out, Article 21 of the Model Treaty (an "other income" clause) eliminates tax by the country of source for all rents not attributable to a permanent establishment or real property, with taxation resulting only in the country of residence of the recipient of the rents. The treaty with the United Kingdom is similar in this regard.[21]

More commonly, treaties leave the taxation of rents in the country of source. This results because the treaties make no specific provision for the taxation of rents and also contain no "other income" clause shielding unspecified income from taxation by the country of source.

Income from Real Property

Under the U.S. Model Treaty, income from real property is taxable in the country in which the property is located.[22] This is the simplest of provisions, and some near-equivalent of it is found in every income tax treaty. It follows that, even under treaties, income from foreign investment in real estate is subject to income tax in the country of source.

In the U.S. Model Treaty, income from real property is defined expansively to include income from agriculture and forestry, while the term "real property" derives its meaning from the law of the country

---

[21]There is further discussion of "Other Income" clauses below.
[22]U.S. Model Treaty, art. 6(1).

imposing the tax.[23] United States tax law (remember section 897) contains a sweeping definition of "real property."[24]

Many income tax treaties expressly identify some of the constituents of the class of real property. Common inclusions are mines, quarries, and all other exploitations of natural resources. Occasional exclusions are ships and aircraft. These would be widespread norms, one imagines, even if the treaties were silent on those items. Less clear is the treatment of livestock and agricultural and forestry equipment when not expressly mentioned. Under U.S. law, some but not all of these items are real property.[25] With all the variations of national law, there is bound to be some uncertainty, which can be resolved only by consulting local counsel.

Another common provision is the exclusion of interest on mortgage debt from the class of real property income. The U.S. Model Treaty contains no explicit rule, but the result is not in doubt.

Gains from the Sale of Real Property

Treaties almost invariably make gains from the *sale* of real property subject to tax in the country in which the real property is located. There is sometimes a separate provision to this effect, as in the U.S. Model Treaty (Article 13(1)), but more commonly there is a single provision for income from real property and gains from the sale of real property. Regardless of the format, the essential rule is always the same: the country in which real property is located retains priority of taxing power.

The U.S. Model Treaty extends the taxation of real estate by a treaty country to sales of shares of corporations (no matter where incorporated) holding assets consisting principally of real estate in that country, as well as to sales of interests in partnerships, trusts, and estates with similar assets.[26] Several recent treaties, including those with Australia, Canada, and the United Kingdom, are similar on this score. This treatment is consistent with section 897 of the Code, which imposes tax on gains of foreign taxpayers from sales of "U.S. real property interests," a class that includes shares of domestic corporations owning U.S. real estate as well as direct holdings of real estate.[27]

---

[23]U.S. Model Treaty, art. 6(2).

[24]See chapter 8.

[25]Property used to *grow* or *harvest* timber or crops is real property, but not property used to process them. See Reg. §1.897-1(b)(4)(i)(A).

[26]U.S. Model Treaty, art. 13(2).

[27]See chapter 8. Unlike the treaties, however, section 897 does not directly reach interests in *foreign* corporations.

Capital and Other Gains from Sales of Personal Property

As a rule, treaties provide that gains from the sale of personal property are taxed only in the seller's country of residence. Capital gains of residents of treaty countries are therefore not subject to U.S. taxation, even when derived from assets, such as investment securities, that have some relation to the U.S. economy. Since the baseline treatment of capital gains of foreign taxpayers under the Code is similarly benign, the treaty regime adds little to what is already there. That being so, the few atypical treaties, such as the treaty with the United Kingdom, that allow each treaty country to tax capital gains in accordance with its own national tax laws, entail in practice a tax regime little different from that enjoyed by residents of countries with more fully developed treaty protection for capital gains.

Treaty protection (like that of the Code) generally extends only to gains from a specific and narrow class of property. Real property, as the discussion above confirms, is not covered. Nor, for the same reason, does the protection reach personal property that represents beneficial ownership of real property (such as shares of corporations owning real property). Contingent gains from dispositions of intangible property are commonly treated as "royalties" rather than as gains from the sale of property.[28] Finally, gains from the sale of personal property attributable to a permanent establishment are never shielded under treaties as "capital gains."

What this means in overview is that the gains protected by treaties consist pretty much of gains from pure investment assets, principally financial assets. Some physical assets, such as art and antiques, are also shielded, but only when they are sold independently of a permanent establishment.

One difference between treaties and the Code is in the treatment of gains from sales of property by a business that does not possess its own permanent establishment in a treaty country. A dealer in property can make sales that are effectively connected with a U.S. business and still avoid U.S. taxation under the treaty regime *if* the gains are not attributable to a permanent establishment. To illustrate the point, consider an artist or an art dealer selling pieces from inventory in the United States. The sales would not generate effectively connected income under the Code if there were no U.S. trade or business. The existence of *any* U.S. trade or business of the seller, however, would alter this result, even if the

---

[28]See, e.g., U.S. Model Treaty, art. 12(2).

trade or business bore no direct relation to the sales of art. The artist could not, for example, present a seminar in the United States, or teach, or give a lecture tour, or perform any personal services in the United States, without exposing the gains from sales of property to becoming effectively connected income under the Code.[29] Treaties, in contrast, normally shield sales of property in the United States by a person who has no U.S. permanent establishment. A foreign antique dealer from a treaty country can therefore mix a few sales with a lecture tour in the United States, whereas one from a nontreaty country must be far more guarded.

"Other Income" Clauses

A provision found in a number of treaties is a residual "other income" clause. In the U.S. Model Treaty it is Article 21(1): "Items of income of a resident of a Contracting State, wherever arising, not dealt with in the foregoing Articles of this Convention shall be taxable only in that State." The only qualification of this provision follows immediately, in Article 21(2), which allows taxation of income attributable to a permanent establishment or fixed base by the country of the permanent establishment's location. Because the Model Treaty blankets most items of income quite thoroughly, the effect of Article 21 is not huge. Some of its pockets are nonetheless worth noting. Because, for example, the Model Treaty makes no specific provision for rentals derived from tangible personal property, Article 21 shields them from tax by the country of source in the hands of a resident of a treaty country. Income from the cancellation of indebtedness, from court-awarded damages, from prizes and awards, and from pure windfalls might also flourish under the umbrella of Article 21.

The "other income" clause of the U.S. Model Treaty also bears importantly on the taxation of dual residents. The tie-breaking rules on residence confer the benefits of residence on individuals who would otherwise be dual residents (and hence exposed to "savings" clauses in both treaty countries) but offer no protection for items of income not actually covered by the treaty. The breadth of the "other income" clause of the Model Treaty, however, makes the protection of dual residents very nearly complete. Only a small handful of treaties, however, have "other income" clauses as expansive as the U.S. Model Treaty's.

---

[29]See §864(c)(3) and further discussion in chapter 7.

Chapter 24

The Rise and Fall of Treaty Tax Shelters: Sandwiches, Conduits, and the Treasury's Response

Twenty years ago, even ten, this chapter might have been a step-by-step user's guide for setting up international tax shelters based on income tax treaties. Now, it is more of a reminiscence tinged with nostalgic yearning. The main reason for going over treaty tax shelters here is as background to understand the battery of measures recently added to the U.S. tax system that restrain or eliminate the use of income tax treaties in international tax shelters.

The Origins of Treaty Tax Havens

Treaty tax havens came about largely by accident. Among the elements abetting their rise were the break-up of the great colonial empires after World War II and the unquenchable thirst of the U.S. economy for foreign capital. During the 1950s the United States entered into income tax treaties with former colonies of the United Kingdom and the Netherlands that had become separate sovereignties. The terms of these treaties were initially the same as those of U.S. treaties with the mother countries, even though the tax systems of the newly independent countries were far different. The U.S. tax treaty with the Netherlands Antilles, for example, when first adopted in 1955 was essentially the same as the existing treaty with the Netherlands. For over 30 years it was the main working part in several treaty tax shelters.

Also part of the landscape during this period were persistent balance-of-payments deficits of the United States with the rest of the world. Beginning in the 1950s, large and increasing amounts of U.S. dollars accumulated outside the United States. Their foreign holders did not invariably return them to the U.S. banking system. Instead, vast quantities of U.S. dollars remained on deposit in foreign banks and became the wherewithal of wholly foreign financial transactions. U.S. dollars on deposit in a bank outside the United States are known as "Eurodollars."[1] The capital markets in which Eurodollar obligations and instruments arise are known as the "Eurodollar market."

---

[1] A "Eurodollar" is a dollar-denominated bank deposit anywhere in the world outside the United States. The term is somewhat misleading. In the period immediately following World War II most Eurodollars were in banking centers such as London, Geneva, and Luxembourg, hence the name "Eurodollar." In the

International Taxation

Because interest rates in the Eurodollar market were often lower than in U.S. capital markets, it became interesting to U.S. companies early on to raise capital by borrowing Eurodollars. A major obstacle to such financing, initially, was the U.S. tax on U.S.-source interest. Before the exemption of U.S.-source "portfolio" interest from U.S. tax in 1984 (now codified in sections 871(h) and 881(c)) foreign persons were subject to 30-percent flat-rate U.S. tax on U.S.-source interest unless protected by a treaty in their country of residence. And to invoke a treaty against the U.S. Treasury might attract unwanted attention from their own national treasuries. The 30-percent flat tax thus put a serious crimp on borrowing by U.S. enterprises on the Eurodollar market (or, for that matter, from any foreign lender).[2]

Netherlands Antilles Finance Corporations

Sometime in the 1950s someone got the wondrous idea that the U.S. flat-rate tax could be eliminated by channeling Eurodollar loans through a Netherlands Antilles corporation. The method was to use a Netherlands Antilles finance corporation as the middle party in "back-to-back" or "mirror-image" debt.

A U.S. enterprise seeking to borrow from foreign holders of dollars would first create a subsidiary corporation chartered in the Netherlands Antilles. The Antilles corporation would issue bonds, typically bearer bonds denominated in U.S. dollars, in some convenient financial center such as Luxembourg or Geneva where Eurodollars congregate. The proceeds of this first borrowing were then re-lent by the Antilles corporation to its U.S. parent (the ultimate borrower) at *nearly* identical interest rates and maturities. The obligation of the U.S. parent to the Antilles corporation in the second borrowing stood as security for the bonds issued by the Antilles corporation to the ultimate lenders. Often the U.S. parent guaranteed the Antilles bonds as well. Coordinated borrowings channeled in this fashion through an Antilles entity are known as "back-to-back" or "mirror-image" debt. The pattern is shown schematically in Diagram I, illustrating a mirror-image arrangement in which Eurodollar bonds are issued to foreign lenders, to whom interest flows from a U.S. borrower through a Netherlands Antilles finance subsidiary.

1970s the term "petrodollar" (reflecting its origin as payment for oil imported by the United States) was sometimes heard.

[2]Bear in mind that it was (and still is) alien to the culture of many potential foreign lenders to suffer any tax whatsoever on interest income.

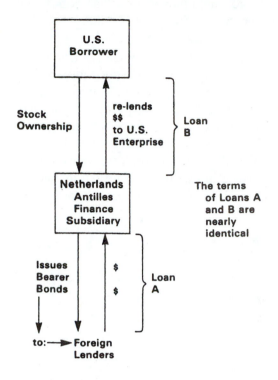

Diagram I. *Interest flows from U.S. Borrower to Finance Subsidiary to Foreign Lenders.*

The income tax treaty between the Netherlands Antilles and the United States eliminated U.S. flat rate tax on the interest paid by the U.S. borrower to the Antilles corporation. The Netherlands Antilles, for its part, does not impose withholding tax on interest paid by Netherlands Antilles corporations to foreign persons. In this structure, therefore, no withholding tax was imposed on interest at any point in the chain.

The Treaty with the Netherlands Antilles thus permitted lenders all over the world to lend to U.S. borrowers through Antilles finance companies at no U.S. tax cost. Observe that nothing much happened in the Netherlands Antilles. The only involvement of the Netherlands Antilles in this structure was the issuance of a corporate charter to the finance subsidiary. Neither the U.S. borrower nor the foreign lender has any economic or other connection to the Netherlands Antilles.[3] The parties to this financing transaction in effect appropriated the Netherlands

---

[3]The finance corporation's accounts were usually kept in a financial center bank—often Luxembourg or Geneva—which was also where the interest on the Eurodollar bonds was paid out.

Antilles treaty to shield interest on a loan coming into the United States from a third country, which could be almost anywhere.

In light of this possibility, the Netherlands Antilles Treaty came to be known as the United States' "income tax treaty with the world." And because the borrower and lender have in effect shopped around for the treaty environment that pacifies U.S. tax on interest, the underlying pattern is known as "treaty-shopping." The structure—in which a treaty-favored finance entity rests between back-to-back loans like corned beef between two slices of rye—is also called a treaty "sandwich." Treaty sandwiches—with some variations in fillings and condiments—flourished in international investing until quite recently, when countermeasures by the U.S. Treasury began to devastate their habitat.

Treaty Sandwiches

Several elements in this sandwich warrant attention. First, consider what makes a country a tax haven in a practical sense. It is not necessarily the absence of an income tax. The Netherlands Antilles was not at the time a zero-tax jurisdiction. It imposed an income tax of roughly 30 percent on Antilles-based corporations. What made the Antilles a tax haven in this sandwich was the absence of any withholding tax on Antilles-source interest paid to foreign persons by Netherlands Antilles corporations, coupled with the provisions of its income tax treaty with the United States. Interest received by the Antilles corporation from the U.S. borrower *was* subject to Antilles income tax. But at the same time interest paid out by the Antilles corporation was deductible in the Netherlands Antilles Because of the matching terms of the back-to-back loans channeled through the Antilles finance subsidiaries, interest deductions largely offset Antilles taxable income. Only the excess of interest received by an intermediate Antilles corporation over the interest it paid out—a relatively small amount—was taxed in the Netherlands Antilles.

You may wonder why the interest rates in both legs of the back-to-back loans weren't exactly the same, which would have eliminated *all* taxable income in the Netherlands Antilles. The answer lies in the need to gain the cooperation of the Netherlands Antilles government. To induce the Netherlands Antilles tax authorities to grant favorable rulings to the mirror-image loan arrangement (needed to secure deductions and forestall taxation in the Netherlands Antilles) it was necessary to build a taxable profit into the operations of the Antilles corporation by leaving a difference between the interest it received and the interest it paid. Thus if the Eurodollar bonds issued by the Antilles corporation paid interest of 10 percent, that entity's own loan to its U.S. parent might yield $10\frac{1}{4}$ percent. The resulting 1/4 percent profit would be subject to Netherlands

Antilles income tax. This tax (sometimes known as the "toll charge") was the compensation exacted by the Netherlands Antilles treasury for the beneficial use of its income tax treaty. Depending on the size of the underlying loan, the required spread ranged from 1/8 to 1/2 percent. In the case of a $100,000,000 loan, for example, a 1/4 percent spread would entail an annual toll charge of roughly $75,000 (a tax of 30 percent imposed on $250,000, which is 1/4 percent of $100,000,000).

Given the palpably artificial connection of the Netherlands Antilles with the overall transaction, the parties had reason for uneasiness about the certainty of the tax benefits of a treaty sandwich. Beyond the "toll charge," no money ever went to the Netherlands Antilles. The Antilles entity did little besides pay and receive nearly matching amounts of interest. This is the type of situation in which the Revenue Service has on occasion been successful in persuading courts to disregard an intermediate entity as a pure conduit lacking in "substance." If channeling of interest through the Netherlands Antilles were ignored the structure would collapse into a direct loan from the United States to the holder of a eurobond, with interest subject to flat rate U.S. tax and withholding.[4]

What gave particular urgency to these concerns was the case of Aiken Industries v. Commissioner.[5] In *Aiken* (simplifying a bit), a Bahamas corporation ("Bahamas") owned all the shares of a U.S. corporation ("U.S.Co") and all the shares of an Ecuadorian corporation. Bahamas lent money to U.S.Co under a note ("U.S.Co note") providing, naturally enough, for the payment of principal and interest. Less than a year later, the Ecuadorian subsidiary of Bahamas created its own wholly-owned Honduran subsidiary ("HavenCo"), to which Bahamas then transferred the U.S.Co note in exchange for nine demand notes, each requiring HavenCo to pay one-ninth of the principal amount owed by U.S.Co under the U.S.Co note, with interest at the same rate. The course of events is illustrated in Diagram II, on the following page.

At the time HavenCo was created (but not today, so don't get any ideas) there was an income tax treaty in force between the United States and Honduras exempting interest "received" by a corporation of a treaty country from withholding tax in the country of source. The point of the exchange of notes between Bahamas and HavenCo was therefore to permit the interest paid by U.S.Co to escape U.S. withholding tax under the treaty with Honduras. HavenCo itself would offset its interest income with interest deductions. The basic pattern is back-to-back mirror-image loans through a treaty country.

---

[4]These were the days before the exemption of portfolio interest. See chapter 5.
[5]56 T.C. 925 (1971), *acq.*, 1972-2 Cum. Bull. 1.

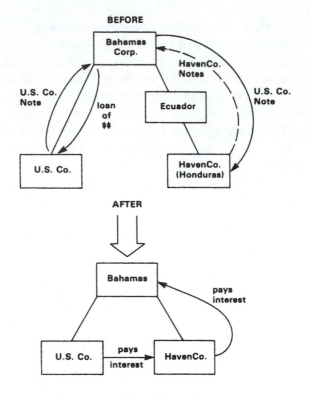

Diagram II—*Aiken* Case

The IRS attacked HavenCo's claimed benefit under the Honduran treaty. The standard approach of the Treasury at the outset in "form and substance" cases is to yell "sham" in a crowded courtroom with the expectation (or the hope at least) that intellectual panic will ensue. *Aiken* was no exception. The first contention of the Revenue Service in the case was that the very existence of HavenCo should be disregarded for tax purposes, with the consequence that the interest paid by U.S.Co would be treated as paid directly to Bahamas and subject to U.S. withholding tax. But HavenCo was demonstrably a real Honduran corporation and the Tax Court correctly declined to deny or ignore its existence.

Although the court acknowledged HavenCo as a real corporation, the taxpayer in *Aiken* still lost. The Tax Court concluded from the perfect identity of the terms of the notes payable *to* and *by* HavenCo that no interest was in fact "received" by HavenCo in the sense of being reduced to its dominion and control. All interest ostensibly received by HavenCo was subject to an immediate obligation to pay it out again. Nothing of value ever vested in HavenCo. The court's holding was underpinned by the "business purpose" doctrine derived from Gregory

v. Helvering[6] to the effect that a transaction with no economic purpose other than income tax reduction may be denied its ostensible character for income tax purposes. The court inferred the absence of a business purpose from the exact symmetry of the transaction and the impossibility of a profit for HavenCo, which "obtained exactly what it gave up in a dollar-for-dollar exchange [and] was committed to pay out exactly what it collected, and . . . made no profit on the acquisition of [U.S.Co's] note in exchange for its own."[7] The court summed up its holding as follows:

> In effect, [HavenCo], while a valid Honduran corporation, was a collection agent with respect to the interest it received from [Bahamas]. [HavenCo] was merely a conduit for the passage of interest payments from [U.S.Co] to [Bahamas], and it cannot be said to have received the interest as its own. [HavenCo] had no actual beneficial interest in the interest payments it received, and in substance, [U.S.Co] was paying the interest to [Bahamas] which "received" the interest within the meaning of [the treaty].[8]

There is an obvious similarity between the pattern struck down in *Aiken* and the sandwiches using Netherlands Antilles finance corporations to bring Eurodollars into U.S. capital markets. Compare the relationship of HavenCo, U.S.Co, and Bahamas with the similar array of entities in the outline of a Eurodollar financing above. You may wonder, in this light, why the Treasury did not invoke *Aiken* in the period before 1984 (when U.S.-source portfolio interest became exempt from U.S. tax for foreign persons) to attack mirror-image loans channeled through Netherlands Antilles finance corporations. There are, to be sure, differences between the latter and *Aiken*. On its facts, *Aiken* applies to interest received by a corporation that does not and cannot derive a profit from the overall transaction. The finance company in the Antilles-based financing, for its part, earned and retained a small profit by virtue of paying out interest at a lower rate than the rate of interest it received from a U.S. borrower. While this distinction proved crucial in a later case, as we shall see below, that is not why the IRS initially held back the *Aiken* card. The IRS simply didn't dare play it, for fear that it would succeed.

In the 1970s and early 1980s U.S. capital markets had become heavily dependent on hundreds of billions of dollars of foreign capital flowing into the United States through the Netherlands Antilles window. The Treasury's pursuit of tax revenue was overwhelmed in this situation by its boundless craving for foreign capital. Benign taxation of Nether-

---

[6]293 U.S. 465 (1935).
[7]56 T.C. 934.
[8]56 T.C. 935.

lands Antilles finance companies was the avenue of foreign capital into the United States.[9] The IRS even issued favorable advance rulings in the 1970s acknowledging treaty exemption for U.S.-source paid to Antilles-based finance intermediaries.

The volume of financings channeled through Netherlands Antilles corporations was so great in the 1960s and 1970s (reaching by some estimates a total of $500 *billion*) that the toll charges became a major underpinning of the Netherlands Antilles economy.

After the exemption from U.S. taxation of U.S.-source "portfolio" interest[10] paid to foreign persons in the 1984 Act U.S. borrowers no longer needed the Netherlands Antilles window to raise capital abroad on favorable tax terms. The Treasury therefore no longer had any reason to look the other way from treaty sandwiches. Before the ink on the 1984 Act was dry, the Service, having apparently awoken to the true meaning of *Aiken*, invoked the case to deny exemption under the treaty with the Netherlands Antilles for interest paid from U.S. sources to a finance corporation chartered in the Netherlands Antilles that was itself an intermediary in a sequence of back-to-back loans.[11]

Active Business Sandwiches

You may wonder why the IRS (or taxpayers) cared about back-to-back debt channeled through the Netherlands Antilles after the exemption of portfolio interest. U.S. borrowers since then have been able to issue their bonds to any foreign person in the world and pay interest exempt from U.S. tax.

The treaty window, however, remained vital for active business operations. Not all U.S.-source interest is exempt portfolio interest. In particular, interest paid to a 10-percent shareholder of a borrowing entity

---

[9]Note further that *Aiken* involved a transfer between related persons of *existing* debt (subject to U.S. taxation) to a treaty-favored environment. The Treasury had no particular reason to care whether foreign investors already subject to U.S. tax had incentives to shift to a more favorable regime, but could not risk shutting down the largest single source of *new* foreign investment in the United States.

[10]§§871(h), 881(c). The exemption reflects Congress's and the Treasury's acknowledgement that the United States could not afford to tax interest derived from foreigners' passive investment in U.S. capital markets.

[11]Rev. Rul. 84-152 and 84-153, 1984-2 Cum. Bull. 381, 383. The question of the reach of the *Aiken* case surfaced in the courts at long last in Northern Indiana Public Service Co. v. Commissioner, 115 F.3d 506 (7th Cir. 1997), *affirming* 105 T.C. 341 (1995), involving a prototypical sandwich of back-to-back loans channeled through a Netherlands Antilles finance company. The IRS flung its entire arsenal at the taxpayer, but lost in both the Tax Court and the court of appeals. By then, however, because recent statutory provisions render back-to-back debt largely ineffective to secure treaty benefits, the outcome no longer mattered much.

is not. Therefore a foreign *equity* owner of a U.S. business cannot extract the earnings from it in the form of exempt portfolio interest simply by placing debt in its capital structure.[12] The tax exemption for interest in treaties, however, is usually broader than the exemption of portfolio interest in the Code. For this reason treaty sandwiches remained essential in sheltering income from active business operations. Consider a further example.

Suppose that in the mid-1980s Marcel (a citizen and resident of Fiscalia, whom you may remember from chapter 3) wanted to acquire and operate a business in the United States. Suppose further that the purchase price was $1.5 million and that Marcel expected annual pre-tax earnings of roughly $250,000. If Marcel simply bought the U.S. business as a sole proprietor, he would have $250,000 of income "effectively connected" with a U.S. business, which would attract U.S. income tax of nearly $80,000.

One way of reducing U.S. income tax is to create a stream of interest deductions as offsets to the U.S. business profits. Marcel might therefore consider acquiring and operating the business through a U.S. corporation capitalized with both stock and debt owned by him. Something like this:

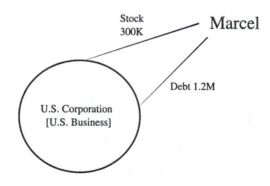

Diagram III

The corporation's income would, of course, be subject to U.S. corporate income tax, but the interest on its debt would provide deductions from taxable income.[13] If Marcel lent the U.S. corporation $1,200,000 at 12.5 percent interest, for example, investing $300,000 as equity capital, the

---

[12]See chapter 5.

[13]Borrowing from a bank or other third party would not achieve the same result for Marcel because he would give up the beneficial ownership of a portion of the income from the venture.

corporation's annual taxable business profits would be only $100,000 ($250,000 minus $150,000 of interest), which would attract U.S. corporate income tax of $22,250, nearly $58,000 less than the U.S. tax on Marcel's profits in the simpler plan of his direct ownership of the business.

The plan of Diagram III by itself, however, would be of little tax benefit. Interest paid to Marcel on the debt of a corporation beneficially owned by Marcel is *not* exempt "portfolio interest," because portfolio interest does not include interest received by owners of substantial equity holdings in the paying corporation.[14] Therefore, if Fiscalia had no income tax treaty with the United States, interest paid by the U.S. corporation to Marcel would be subject to U.S. withholding tax of 30 percent, which would bring the annual U.S. tax cost of the venture back to roughly $67,000. If Fiscalia did have an income tax treaty with the United States, the interest paid by the corporation to Marcel (who is a Fiscalian resident) might escape U.S. tax, but would then be subject to Fiscalian income tax in Marcel's hands. Marcel would only have traded U.S. taxes for Fiscalian ones.

Marcel's Sandwich

Until the repeal of the U.S. treaty with the Netherlands Antilles in 1988, the solution to Marcel's tax problem took the form of a back-to-back loan channeled through a Netherlands Antilles corporation. Marcel could eliminate the U.S. withholding tax on the interest paid by the U.S. corporation, without exposing himself to current taxation overseas, by interposing one or more well-chosen corporations in the chain of ownership. Marcel might, for example, borrow $1.5 million in Fiscalia and contribute that amount in exchange for stock to the capital of a Bermuda corporation, which would in turn contribute $300,000 to the capital of a Netherlands Antilles corporation in exchange for its stock and lend to it the balance of $1.2 million for a note bearing interest at, say, 12 percent. The Netherlands Antilles corporation would then create a U.S. corporation with the same capital structure (that is, $300,000 of stock and $1.2 million of debt—at 12.5 percent—both held by the Netherlands Antilles corporation), which in turn would acquire and operate the target U.S. business. The overall pattern is in Diagram IV.

The hoped-for consequences of this structure were the following. The U.S. corporation would pay and deduct interest of $150,000 to the Netherlands Antilles corporation, reducing its taxable income to $100,000, on which it would pay U.S. corporate income tax of $22,250.

---

[14]See chapter 5.

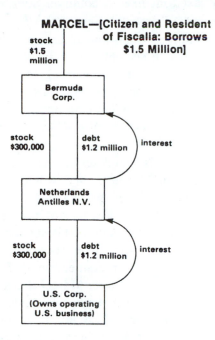

MARCEL—[Citizen and Resident of Fiscalia: Borrows $1.5 Million]

stock $1.5 million

Bermuda Corp.

stock $300,000

debt $1.2 million

interest

Netherlands Antilles N.V.

stock $300,000

debt $1.2 million

interest

U.S. Corp. (Owns operating U.S. business)

Diagram IV

The $150,000 of interest paid out would be free of U.S. withholding tax under the treaty with the Netherlands Antilles. The interest income of the Netherlands Antilles corporation would be largely offset by deductions for interest paid to the Bermuda corporation (which would also be free of withholding tax in the Netherlands Antilles). The relatively small spread between the interest received and the interest paid by the Netherlands Antilles corporation (1/2 percent of the $1.2 principal, or $6000) would be the only income subject to tax there.[15] Finally, the interest income received by the Bermuda corporation would accumulate there free of income tax.

The upshot of the structure is that a portion of the income derived from a business in the United States is removed from the reach of the U.S. taxing power and comes to rest offshore beyond the taxing power of any country. If Fiscalia is itself a high-tax jurisdiction, interest paid by Marcel on his borrowings there might also offset Fiscalian taxes. The result is a tax-free income stream (derived from economic activity in a high-tax country) sandwiched between two streams of deductions

---

[15]The annual tax cost at the Netherlands Antilles rate of 30 percent would be less than $2,000.

offsetting highly taxed income. A common sobriquet for this type of structure was in fact a "Bermuda Sandwich."[16]

The Bermuda entity is often known as a foreign (or "offshore") "base company" in which accumulates untaxed income carved out of a stream of high-taxed income. The earnings of the base company can be used to start other international ventures (including more sandwiches). If Fiscalia doesn't tax the earnings of offshore corporations until they are repatriated, taxation of the base company's income may be deferred indefinitely.[17]

This type of structure is also described as "earnings-stripping" or "interest-stripping." Business profits that would otherwise be subject to U.S. taxation are stripped out of the U.S. tax environment by interest deductions and come to rest in a low-tax environment instead. All treaty sandwiches and most other international tax shelters are variant forms of earnings-stripping. We have already encountered a simple earnings-stripping pattern in chapter 3, in connection with the source rule for interest paid by an individual. There, Marcel deducted from U.S. business profits a stream of interest payments made to his own foreign finance company that suffered no U.S. tax on the interest because under the source rules the interest paid by Marcel has *foreign* source.

Several elements of the sandwich structure warrant further attention. First, don't try this at home. A *U.S.* person cannot use a structure of this type to strip business profits earnings away from U.S. taxation. If Marcel were a U.S. person there would be no U.S. tax benefit whatsoever. Reflect on Subpart F and the PFIC rules.[18] If Marcel were a U.S. person the Bermuda corporation would be a controlled foreign corporation (and probably a PFIC too). As a U.S. person Marcel would be subject to immediate U.S. taxation on the earnings of the Bermuda corporation as though he had received them directly. Therefore *only* a foreign person can use a treaty sandwich to shelter the earnings of a U.S. business.

Second, if Fiscalia is a high-tax country, Marcel has the further problem of dealing with Fiscalian taxes. Whether he can do so depends on how aggressively Fiscalia taxes the controlled foreign corporations

---

[16]There were further elaborations of sandwich structures depending on the specific tax, financial, and currency rules in the country of the ultimate investor (here Fiscalia). Another part of the filling (between Bermuda and Marcel) might be, for example, a Swiss bank trust account or a Liechtenstein Anstalt or Stiftung. You may not know what these are (and that reflects well on you) but anyone likely to use them in a sandwich probably did.

[17]Of course Marcel may have to put off spending those earnings as well. But if consumer interest is tax deductible in Fiscalia, Marcel can gain further tax advantage by borrowing to consume immediately and repaying the debt with delayed repatriation of earnings, having enjoyed the benefit of the interest deductions in the interim.

[18]See chapters 15 and 16 to refresh your memory.

and other "offshore" operations of Fiscalian persons. It depends, in other words, on the extent of possible "deferral" of *Fiscalian* tax on foreign income. If Fiscalia has rules similar to the United States, such as Subpart F and the PFIC rules, Marcel cannot succeed. The interest income of the Bermuda corporation (being passive investment income) would be subject to full current taxation in the hands of its controlling shareholder. If on the other hand Fiscalia does not look through the controlled foreign corporations of its own citizens and residents, then the sandwich works for Marcel in Fiscalia.

Until about 25 years ago, the United States was the only country that systematically imposed current taxation on controlled foreign corporations owned by its citizens and residents. It still goes the furthest in that direction. But many other high-tax countries have sharply curtailed the possibility of deferral of taxation through controlled foreign corporations. France and Germany, for example, have provisions similar to Subpart F capturing the passive income of controlled foreign corporations. Other high-tax countries, such as the Netherlands and Switzerland, still allow extensive deferral. The U.K., once surprisingly easygoing, now has quite a severe regime for controlled foreign corporations.

In sum, if Marcel is from a high-tax environment a treaty sandwich will not avail him unless he can pacify both U.S. taxes and his own national taxes. In recent years both objectives have become more difficult.

This is the point in the story to introduce some of the countermeasures mobilized by the U.S. Treasury against treaty sandwiches and other international tax shelters. [I shall work them into the narrative in roughly chronological order.] After a slow start in the 1980s the Treasury's arsenal at the turn of the Millennium has reduced the treaty tax haven to near-extinction.

Limitations on Treaty Benefits

The Treasury's first point of attack on treaty shopping during the 1980s came in the negotiation of new treaties. The U.S. Model Treaty has contained since 1977 a provision limiting the benefit of the treaty to corporations that have some real economic connection with the treaty countries beyond the formality of a corporate charter. The limitation on benefits in the current (1996) version of the U.S. Model Treaty is somewhat more elaborated. Article 22 of the U.S. Model Treaty, ominously headed "Limitation on Benefits," reads (in part) as follows:

1. A resident of a Contracting State shall be entitled to benefits otherwise accorded to residents of a Contracting State by this Convention only to the extent provided in this Article.

2. A resident of a Contracting State shall be entitled to all the benefits of this Convention if the resident is:

   a) an individual;

   . . .

   c) a company, if

       i) all the shares in the class or classes of shares representing more than 50 percent of the voting power and value of the company are regularly traded on a recognized stock exchange, or

       ii) at least 50 percent of each class of shares in the company is owned directly or indirectly by companies entitled to benefits under clause i), provided that in the case of indirect ownership, each intermediate owner is a person entitled to benefits of the Convention under this paragraph;

More simply put, this provision limits treaty benefits to actual individual residents of the treaty country and to corporations that are more than 50-percent owned by actual individual residents. As well you can imagine, this provision would seriously inhibit treaty shopping. Relatively few people will uproot themselves just to set up a tax shelter.[19] Consider the effect of Article 22 on Marcel's sandwich. If part of the Netherlands Antilles treaty, it would have rendered Marcel's sandwich useless unless Marcel had become an actual resident of the Netherlands Antilles.

The End of the Antilles Treaty

The treaty with the Netherlands Antilles, of course, contained no such limitation on benefits. When the U.S. Treasury asked the Netherlands Antilles to renegotiate its income tax treaty to include a limitation on benefits, the Netherlands Antilles naturally refused. The Treasury coun-

---

[19]Treaty sandwiches using Netherlands Antilles corporations were almost always owned by *non*residents of the Netherlands Antilles.

tered in mid-1987 simply by terminating the treaty, effective January 1, 1988.[20]

The demise of the treaty with the Netherlands Antilles brought one of the classic tax-haven possibilities to an end. The spread of anti-treaty-shopping clauses in the treaty network of the United States also narrowed the range of alternatives. But limitations on benefits in treaties are of little effect unless they are universal. It hardly mattered how many treaties had restraints on treaty shopping as long as there was at least *one* treaty with a potential tax haven country that did not. And even as the environment for treaty-shopping grew less hospitable in the late 1980s, treaty tax havens hung on as the tax-averse combed the U.S. treaty network for a good host.

The Dutch Sandwich

It remained possible until 1994 to use the treaty between the United States and the Netherlands, which offered its guests surprisingly broad protections. What made the Netherlands a tax haven was (surprise!) its own income tax treaty with its former colony, the Netherlands Antilles. A combination of entities organized in the Netherlands and the Netherlands Antilles was for a time the most promising structure for treaty-favored investment in the United States. There were several variations. One of the simpler entailed ownership of a U.S. business corporation by a Netherlands corporation, itself owned by a Netherlands Antilles corporation, in turn owned by the ultimate investor (in our case, Marcel). As in the sandwich described above, the capital structure of the Netherlands corporation would mirror that of the U.S. corporation with back-to-back debt, so that U.S.-source interest flowing to the Netherlands corporation would be exempt under the U.S.-Netherlands treaty, while interest paid out by the Netherlands corporation would be deductible from taxable income in the Netherlands and exempt from Dutch withholding tax under the Netherlands' own treaty with the Netherlands Antilles. The pattern is in Diagram V, on the following page.

This type of structure was called a "Dutch sandwich," because it cradled a Dutch entity between two others.[21] Between the mid-1980s and 1994 the Dutch sandwich was the top treaty tax haven. Then in 1992,

---

[20]The treaty exemption for interest on *existing* debt was preserved, however, by separate tax legislation.

[21]There was no need for a tax haven entity (Bermuda or Cayman Islands) above the Netherlands Antilles corporation in a Dutch sandwich. After the repeal of the Netherlands Antilles' treaty with the United States, the Netherlands Antilles dispensed with its own income tax, which it had previously maintained solely to avoid the appearance of being a pure tax haven.

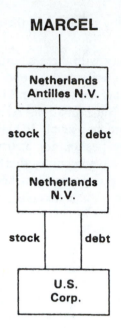

A Dutch Sandwich

Diagram V

after more than 10 years of negotiations, the United States and the Netherlands agreed on a new income tax treaty, containing a limitation on benefits aimed at treaty-shopping, which became effective in 1994.[22] This did not spell the end of treaty sandwiches, though, because the U.S. treaty with Luxembourg (which also had a treaty with the Netherlands Antilles) still had no limitation on benefits. The Dutch sandwich for a time became the Luxembourg sandwich.[23]

The U.S. Treasury set out to renegotiate the treaty with Luxembourg. A new Luxembourg treaty (with limitation on benefits, naturally) was signed in 1997. The new treaty will go into effect in 2001 (or went into effect in 2001, depending on when you are reading this). The Luxembourg sandwich therefore enjoyed a significant career. The composition of the sandwich required considerable modification at various points, however, because of several additional statutory countermeasures against

---

[22]The United States could not simply terminate the treaty with Holland unilaterally, as it had done with the Netherlands Antilles. Given the large trade between Holland and the United States and the high level of Dutch investment in the United States (the highest of any country, per capita), the United States *must* have a tax treaty in effect with Holland.

[23]To picture a Luxembourg sandwich, just substitute a Luxembourg corporation for the Dutch corporation in Diagram V.

international tax shelters added to the Treasury's arsenal in the 1990s. The next step in this historical traversal of treaty sandwiches is an excursion into these measures. The first of these is the limitation on "earnings-stripping" in section 163(j).

Section 163(j)

It is evident from the preceding discussion, I am sure, that debt artfully placed in the capital structure of a corporation can be a powerful instrument for containing U.S. taxation. In the international setting it permits the reduction of income exposed to U.S. tax by interest payments that are not subject to U.S. tax in the hands of those receiving them. In the classic Dutch sandwich the entities involved were all under the same beneficial ownership. The core of the sandwich structure, it turns out, is the same sort of self-loan that our friend Marcel carried out in chapter 3[24] in pursuit of untaxed foreign source interest that could nonetheless be deducted from U.S. taxable income. The channeling of interest deducted from U.S. taxable income through a treaty-favored entity is similarly a form of earnings-stripping, consisting of the deduction of interest payments from a stream of business profits that would otherwise be subject to U.S. taxation and their deflection to a tax-favored environment.

The 1989 and 1993 Acts brought a specific statutory restriction on earnings-stripping in the form of section 163(j). The explanation of section 163(j) given by a congressional committee underscores the element of self-loan in the earnings-stripping pattern:

> [I]t is appropriate to limit the deduction for interest that a taxable person pays or accrues to a tax-exempt entity whose economic interests coincide with those of the payor. To allow an unlimited deduction for such interest permits significant erosion of the tax base. Allowance of unlimited deductions permits an economic unit that consists of more than one legal entity to contract with itself at the expense of the government ... [A] limitation on the ability to 'strip' earnings out of this country through interest payments in lieu of dividend distributions is appropriate. The uncertainty of present law (particularly the debt-equity distinction) may allow taxpayers to take aggressive positions that inappropriately erode the U.S. tax base.[25]

---

[24]There the earnings-stripping resulted simply from the source rule for interest paid by an individual. Marcel deducted from U.S. business profits a stream of interest payments made to his own foreign finance company that suffered no U.S. tax on the interest because under the source rules the interest paid by Marcel has *foreign* source.

[25]H. Rep. No. 247, 101st Cong., 1st Sess. 1241-1242 (1989) (1989 House Report).

Section 163(j) does not deny treaty benefits directly. Instead, it disallows certain earnings-stripping deductions from a stream of income exposed to U.S. taxation. Section 163(j) limits the *deduction* of earnings-stripping interest payments from a corporation to a related person, thus limiting *other* tax benefits (specifically, the deduction by the paying corporation) that would otherwise follow from the payment of interest favored by an income tax treaty. Section 163(j) is a complex provision of which I shall summarize only the broad elements here.

Deduction of "excess" interest paid by a corporation to a related person is disallowed under section 163(j) if

1) the corporation paying the interest has a debt-equity ratio greater than 1.5 to 1, and
2) the recipient of the interest is shielded from U.S. taxation, and
3) the corporation's interest expense exceeds 50 percent of its pre-interest income.

The non-deductible interest is the amount of interest paid or accrued *exceeding* 50 percent of the paying corporation's pre-interest income, to the extent it is paid to a related person not subject to U.S. taxation. Thus if a corporation's debt is more than 1.5 times its equity capital, it cannot deduct more than one-half of its taxable income in the form of interest paid to an untaxed related person.

This may be easier to fathom through an example. Consider Marcel's Dutch sandwich in Diagrams IV and V. Because the debt-to-equity ratio of the U.S. corporation conducting business in the United States is 4 to 1 (which is greater than 1.5 to 1), section 163(j) would apply to interest paid to its treaty-favored Netherlands affiliate. The "excess" interest here is $25,000 (the amount by which the interest paid of $150,000 exceeds one-half of the corporation's taxable income of $150,000). The corporation's interest deduction would be limited to $125,000. While this may not seem intolerably painful, there is more. Any other debt in its capital structure—even owed to an unrelated person—would further reduce its earnings-stripping deduction. If the corporation also paid interest of $50,000 on debt to an unrelated bank, for example, the deduction for interest paid to the Netherlands corporation would be limited to $75,000.

If it had no third-party debt (a somewhat unrealistic assumption), the U.S. corporation could avoid the bite of section 163(j) either by reducing its interest payments $125,000 or lowering its debt-equity ratio. A reduction of debt to $900,000 (combined with an increase in equity capital to $600,000) would bring its debt-equity ratio within the statutory safe harbor. At the same interest rate (12.5 percent) the interest deduction would be $112,500. It might occur to you to increase the interest rate to, say, 20 percent, which would increase the annual interest deductions to $180,000. That, however, would be extremely hazardous. If the U.S. corporation's debt structure is overextended under established administrative practice and case law concerning debt and equity, the IRS might succeed in recharacterizing the entire ostensible "debt" as equity, with disastrous tax consequences. To avoid problems Marcel would have to keep both the amount and terms of the debt used in his sandwich structure within the range that could have been entered into at arm's length with an unrelated borrower without creating an unreasonable risk of default.

Section 163(j) rations earnings-stripping interest deductions rather than disallow them altogether. It is also a somewhat blunt, all-purpose weapon. Its effect is by no means limited to tax haven operations. It disallows earnings-stripping deductions of interest that is shielded from further *U.S.* taxation, whether the interest payments are deflected to a tax-haven environment *or* are exposed to high foreign taxes where they finally come to rest. Section 163(j) preserves a certain amount of business profits for U.S. taxation whether they would be subject to high foreign taxes elsewhere or not at all. Section 163(j) thus both constrains treaty tax havens *and* apportions the taxation of business profits between the United States and other high-tax jurisdictions with which it has income tax treaties.[26]

Conduit Regulations Under Section 7701(l)

The 1993 Act brought the Treasury another weapon in its campaign against sandwiches and other international tax havens: section 7701(l). Understated in form, section 7701(l) is potent in reach. Under the somewhat cryptic heading "Regulations Relating to Conduit Arrangements," section 7701(l) reads: "The Secretary may prescribe regulations recharacterizing any multiple-party financing transaction as a transaction directly among any 2 or more of such parties where the Secretary determines that such recharacterization is appropriate to prevent avoidance of any tax imposed by this title." Someone who did not have in mind the history of sandwiches and other tax-favored structures using finance intermediaries would be hard pressed to divine what section 7701(l) is about. In fact this single sentence changes the balance of power between

---

[26]For this reason, several high-tax treaty partners of the United States have taken a jaundiced view of section 163(j).

taxpayers and the Treasury in the matter of conduits, earnings-stripping, and back-to-back debt.

Reread section 7701(l). It gives the Treasury the power to recharacterize certain "multi-party financing" transactions. To understand what that means consider the outcome of the *Aiken* case, discussed above, where a court in effect excised a treaty-favored Honduran corporation from a chain of back-to-back loans on the ground that it was a "conduit." In consequence the structure was recast as a loan directly from a Bahamas corporation to a U.S. corporation, with interest (subject to flat rate tax, naturally) flowing the other way. With section 7701(l) in place the Service can reshuffle back-to-back loans systematically and cut treaty-favored entities out of sandwich structures altogether.

The regulations under section 7701(l) are known as the "Conduit Regulations." These regulations are a decidedly fierce read. What you should glean from them at a minimum is that they treat most chains of debt and many combinations of debt and leases or licenses as multiparty financing transactions. If there is a significant possibility of tax avoidance, the IRS can disregard the participation of any intermediate entity as a "conduit." Here also, an example may make things easier to understand. Turn to the Dutch sandwich in Diagram V. The back-to-back debt binds together a multiparty financing involving three entities. The Treasury can therefore recharacterize the transaction as a debt running directly between the U.S. corporation and the Netherlands Antilles corporation. Because there is no longer a U.S. treaty with the Netherlands Antilles, interest on the loan as recharacterized (which is not exempt portfolio interest, because of Marcel's stock ownership) is subject to flat rate U.S. tax.

Therefore, even without limitations on benefits in U.S. income tax treaties, the Conduit Regulations under section 7701(l) would have defeated treaty sandwiches built on back-to-back debt. The substitution of a Luxembourg corporation for the Netherlands corporation in the classic Dutch sandwich after a limitation on benefits was added to the Netherlands treaty would avail nothing. The Luxembourg variant would be cast as payment of interest from the United States straight to the Netherlands Antilles.

The Last Incarnation of the Treaty Sandwich

You might think, in this light, that section 7701(l) finished off treaty sandwiches once and for all. But it didn't. The Conduit Regulations, to be sure, drove the final stake in the heart of treaty sandwiches built on back-to-back debt.[27] Treaty tax havens were not entirely finished off, however. Even with the Conduit Regulations, there remained a way to set-up a treaty-based tax shelter haven, if the underlying treaty had no limitation on benefits.

The design of this structure eliminates the back-to-back debt, so that no "multi-party financing" is involved. The structure makes use of the U.S. treaty with Luxembourg combined with helpful elements of the national tax systems of Luxembourg and Switzerland. Luxembourg does not tax income derived from financing operations by foreign branches of Luxembourg corporations. Switzerland, for its part, also does not tax the income from financing operations of Swiss branches of Luxembourg corporations.

To work around section 7701(l) Marcel might therefore set up the following structure of ownership of business assets in the United States. Marcel would create, entirely with *equity* capital, a Luxembourg corporation with a branch in Switzerland engaged in lending money. The Luxembourg entity would lend through its Swiss branch to another entity, also beneficially owned by Marcel, engaged in Marcel's U.S. business. Under the treaty between the United States and Luxembourg, the interest paid to the Luxembourg corporation would be free of U.S. tax, within the limits imposed by the earnings-stripping rules of section 163(j). Meanwhile, neither Luxembourg nor Switzerland would impose significant tax on the interest income. Diagram VI contains a simplified version of the structure.

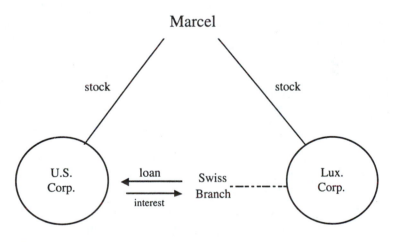

Diagram VI

---

[27]Earlier provisions such as section 163(j) were more like steaks in the heart. They killed through a build-up of cholesterol rather than a single sharp blow.

While it may look vulnerable, this structure is not readily assimilable to a "multi-party financing transaction" subject to the conduit rules. The key element is Marcel's all-equity interest in the Luxembourg corporation. There is no back-to-back debt. Because the interest income accumulates in the Luxembourg entity rather than flowing through it along a chain of debt, there is no evident "multiple-party financing transaction" for the Treasury to recombine under the Conduit Regulations. A multiparty financing must have at least three parties and *two* legs of debt. In its final incarnation the treaty sandwich has only one slice of bread.

At this writing (mid-2000) the open-faced sandwich still works. But, although for illustrative purposes I set one up for our friend Marcel, this structure is in fact wholly impractical for a small player like Marcel. In order to satisfy requirements of Luxembourg law the Swiss branch must have a certain substance, including an actual staff, which would make it prohibitively expensive to shield from tax an income stream of $250,000 per year. For large enterprises, however, it provides the last best avenue of foreign investment in U.S. business operations.

Not for long, though. The Luxembourg open-faced sandwich will soon be only a lingering aftertaste. As noted above, a new treaty negotiated with Luxembourg in 1997 contains a limitation on benefits more than sufficient to defeat this maneuver. Final ratification and entry into force of the new Luxembourg treaty has been held up by various wrangles in Congress and the Luxembourg Parliament. But the new Millennium—as likely as not even before this book reaches print—will almost surely consign this surviving treaty half-sandwich to oblivion.

So, is there anything left? International tax specialists are doubtless scouring the U.S. treaty network for a venue that can substitute for Luxembourg in the half-sandwich with the all-equity topping. If they find one, however, a limitation on benefits in the pertinent treaty is probably not far behind.

Back to Basics

Interestingly, though, a basic, almost primitive, earnings-stripping possibility survives. It rests on the use by a foreign individual of the source rule for interest to strip business profits away from the U.S. tax environment, a pattern we first encountered in chapter 3. None of the recent developments canvassed here, including section 163(j), the conduit regulations, and limitations on treaty benefits, lays a glove on this maneuver. Review the pattern in chapter 3. No interest is paid by a corporation; therefore section 163(j) does not come into play. There is no multi-party financing, just a single debt between two parties that cannot be recombined. And no treaty exemption or other benefit is invoked by anyone.

In the pattern observed in chapter 3, this maneuver suffers from constraining nontax limitations. There can be only one owner who must, from the perspective of the U.S. tax system, be a direct proprietor. Direct ownership by an individual is not a flexible form of ownership of a U.S. business. Historically this has severely limited the type and size of businesses that could avail themselves of the tax advantage. The problems include difficulties of management and the owner's unlimited liability. It is hard to imagine an automobile assembly plant or a chain of retail stores organized as a directly-owned sole individual proprietorship.

Check the Box

A recent development in a different area of tax law, however, may considerably have enlarged the potential range of this form of investment in U.S. business assets. The check-the-box regulations on the tax character of entities[28] allow a foreign owner of a U.S. business in Marcel's position to hold assets in a separate entity and still be taxed as an individual proprietor. Let's revisit Marcel's purchase of a U.S. business in chapter 3 in this light.

This time, instead of acquiring the U.S. business directly Marcel forms a Limited Liability Company (LLC), to which he transfers $200,000 as equity capital. The LLC elects to be fiscally transparent under the check-the-box regulations. The LLC borrows $800,000 from a foreign corporation also owned by Marcel, and purchases the U.S. business for $1 million, securing the $800,000 loan from Marcel's finance corporation with the U.S. business assets. The structure is illustrated in Diagram VII.

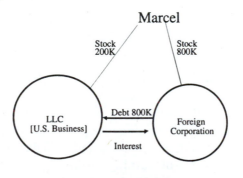

Diagram VII

---

[28]See chapter 10.

Diagram VII may remind you of a pattern of ownership we have already encountered, although in the diagram it is somewhat disguised. Think back to Marcel's form of ownership of a U.S. business in chapter 3, which there was coupled with a loan to Marcel from his own foreign finance corporation. When you take into account the effect of the check-the-box election, the two forms of ownership are exactly the same from the perspective of the U.S. tax system. The LLC is a single-owner entity that has checked the box (i.e., has elected to be fiscally transparent). It is therefore, for U.S. tax purposes, a form of direct ownership of assets by Marcel. The loan from the foreign finance company to the LLC is simply a loan directly to Marcel. The interest paid by the LLC has foreign source, just as though it had been paid by Marcel (which for tax purposes it has been). If indeed we eliminate the LLC from this pattern (which is what happens in effect when Marcel checks the box of fiscal transparency) we can redraw the relations between the players and events as in Diagram VIII:

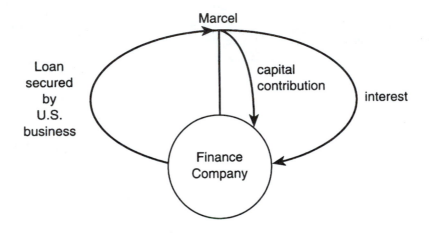

Diagram VIII

Look familiar? The check-the-box regulations let Marcel have his cake and eat it. Marcel can preserve the advantage of the corporate form of ownership—limited liability with more flexible capital and management structure—while retaining the earnings-stripping tax advantage resulting from the source rule for interest paid by individuals. With an LLC, in fact, the range of this type of earnings-stripping pattern structure is considerably extended. The electing LLC can have only one owner (or it would be a partnership for U.S. tax purposes and the interest it paid would have U.S. source), but it can have varied and far-flung business operations. As long as Marcel is the sole owner (and not a U.S. resident), the business can be a chain of restaurants or retail stores, a fashion business, a high-tech electronic commerce or software development business, or even a conglomerate. In our example, multiply the numbers by 100 or a 1,000. If the LLC operates a billion-dollar U.S. business subject to $800 million of debt, the interest paid out (because in tax effect paid by Marcel) still has foreign source.

We have come full circle. The last best remaining international tax shelter is the one we encountered first. It is built, somewhat prosaically, on the source rule for interest paid by individuals. Perhaps because of the very lack of moving parts—it involves no treaties or mirror-image debt—it has held up better than the others.

Like all the others, however, its future career is tenuous. This is not because the structure can easily be attacked—it is surprisingly sturdy—but because it can fall to a statutory stroke of the pen. A small change in the source rule for interest would stop it cold. Rather than spell it out, I'll leave to you to ponder what that might be. In a subject with so transitory a form as international taxation it is natural to end with an unanswered question.

Table of Cases

References are to Pages

Index

References are to Pages

Index

Index